Businessmen and Politics

Businessmen and Politics

Studies of business activity in British politics, 1900–1945

Edited by John Turner

Heinemann · London and Exeter (NH)

Heinemann Educational Books Ltd
22 Bedford Square, London WC1B 3HH
LONDON EDINBURGH MELBOURNE AUCKLAND
HONG KONG SINGAPORE KUALA LUMPUR NEW DELHI
IBADAN NAIROBI JOHANNESBURG
EXETER (NH) KINGSTON PORT OF SPAIN

First published 1984

British Library Cataloguing in Publication Data
Businessmen and politics
1. Businessmen—Great Britain—Political activity 2. Great Britain—Politics and government—20th century.
I. Turner, John
322'.3'0941 HF499
ISBN 0-435-32870-0

Typeset by Inforum Ltd, Portsmouth
Printed in Great Britain by Biddles Ltd, Guildford, Surrey

Contents

Preface and Acknowledgements

This book is the outcome of a symposium on 'Businessmen and Politics' which was held in London in 1980. The organisers wished to bring together economic and political historians to discuss a subject of common concern and great importance to twentieth century historiography; they believed that historians of twentieth century Britain have accepted too readily the distinction between economic and political history, which clouds understanding of the development of modern industrial society. The programme emphasised questions of current research interest which called for a synthesis of the two sub-disciplines. Five of the chapters in this volume were first presented as papers at the symposium, and a further two were written by participants in response to issues raised at the meetings. The authors are therefore indebted for stimulus, criticism and advice to more than sixty fellow scholars who attended the two sessions; particular gratitude is owed to the two chairmen, Donald Coleman and Eric Hobsbawm, and the *rapporteurs* who led discussion, Forrest Capie, T.A.B. Corley, Jose Harris and John Ramsden. Frank Longstreth, Keith Middlemas and Terence Rodgers, whose conference papers are not represented here, nevertheless made valuable contributions and helped to give direction to the discussions. As editor I must also express my deep sense of obligation to Leslie Hannah, Director of the Business History Unit, who shared the work of organising the symposium and the first editorial revision of the papers. Although other commitments forced him to withdraw from the joint editorship of this book, he has been generous with his time in discussion, and parts of the introductory chapter rest heavily on our conversations. For errors, omissions and the general interpretation in that chapter I nevertheless take full responsibility, as does each contributor in respect of his chapter.

The contributors' debts to the owners and curators of archival collections are acknowledged in the footnotes to each chapter; we apologise for any omissions, which are unwitting, for historical work of this kind depends heavily on access to private archives.

In preparing this book for press I have been much helped by Sheelagh Taylor. David Hill, of Heinemann Educational Books, has shown astonishing forbearance. My greatest debt, as ever, is to Sara Turner for unfailing advice and support.

John Turner
Bedford College, London

1 The Politics of Business
John Turner

Politics, in Lasswell's words, is about 'who gets what, when, how'.[1] This book is about the politics of British businessmen in the first half of the twentieth century. During this period industrial decline and its consequences occupied the centre of the political stage in peacetime. Yet the special political contribution of businessmen, who were after all intimately concerned with industry's problems, has never had the attention in Britain which has been accorded to it in other industrial countries.[2] Trade unions have been studied at length, but research on the politics of other economic interests has only recently begun to appear.[3] This collection of studies, by economic and political historians, is an attempt to redress the balance by shifting attention towards business politics.

The individual chapters, arranged in roughly chronological order, are chosen to illustrate important facets of the subject. This, introductory chapter examines the politics of business in Victorian Britain, then proceeds to an analysis of twentieth century business politics both inside and outside the parliamentary framework. The second chapter, by Richard Roberts, examines the business lobby against municipal socialism at the turn of the century, illustrating the role of pressure groups working on parliament and public opinion. My own chapter describes the growth of representative 'peak' organisations during the First World War. Stephen Tolliday then examines the inter-war steel industry and the part played by companies and trade associations in negotiation with the government. Michael Dintenfass challenges the theory of 'corporate bias' in inter-war politics, put forward by Keith Middlemas in his book on *Politics in Industrial Society*, by an analysis of the tripartite talks between the TUC, employers' associations, and the government between 1927 and 1933. The second Richard Roberts argues that informal relationships between businessmen and civil servants in the early 1930s both eased the way towards state intervention in declining industries and protected the parliamentary process against 'corporate bias'. The last three chapters take a different approach, examining three industries whose political activities were especially controversial. Philip Williamson documents the political acts and attitudes of bankers between the return to the Gold Standard in 1925 and its abandonment in 1931. George Peden, discussing the aircraft industry in the late 1930s, concludes that businessmen, like politicians, were subject to a system of political checks and balances. Finally, Geoffrey Jones examines the oil industry, comparing the British experience with that of other major oil-users and oil-producers, and suggests that contrary to polemical convention, politicians rather than businessmen usually retained the upper hand.

These are empirical studies, but students of business politics cannot ignore the theoretical questions raised by political sociologists. The Marxist tradition, besides its emphasis on economically determined class divisions, suggests that state power, in one way or another, promotes capitalist economic relationships.[4] The Anglo-American pluralist tradition offers the picture of a political system as a neutral switchboard between competing economic interests, though in a recent revision Charles Lindblom has emphasised the likelihood that in any free-enterprise system business interests will wield great political power.[5] The recently fashionable 'corporatist' school, originating in Germany, sees industrial society as a competition between economic interests organised into representative institutions such as trade unions and employers' associations. The common assumption is a very diffuse body of thought is that corporate activity reduces political conflict, and that functions reserved by classical political theory to the state do in fact fall upon organisations which correspond to functional economic divisions in society. These may be voluntary, private organisations which actively seek governing functions, or bodies established by the state in which membership may be compulsory.[6] In either case, corporatism bypasses representative democracy.

It is convenient to write the history of industrialised Germany in these terms,[7] but rather more difficult to apply the theory to Great Britain. Keith Middlemas has made a valiant attempt, describing a system of 'corporate bias' in British politics since the early twentieth century. According to Middlemas the Federation of British Industries and the National Confederation of Employers' Organisations helped to manage British politics through a 'continuous contract' with government and the Trades Union Congress, by which the political parties were largely excluded from economic management and the political extremes of communism and fascism were kept weak. The evidence for this is very ambiguous, but his analysis, like an earlier study by Samuel Beer,[8] rightly emphasises the political importance of non-party, non-parliamentary activity.

The corporatist tide is ebbing, even in German historiography,[9] but the fundamental questions posed by Marxist and pluralist writers remain. How far do capitalists control the apparatus of government in capitalist societies? How do they do it, and what opposition do they face? Are divisions within the capitalist classes more or less important than differences between capitalists and other social groups? All these questions are met in one form or another in the chapters that follow. A number of important common points emerge from the studies, which help to describe the industrial polity of early twentieth century Britain.

The first is that the interests of British businessmen were multifarious and often contradictory: a good example of this is the range of opinions in industry about tariff protection. A second, related point is that the ideologies developed by party politicians to mobilise the mass electorate often cut across businessmen's views about their own interests. A case in point is the 'social imperialism' of the Edwardian decade. Some industrialists supported it as a means to tariff reform, others because it offered a bulwark against socialism.[10] Some of those who had seen it as a vehicle for protectionism were outspoken in their disgust when the Conservative party abandoned Tariff Reform in 1913 for the politically excellent reason that it had become an electoral liability.[11] The third common point is that business interests did not capture the apparatus of the state, though it was often possible for industrial or financial interests to exercise a veto over policies. In his study of the aircraft industry, Peden quotes Sir N. Warren Fisher's almost Hegelian dictum that 'the supreme interest of the stockholders is the integrity of the State . . . from destruction by external force'.[12] In the end, reasons of state took priority over private economic concerns. To return to Lasswell's aphorism, one can say that businessmen got much of what they wanted in Britain in the first half of the twentieth century. They were able to do so because the 'business interest' constituted a loose coalition of groups, which could sometimes be effective. The relationship between business and the state was not one of domination by either side, but of bargaining between two weak entities which often did not know their own minds. In bargaining with other groups, business did about as well as its principal competitor, the trade union movement. If only for that reason, it is surely right to treat business politics as seriously as labour politics is normally treated by British historians.

The Victorian and Edwardian background

Businessmen were active in nineteenth and early twentieth century politics for many reasons – altruistic, sectarian and social – which did not directly involve their businesses. But the expansion of the Victorian state touched their economic interests at many points and thus created a distinctive business presence in politics. The most direct index of the political activity of businessmen is the number of businessmen who were MPs. Recent studies suggest that businessmen were never in the majority in the pre-1914 House of Commons, but that there was a steady growth in numbers so that by 1914 there were 94 manufacturers

(64 Liberal and 30 Unionist) and 81 MPs from commercial or financial backgrounds (41 Liberal and 40 Unionist).[13] During the nineteenth century the Liberal predominance among businessmen was steadily eroded, with a particularly marked swing to the Conservatives after the Liberal split over Home Rule in 1886; but only the First World War, and the near-fatal Liberal split of 1916–18, made the Conservative party pre-eminently the 'bosses party'.[14] Meanwhile the difficulties of combining business careers and political ambitions began to deter leading businessmen from active politics.[15]

Late Victorian Parliaments had obvious attractions for the successful businessman. Parliament was the pinnacle of social achievement, and a seat in the Commons served for those who lacked the wealth or distinction to command a peerage. There were well-trodden paths to Westminster: employers who dominated the society of factory towns could count on the support of 'their' workpeople, with little substantial exception before 1914, while for those in larger conurbations the Liberal political machine was in business hands until the end of the century.[16] The emergence of the Liberal party in the late nineteenth century as a radical popular party with marked collectivist impulses alienated many businessmen, but those who wished could readily shift to the Conservative party, whose electoral position in urban England was strengthened by the 1885 redistribution of seats.[17] But Parliament was dominated by party organisations which often resisted pressure from businessmen on questions of business importance. A range of extra-parliamentary organisations therefore grew up to deal with this situation.

The first notable extra-parliamentary organisations of businessmen which can claim 'political' status appeared in the 1840s, and were concerned with the Factory Acts. These included the National Association of Factory Occupiers, immortalised by Dickens as the 'Society for Mangling Operatives'. The early bodies were succeeded, with intervals of inanition, by the National Federation of Associated Employers of Labour (1871–81), the Employers' Parliamentary Council (1894–c.1896), the Liberal and Property Defence League, and the Employers' Parliamentary Association (1911–16).[18] With financial support from industrialists, all these bodies did their main work by lobbying Parliament against measures hostile to employers' interests. They also produced extensive propaganda, in every form from broadsheets to books, and thrust their views on Royal Commissions and other public inquiries. Their areas of concern included factory legislation; workmen's compensation; trade union legislation; the regulation of public utilities; social welfare legislation, and its impact on taxation; and occasionally the tariff question.

The lobbying organisations, which claimed with more or less conviction to represent employers as a whole, were closely associated with trade and employers' associations and chambers of commerce, whose ostensible purposes were 'functional' rather than 'political'. These organisations had various origins. The Chambers of Commerce had first appeared in the late eighteenth century in leading market and industrial towns to represent the common interests of merchants and manufacturers in local affairs; a national body, the Associated British Chambers of Commerce, was set up in 1860, explicitly to lobby parliament and government departments.[19] Trade and employers' associations had their roots in combinations of masters in particular trades, also in the late eighteenth century, which were set up to fix prices and maintain a common front against wage demands. Most such groups were local in scope at least until the late nineteenth century, and by no means every trade had robust local price or wage agreements, let alone national ones, even at the end of the century. But especially after the commercial slump of the 1870s regional and national price agreements became more common in such industries as iron and steel manufacture and heavy chemicals. Price agreements were rarely stable, and in trades where price stability was very important it was common for trusts or loose combines to take the place of ineffectual price agreements: good examples are the United Alkali Company and the Salt Union.[20] Yet some trade associations remained in being and often undertook political functions on their members' behalf. Contrasting examples are the British Iron Trades Association, which was founded in 1875 to advance the industry's interests but constantly stumbled on the fact that the industry was divided in its attitude to protective tariffs; and the British Electrical and Allied Manufacturers' Association, founded in 1906, which was a united and strident tariff reform body, highly influential in the creation of more elaborate business representative organisations during the First World War.[21]

In the later nineteenth century, though, the trade associations were overshadowed by employers' associations for dealing with labour questions. Loosely organised employers' groups became more formal in organisation, and somewhat more coherent in policy, as collective bargaining was gradually accepted as the norm in the period after 1870. The development of 'New Unionism' among semi-skilled and unskilled workers in the late 1880s, together with pressure on profits, brought further change. Employers responded with national federations of employers' associations such as the Shipping Federation, the Shipbuilding Employers' Federation and the Employers' Federation of Engineering Associations (later the Engineering Employers' Federation), all of which were prepared to use national lock-outs to coerce recalcitrant unions. The 'employers' backlash' of the 1890s involved not only the exertion of sheer industrial power to weaken unions by the use of lockouts and 'free labour' strike-breakers, but also a political, legal and ideological effort.

The employers' federations gave evidence to the Royal Commission on Trade Unions in 1893–4, urging the limitation of trade union privileges, and employers spoke in Parliament in support of the Commission's recommendations, which emphasised the value of voluntary conciliation agreements between employers' associations and unions.[22] The Employers' Parliamentary Council, formed in Manchester in 1894 to counteract the Parliamentary Committee of the TUC, concentrated on parliamentary lobbying for voluntary collective bargaining. Both large firms and employers' associations were concerned in bringing the legal actions – Temperton vs. Russell, 1893; Trollopes vs. the London Building Trades Federation, 1896; and Lyon vs. Wilkins, 1899 – which prepared the ground for the best known, in which the Taff Vale Railway Company, with tacit support from the Railway Companies' Association and the Employers' Parliamentary Council, successfully sued the Amalgamated Society of Railway Servants in 1901.[23] At the ideological level, the Liberty and Property Defence League, besides acting as an umbrella organisation for free labour recruitment, was the centre of a publicity effort which insisted on the rights of employers and the iniquities of both trade unionism and any form of state intervention in industrial relations matters.[24] Although the major employers' federations differed about tactics, as for example towards national collective bargaining or arbitration, they had established themselves by 1914 as a major force in business politics.

Despite the vigour of business organisations and the steadily growing numbers of businessmen in parliament, business politics on the eve of the First World War was defensive and divided. The demand for tariff protection, for example, reflected some businessmen's fear of national economic decline. It also divided business opinion: while steelmakers contributed heavily to the support of the Tariff Commission, the cotton textile industries were equally firm in defence of Free Trade, and there was a vocal Free Trade minority in the steel and other metal trades. On social welfare issues, some businessmen supported state welfare schemes to stave off social unrest; others promoted their own private welfare schemes as part of an industrial relations strategy directed against trade unions; others rejected any form of welfare activity, public or private.[25] The usual result was that, on parliamentary issues at least, professional politicians ran rings around businessmen, who fought back ineffectually by parliamentary lobbying organised through such bodies as the Liberty and Property Defence League. Direct consultation between government departments and the business community, which was to be very important during and after the First World War, was confined to a few sectors: there were close links between the armaments and shipbuilding industries and the defence departments, though this generally meant that industry became the tool of government rather than vice versa; and the financial community, through the Bank of England, had very great influence over some aspects of monetary policy.[26] Dissatisfaction within the business community was the spring of action which was to be released by the First World War. The institutions of business politics – lobby groups, and trade and employers' associations – were ready to go to work on the issues of business politics – industrial relations, social welfare, commercial policy and tariffs, and state regulation of industry.

The First World War and its aftermath: institutions and issues

The Great War and 'reconstruction' shifted business opinion and the institutions through which it was expressed. The four themes of commercial policy, industrial relations, welfare, and state regulation were joined by an increased concern with direct state intervention in the economy. Although the most striking wartime innovations were also the most evanescent, the shock of controls during the war mobilised businessmen for post-war political activity. Familiar problems of declining staple exports and difficult industrial relations returned with the return of peace; and the party-political system was recast so that businessmen gravitated more naturally to the Conservative party, while the Labour party focused radical and socialist opposition.

In business politics the war's major events were the appearances of two 'peak organisations'. The Federation of British Industries, seeking to represent the whole of British industry in its relations with government, was set up in 1916. The National Confederation of Employers' Organisations appeared in 1919 to co-ordinate the views of the employers' associations in negotiations with the government and the TUC; its founders were suspicious of the steadfastness of the FBI. These developments are examined in chapter 3 below. Meanwhile trade and employers' associations grew in number and scope to meet post-war challenges in foreign trade[27] and industrial relations.[28] Between the wars government departments looked to representative associations for information: consultation with them could also lend legitimacy to government policy. In implementing the 1921 Safeguarding of Industry Act[29] and the 1932 Import Duties Act[30] the Board of Trade and the Import Duties Advisory Committee emphasised that submissions from industry would carry most weight if they were made by representative associations.

Consultation of this sort was largely cosmetic. As Tolliday shows in chapter 4, civil servants could easily play off one industrial interest against another and thus resist any pressure for a change of policy. Nevertheless, to the advocates of a 'middle way' of non-socialist economic planning in the 1930s, trade associations seemed a natural vehicle for devolved planning. In practice trade associations themselves resisted proposals made in 1934 by Harold Macmillan and Lord Melchett which would have associated them with the state by legislating for compulsory reorganisation by amalgamations if the majority in an industry desired such a course.[31] Where economic conditions justified it, trade associations were already taking the initiative in the reduction of competition, without involving the state except at arm's length: National Shipbuilders Securities Ltd., an offshoot of the secretive Shipbuilding Conference, bought up and scrapped redundant shipyards throughout the 1930s.[32] In other industries, where no consensus existed on the need for rationalisation, trade associations could be found as the focus of resistance to change.[33] During the Second World War the associations were drawn into the implementation of policy – a role which had sometimes been adopted in peacetime, for example over the 1921 Dyestuffs Act[34] – and this revived interest in their use for devolved planning. But the post-war Labour government was more concerned with nationalisation than with setting up a corporatist political framework: the 1947 Industrial Organisation and Development Act gave only trivial opportunities for trade associations, while the 1948 Monopolies Act invalidated the price-fixing role which had justified the existence of many associations.[35] Trade associations were to remain in the background until the creation of the National Economic Development Council in 1961.

Employers' associations fared rather better between the wars. The major federations dominated the NCEO and took advantage of the slump to roll back the position which the trade unions had established during the war.[36] The Engineering Employers' Federation, for example, reasserted the 'power to manage' in a high-handed lock-out in 1922,[37] and the National Federation of Building Trades Employers went from strength to strength while the builders' unions fragmented.[38] Outside the traditional industries such combative postures were less common. Dealing with assembly-line or continuous process work, outside the traditional management structures and craft allegiances which had shaped industrial relations before the war, large firms in such new industries as car assembly and chemicals could take a more flexible attitude.[39] Such firms were prominent also in the Mond–Turner talks in 1927, in which a group of businessmen led by Sir Alfred Mond of ICI discussed with leading trade unionists the broad principles of industrial change, an event which the major federations greeted coolly.[40]

The FBI and the NCEO both had to modify their early expectations of great political influence. Until 1930 the FBI was internally divided over the tariff issue;[41] its major political initiative was a yearly submission to the Chancellor asking for lower taxes, and it was consulted over details of commercial policy in the 1930s but over little else.[42] The NCEO was set up in the expectation that tripartite bargaining between government, employers and trade unions would become institutionalised. As the government withdrew from industrial relations it became a well-organised lobby. It dealt directly and in private with the Ministry of Labour and the Home Office over such matters as working hours and factory safety, where its influence was negative.[43] In public its leaders spoke out against policies which threatened to impose costs or restrictions on employers. Such attitudes were congenial to a large bloc in the parliamentary Conservative party, and it is hard to separate the industrial influence of the NCEO from a strong right-wing current of Conservative opinion, though NCEO leaders routinely claimed great influence over legislation. The FBI had a less obvious partisan role, especially because its leaders eschewed the partisan identification with 'capital' against 'labour' which the NCEO embraced.[44]

Business attitudes between the wars, especially to the state, reflect wartime turmoil. After the establishment of the Ministry of Munitions in 1915 raw material, price and wage controls were extended, somewhat haphazardly, to most of British industry.[45] Businessmen were recruited as temporary civil servants and even, after Lloyd George became prime minister in December 1916, as ministers. This gave real influence to leading businessmen in the management of the war economy, and launched a number of them on public careers which enhanced the overall influence of business in politics after the war. But even during the war most business recruits to government were convinced that the close relationship between business and government should not last beyond the armistice. On the other hand, the war seemed to strengthen the labour movement[46] and reinforce the arguments for an active trade policy: and here, the state might be the ally of business.

A number of minor demands for state intervention to support industry against foreign competitors were conceded by legislation in the early post-war years, but the tariff question stayed open. Business attitudes, as ever, were mixed. Even before 1914 the tariff debate had not divided businessmen on simple lines: not all steelmakers were protectionist, nor all cotton manufacturers Free Trade. Even the polarisation of attitudes between 'cosmopolitan' finance and protectionist heavy industry was rapidly breaking down, as banks and large industrial firms began to exchange directors who carried their opinions with them. The war accelerated a general drift towards protectionist sentiment, and in particular brought to prominence a number of banker–industrialists[48] who were well represented on official committees during the war and who took up leading positions in the peak organisations after the war, from which they pressed the protectionist case.[49] The blurring of distinctions between 'finance' and 'industry' was especially important in the 1920s. The two major economic policy issues were the tariff and the return to the Gold Standard. On grounds of economic theory one would expect a sharp clash over the return to Gold between protectionist industrialists and bankers who realised that a free market in gold implied a free market in everything else.[50] As Philip Williamson shows in chapter 7, no such clear division appeared: bankers, albeit in private, worried that the return to Gold at a parity of $4.86 would damage industry, and after 1929 were even prepared to press for protection and imperial preference. Industrialists complained about the timing of the return in 1925, but did not question the economic – and moral – logic of 'shackling ourselves to reality'[51] on which the policy decision was based.

Business attitudes to the tariff, similarly, were not clear cut between the wars. The post-war boom muted tariff demands even in the traditionally tariff-conscious steel industry. With the coming of recession, tariff calls were renewed, but pre-war divisions within industry were evident once more. The 1921 Safeguarding of Industries Act originated in wartime planning for a post-war economic struggle against Germany, but like other proposals made in that vein it was shelved in 1919 when it became clear that Germany was not a threat to British industry. When the economy slumped in 1921 it was hurriedly dusted off and presented to Parliament as a specific for unemployment. In Parliament it recreated the division between doctrinaire Free Traders and Tariff Reformers which had lain dormant since 1915; but as a tariff measure its effects were limited to a few minor industries. Nevertheless the steel producers, with the support of some leading Conservative politicians, pressed for its exploitation as a comprehensive protective measure. This was successfully resisted by cabinets of both parties, who had learned from the Conservative defeat in the 1923 election on a tariff platform that the electorate would not stand for a general tariff.[52]

Opinion moved steadily in favour of a tariff in the 1920s, led by the iron and steel industries. The 1929 crash was very persuasive, most notably in the FBI, where Free Trade opposition crumbled in 1930.[53] The economic emergency allowed Free Traders and Gold Standard bankers to abandon their economic principles, temporarily, with a clear conscience. Once the 1932 Import Duties Act had imposed tariffs, they were accepted by British industrialists and bankers as the foundation of policy. International cartel arrangements, favoured in many sectors as a defence against the aggressive trade policies of Japan and Germany, where predicated on the tariff.[54] The Government's policy of bilateral trade negotiations, which trade associations and the FBI supported by giving advice, used tariff reductions as bargaining counters.[55] Indeed, the 1932 Import Duties Act took the tariff question out of politics, not only in the sense that tariff-setting was delegated to the 'non-political' Import Duties Advisory Committee, but also in the sense that the tariff was henceforth taken for granted.

Business attitudes to state intervention between the wars were no less mixed than attitudes to the Gold Standard and the tariff. The FBI and other bodies during the war wanted government effort channelled through a Ministry of Industry which would somehow be responsible to industrialists as well as (or instead of) to Parliament. Nothing came of these initiatives.[56] Moreover as the fever of 'decontrol' spread in 1919 the business community seemed able to unite only on negatives. Sir Eric Geddes, himself a 'businessman in politics', laid plans for a Ministry of Transport which would improve the transport infrastructure by integrating road, rail, canal, and port services in government ownership. Bad transport facilities had been condemned by businessmen since the nineteenth century, but still a working coalition of industrialists, led by the transport interests, forced Geddes to withdraw his bill. Private electricity companies led another successful campaign against Geddes's scheme for a national reconstruction of the electricity supply industry.[57]

Thereafter, relations between government and industry began to thaw. The Lloyd George coalition, especially in its latter years, took a tough line with trade unions and succumbed to pressures for economy. Geddes's celebrated axe cut down even further what was left of his transport schemes. For the rest of the inter-war period Conservative governments predominated, and short-lived Labour governments were strikingly timid in their dealings with industry. After 1922 state intervention in the economy grew steadily but very slowly because neither politicians, officials, nor businessmen wanted it to grow any faster. The first major public investment in industry was the establishment of the National Grid as a result of the Electricity Supply Act of 1926. To appease the free-enterprise faithful, the Act committed the Grid to the care of a Central Electricity Board which, though a public body, was almost entirely beyond ministerial (and hence political) control. This was consistent with a pattern of government which Leslie Hannah has called 'government by subcontract': governments of all political colours, when forced to intervene in industry, preferred to devolve control of spending, or of the allocation of tariffs or licences, to bodies on which industry or banking were strongly represented.[58] Thus state intervention was able to grow steadily, despite a mock-battle between Conservative and Labour politicians about the respective merits of 'capitalism' and 'socialism'. Businessmen shared with politicians and civil servants the assumption that the state had a role, but a very limited one, in industry.

State intervention was sometimes so covert that its effect was blunted. After 1924 the Conservative Cabinet badly wanted to reconstruct the steel industry, but preferred to leave the work to the Bank of England. The Bank eventually set up the Securities Management Trust, an internal department to deal with industrial problems. The establishment of SMT at that time was in part a device to divert the newly installed Labour government from nationalising the Bank. In fact Philip Snowden, the new Chancellor, did not want the responsibility of helping the steel industry directly, and welcomed not only SMT but also the Bankers Industrial Development Company, set up in April 1930 as a consortium of private banks led by the Bank of England to provide capital for industrial reconstruction. The 1929 Labour government and its National successors had other ways to make an active industrial policy acceptable to industrialists. One such method is described by Richard Roberts in chapter 6 below. Sir Horace Wilson's practice of 'industrial diplomacy' made it possible to represent major initiatives such as the 1939 Cotton Spinning Industry Act simply as responses to industrial demands, when their provenance was in reality far more complicated. But the consequence of these methods was that the state could do only what the Bank of England or industry itself would do, and this was not usually very much.[59]

Indirect methods made state intervention acceptable to many industrialists in the staple trades, though the coal-owners throughout the period maintained a magnificent obstinacy in the face of economic disaster. In some of the newer industries the desire for state intervention was more positive, and was reciprocated by the government. Oil was an example, discussed below by Geoffrey Jones in chapter 9. Another was Imperial Chemical Industries, set up with government encouragement in 1926 as an alternative to an Anglo-American heavy chemical combine. A distinctive feature of ICI was its willingness to accept quasi-public responsibilities, such as building the Billingham plant in the 1930s to produce fertilisers for an imperial market which never materialised. Conversely, the National Government was prepared to help ICI with its plans to produce fuel oil by hydrogenating coal.[60] ICI could make profits with or without state support: other new industries looked for state support as a condition of existence. These included the small 'strategic' industries protected by the 1921 Safeguarding of Industries Act – such as optical glass and fine chemicals – and delicate new industries such as aircraft manufacture and air transport. The airframe industry survived entirely on the charity of the Air Ministry until the tables were turned by re-armament in the period discussed by George Peden in chapter 8 below. Air transport was the subject of a series of official committees, on which business was heavily represented, which consistently recommended the creation of a state-subsidised monopoly carrier on overseas routes. The outcome, in 1924, was Imperial Airways, which despite its lack of commercial success attracted no serious criticism from private industrialists.[61]

The creation of Imperial Airways, like the establishment of the National Grid, of ICI or of the Bank of England's industrial organs, was made possible by a network of businessmen, politicians and civil servants who co-operated to promote, but also control, state intervention in the economy.[62] Many of the businessmen concerned had risen to prominence in the First World War: Weir at the Air Ministry, Geddes at the Admiralty, Stanley at the Board of Trade and Sir Joseph Maclay at the Ministry of Shipping had all interrupted business careers to take ministerial office; Reginald McKenna, chairman of the Midland Bank during the 1920s, had been ejected from the Exchequer on the fall of Asquith's government in 1916. The accountants Sir William Peat and Sir William Plender had both given advice to wartime official committees. Peat also helped to found the Federation of British Industries, as did Harry McGowan, later of ICI. Weir, too, like Geddes, soon acquired a prominent position in the peak organisations, and also advised the government extensively after 1932 on armaments questions. Other notable members of this subset of the Great and the Good were of a younger generation. Sir Andrew Duncan, who became chairman of the British Iron and Steel Federation in 1934 after the transactions described below by Tolliday, and Sir Charles Bruce Gardner, who was imposed as President of the Society of British Aircraft Constructors by Neville Chamberlain in 1937, had both been associated with industry and the Bank of England's industrial departments.

A sociological analysis of such a small and heterogeneous group of businessmen would be fruitless, but some general points can be made about it. First, its members had no doctrinaire commitment to free enterprise *a l'outrance*, only to efficiency and managerial competence. Second, they were prepared to try any form of intervention, short of expropriation, to which businessmen would consent. Almost always governments were prepared to take their advice because they were confident that such men represented the business community. Conversely Geddes, Weir and others won businessmen's respect because they had the ear of government. Through this group British business between the wars was partly reconciled to state intervention in industry. In that way, much more than in its direct effect on the proportion of GNP accounted for by government spending, or in the models it threw up of interventionist institutions, the First World War helped to change the relationship between British industry and the state.

Finally one must consider the effects of the War on social welfare. Two conflicting strategies emerged among business organisations at the end of the war. The FBI put forward a scheme of generous benefits administered jointly by employers and workers and independent of the state: this reflected the traditions of pre-war welfare capitalism, and some of its protagonists had been prominent in the 1911 campaign against the National Insurance Act. The EEF explicitly rejected the notion of a comprehensive scheme run by employers, and declared that welfare, and especially unemployment provision, was the responsibility of the state and must be run as cheaply as possible.[63] Correspondingly, businessmen between the wars exhibited a spectrum of attitudes to welfare as a political end. The neo-paternalist expedient of running generous employers' welfare schemes was fairly common as an anti-union, anti-Labour device. Together with schemes of profit-sharing and employee shareholding, it was associated with 'new' industries such as chemicals and motor manufacture, as well as the growing multiple retailing sector; and enlightened employers such as Mond and Marcus Sieff were also prominent in the movement for rationalisation in the late 1920s and 'planning' in the 1930s. As in the pre-war period, affection for a welfare state run by and for private enterprise was characteristic of companies with profits to spare.[64]

Perhaps a more typical response, expressed between the wars by the National Confederation of Employers' Organisations, was a simple resistance to welfare schemes on the grounds that the cost would bear too heavily on industries struggling to survive against severe international competition. This range of views persisted until the Second World War. The Shipbuilding Employers' Federation and the Mining Association in evidence to the Beveridge Committee argued that the extensive welfare schemes envisaged were simply too expensive. The director of the British Employers' Confederation (the renamed NCEO) urged simply that 'we did not start this war to improve our social services'; an observation which could easily have fallen from the lips of Sir Allan Smith, the NCEO's co-founder, in 1918. On the other hand, McGowan and other directors of ICI were signatories of the 1942 'National Policy for Industry', which closely resembled the FBI's 1917 suggestions for corporate, rather than state paternalism. Ultimately, business attitudes to welfare depended largely on an estimate of whether the political benefit was worth the economic cost. By 1943, faced with the Beveridge Report and its public reception, 73% of businessmen believed the price was worth paying.[65]

The First World War and its aftermath: business and party politics

'Business methods' became a shibboleth for critics of the status quo in British politics during the First World War, but party politics did not fall hostage to a rampant capitalism. The Unionist Business Committee, led by the arch-Tariff Reformer W.A.S. Hewins, challenged the Unionist leadership on behalf of the back-benches and, *inter alia*, pressed for aggressive post-war measures against German trade.[66] A majority of members were businessmen-MPs, but its leaders were professional politicians, refighting the Tariff Reform argument within the Conservative party. Hewins was snubbed by businessmen when he tried to impose the 'scientific tariff' on the Balfour of Burleigh committee on post-war industrial policy.[67] After the 1918 Election the UBC fell into the background.

The 'Coupon' Election returned a higher proportion of businessmen to the House of Commons than ever before. The 'hard-faced men' had mostly been selected before the war, in readiness for the election expected in 1915.[68] Many Liberal businessman retired from politics, voluntarily or involuntarily, because of the Asquith–Lloyd George split in the Liberal party, but in their place a number of business candidates were recruited for the Coalition Liberals by Christopher Addison, the former Minister of Munitions who was Lloyd George's chief Liberal henchman.[69] After 1918, though, most business MPs were Conservatives and Liberal businessmen were prominent among defectors to the Conservatives in the 1920s. The businessmen, who made up 40.8% of the parliamentary Conservative party in the 1919 Parliament (compared with 24.8% in 1914), were exceptional in a number of ways. Representatives of manufacturing industry outnumbered representatives of commerce and finance (by 85 to 71) for the first time. Too old to expect ministerial advancement, and too inexperienced to offer a very sophisticated contribution to parliamentary politics in the turmoil of the post-war Coalition government, the new business MPs tended to leave politics rapidly, and the great majority of the 1918 cohort of 83 businessmen had retired from politics by 1924. Indeed the turnover of all businessmen in the Conservative party was very rapid in these years, with 204 businessmen entering in the four elections of 1918, 1922, 1923 and 1924, and 200 leaving in the same elections. After 1924 the proportion of businessmen in the parliamentary party settled to around 35% for the remainder of the inter-war period.[70]

These figures are a strong justification for treating the period 1918 to 1924 as exceptional in the history of business activity in Parliament, and the organisation and activity of businessmen-MPs in those years confirms this view. The Federation of British Industries and its close political ally, the British Commonwealth Union, both espoused the belief that businessmen, to obtain the influence they needed, must work outside normal party structures. Together these two bodies set up the Parliamentary Industrial Group, which was concerned in many of the attacks on the Government's industrial policy discussed above on pp. 11–12. Although the PIG continued to hold meetings until 1929, its period of greatest activity was between 1919 and 1923, when it agitated for decontrol, safeguarding, and a firm line against the trade union movement. Before 1924, when the 1918 cohort of businessmen-MPs ceased to be a significant factor on the Conservative back-bench, relations between business and the Conservative leadership were strained: Baldwin was especially distrusted by outspoken business representatives.[71]

After 1924 businessmen-MPs concentrated either on specific issues, such as the 1926 Electricity Supply Bill or the MacQuisten Bill in March 1925, which would have outlawed the trade union political levy, or worked through organisations that had a specific commitment to the tariff. In neither case could a distinct 'business lobby' be discerned, and businessmen-MPs were to be found on both sides of the intra-party debate. Both the National Union of Manufacturers, an organisation of mostly small or medium-sized firms committed to a tariff policy, and the British Commonwealth Union, which drew its support from larger firms but shared a commitment to tariffs and an anti-union policy, were drawn into the running battle between protectionists and Free Traders in Baldwin's 1924–29 cabinet. A critical step in the involvement of the BCU was the formation of the Empire Industries Association late in 1924, which drew much of its early support from the BCU and the Parliamentary Industrial Group. In 1926 the EIA absorbed the BCU, making itself the leading protectionist pressure group operating at Westminster.[72] It was, however, far more than a business interest group. Its leaders included former leaders of the Tariff Reform League such as Leopold Amery and Henry Page Croft, and also W.A.S. Hewins from the old Unionist Business Committee. Moreover, these were not merely disgruntled back-benchers: Amery was in the Cabinet, prominent among those who were pressing Baldwin to abandon the pledges made at the 1924 election against the introduction of a general tariff. With Neville Chamberlain, who played a large part behind the scenes in the EIA, Amery used the EIA as a lever against Baldwin. By attracting as many as two hundred Conservative back-benchers, including prominent former ministers such as Sir Robert Horne, to his cause, he gravely threatened the security of Baldwin's leadership of the party in 1928, which was apparently his principal aim. In pursuit of that aim, he was also prepared to manipulate the activities of the EIA according to a political rather than an industrial logic, withholding public support for protectionist demands when he judged that they did not suit his cabinet tactics. Nevertheless, industry paid well for the propagation of Tariff Reform in the late 1920s, and, when Baldwin's Government fell, gave Amery further support to found the Empire Economic Union, an ally of Lord Beaverbrook's 'Empire Free Trade' campaign which was also designed principally to remove Baldwin from the Conservative leadership.[73]

The passage of the Import Duties Act in 1932 defused the parliamentary tariff controversy, leaving businessmen in Parliament without a great issue around which to combine. But this was hardly a source of weakness. The industrial policy of the National Government, predicated on tariffs and an arm's-length relationship with industry, gave little offence to any industrial interest, and little trouble came from a weak Labour opposition. The Government's manifest willingness to help protesting industries with measures such as the tramp shipping subsidy of 1935 was recognised. For the ideologically minded, ministers made ringing declarations of support for free enterprise; few were as anxious as Sir Jonah Walker Smith, director of the National Federation of Building Trades Employers and Conservative MP for Barrow from 1931 to 1935, who took fright in 1934 that even the National Government might bow to the pressures of democracy and nationalise the building industry.[74] The power of business in parliament was therefore defined and used negatively in the 1930s: one of the few significant examples of a business challenge to government policy was the rejection of Neville Chamberlain's proposed armaments levy in 1937, and that challenge was immediately successful.[75] For the most part, business wishes were met by the Government's cautious expansion of social services expenditure, modest encouragement to specific industries, and open commitment to non-interference. Conservative party policy for industry, as defined in election programmes, was elaborated in consultation with industrialists.[76] In Parliament, business was strong enough to remain passive.

The structure of the Conservative party in Parliament also made for business passivity after the tariff question was settled. Landowners had suffered a sharp decline in wealth and status immediately after the First World War; one result was that they were taking industrial, banking and commercial directorships to augment falling incomes and investing the proceeds of land sales in industrial securities. Within the business community, as well, diversity of interests had become more common. As a result of these changes in the structure of wealth-holding, a majority of Conservative (and National Liberal) MPs – far more than those defined by McEwen as 'businessmen' – had substantial business interests, and these interests were not so clearly confined to single industries or to industry rather than finance as before 1914.[77] But at the same time leading businessmen were less likely to be MPs than before the First World War: the inter-war merger movement put ever larger sections of British industry under the control of a few men who were very unlikely indeed to find the time to be MPs though many of them (McGowan of ICI is a prime example) accepted peerages. Thus while the social and economic background of the business and the political elites converged, the two remained separate at the highest level; and businessmen-MPs no longer combined political activity with entrepreneurial control so completely as they had done before 1914. More and more, MPs were professional politicians using – often using up – personal wealth gained from family businesses as a foundation for a political career which would be longer and more demanding than the relaxing sojourn on the back-benches which had been for many Victorian businessmen the distraction of late middle age. Parliamentary businessmen, more than ever, accepted the twin political disciplines of the electorate and the party whip. It was therefore outside Parliament, in the activities of business associations and in the private meetings of leading businessmen with ministers and officials, that British business took political action between the wars.

Business and politics: the future for research

There can be no simple summary of the role of businessmen in British politics in the first half of the twentieth century, as the account above makes clear. Nor is it possible to discuss with finality the impact of politics on the industrial economy in that period. Political intervention in business affairs, whether at the insistance of businessmen or of their political opponents, undeniably had ambiguous effects, as in the case of ICI's unhappy fertiliser ventures; but some of the initiatives of the inter-war period, such as the National Grid, have had more praise from historians than they ever had at the time. It is easy to show that political decisions had few good effects on economic activity and that well-publicised 'corporatist' agreements between the government and the two sides of industry did not solve the economic problems of low productivity and high costs which had first inspired them: but historians must be interested in unintended ill effects just as much as in unfulfilled expectations. Considering the importance to twentieth century Britain of industry and its performance, there is clearly a great deal of research yet to be done on business politics.

The greatest obstacle is institutional: economic and political historians are trained separately, often work in separate university departments, rarely read each other's books, use different sources and methods, and often fail to appreciate the complexities of each other's work. Yet there are obvious areas in which they could and should co-operate.

Perhaps the greatest need is for more study of the evolution of government policy towards industry. This would require research in all the traditional sources for political and administrative history, but there is a wealth of material in the archives of companies and business organisations which conventionally falls to economic historians to exploit. Work has already been published on the nationalised industries, but the subject of government policy towards private industry, and the influence of private industry on the making of policy, is barely touched.[78] Another major area for exploration is business political activity about labour relations and welfare legislation. Recent work on the labour and welfare policies of company managements has reminded us that employers rather than the government created the framework of modern industrial relations: the worker dealt first with his boss. But the political conditions that allowed this to come about did not happen by accident. Employers, sometimes working as individuals but often through representative associations, were constantly alert to keep the government out of industrial relations and welfare. Such activities by the 'peak associations' were probably less important than Middlemas has suggested but the efforts of individuals and industry-level employers' federations are largely unexplored.[79] Such studies could reveal a much more convincing picture of the relations between 'capital' and 'the state' than either conventional Marxism or the 'corporate bias' theories which have recently been fashionable. Finally there is the area of party politics, which suffers greatly from polemic. An account of the industrial and financial policy of the Conservative party in the early twentieth century is long overdue: it would demand an examination of the role of businessmen not only in Parliament but also in local and national party organisations. Business financing of the Conservative and Liberal parties (and the SDP in our own time) would repay a dispassionate examination, using both company and conventional political records. Here again the relationship of 'capital' and 'the state' can be reduced to empirically testable questions on which historians of different specialisms can co-operate.

Readers from many disciplines will be able to add to this preliminary list. The study of business politics, at the intersection of economic and political history, has far to go. The essays that follow are at the beginning, not the end of the road.

2 Business, Politics, and Municipal Socialism

Richard Roberts

I

'Municipal trading seems a very simple matter of business', wrote playwright and radical pamphleteer George Bernard Shaw, 'yet it is conceivable by a sensible man that the political struggle over it may come nearer to a civil war than any issue raised in England since the Reform Bill of 1832'.[1] Shaw's statement, though knowingly exaggerated, reflects the impassioned temper of the public debate on municipal trading which took place in the last years of the 1890s and the first decade of the twentieth century. The point of principle around which the controversy revolved was the limit to the legitimate extent of the economic undertakings of public bodies. The immediate issue was whether the utility industries were to remain in private hands or be taken over by local authorities. Although it was local government which threatened the private utility undertakings the political controversy was conducted at the national level and it was to Parliament that those seeking to curb the economic activities of local authorities looked. The episode is of interest as an early attempt on the part of certain business interests and militant anti-socialists to stifle the emergent municipal public sector.

II

The business context to the controversy was the rapid extension of municipal trading – the ownership and operation of commercial undertakings by local authorities – which was taking place at the time.[2] Between the mid-1890s and mid-1900s the number of towns of England and Wales in which consumers received municipal supply of water increased from approximately 495 to 620, of gas from 200 to 270, of electricity from 25 to 240, and of tramway services from 30 to 160. Simultaneous with the unprecedented growth of the municipal ownership of utility undertakings was an upsurge in the applications of local authorities for 'novel powers' – powers sought in local bills for which there was no existing statutory consent – to engage in new economic activities.[3] A 'remarkable programme of municipal adventure', commented the compiler of a catalogue of recent applications for novel powers in 1903, upon the proposed extensions to the economic activities of local authorities.[4]

The political context was the growing acceptance of 'collectivism' in Britain. Dicey's account of the rise of collectivism, the increasing interference of public bodies in the lives of the individual members of society, published in 1905, cited municipal trading as another manifestation of the trend which he observed in the framing of legislation.[5] The spectre of collectivism provoked a political reaction and led to the formation of anti-collectivist and anti-socialist organisations, such as the Liberty and Property Defence League, to champion 'individualism'.[6] When the rapid increase in municipal trading was publicly exposed, at the end of the 1890s, the anti-collectivist activists quickly turned it into a political issue.

The municipal ownership of utilities had long been urged by radicals. In 1834 Thomas Hopkins of Manchester, for instance, had advocated that 'all public works should belong to the town . . . for they generally acted under the influence of more elevated feelings than those whose principal aim was profit'.[7] Joseph Chamberlain, while mayor of Birmingham between 1873 and 1876, had pushed through the takeover of the local gas and water supply, and later as President of the Board of Trade had been responsible for the passage of an act governing the establishment of electricity undertakings generally regarded as highly favourable to local authorities.[8] J.F.B. Firth, a leading London radical of the 1860s and 1870s, was also an enthusiast for the municipal supply of utilities and expressed the hope that it would be one of the benefits which would derive from the achievement of the reform of the capital's local government, for which he worked for so long.[9]

The provision of utility supply by the newly established London County Council was an important platform of Sidney Webb's *London Programme* published in 1891 as the Fabian manifesto for the future government of the metropolis. Webb, however, added a socialist dimension to the calls for local authority ownership of utilities by his presentation of the achievement of municipal proprietorship as a step towards the collective ownership of the means of production.[10] The Fabian Society's two 'Municipal Series' of tracts, published in 1891 and in 1897–1900, were among their most widely read publications.[11] They argued the case for the municipal ownership of water, gas, tramways and markets, and, more controversially, the drink trade, milk supply, pawn shops, slaughterhouses, bakeries, hospitals, insurance, and the River Thames steamboats, and attracted public attention, particularly in London, to the proposals. The tracts disseminated the Fabian idea of 'municipal socialism' and began the association in the public mind between municipal trading and socialism.

Webb himself had no illusions that a deliberately socialist intention had motivated local authorities to take over utility undertakings. 'No scientific policy or consistent theory has inspired our town and country councillors in all their manifold action', he wrote in his review of 'The course of municipal socialism' which appeared in the *Labour Annual* of 1896. 'Where they have been socialistic, they have, in nearly every case, been so without knowing it, the unconscious results of a stream of tendency beyond their ken.'[12] For those in search of an explanation for the simultaneous widespread increase in the municipal ownership of utilities, however, municipal socialism offered a plausible answer. It appeared that the phenomenon was the result of the common conversion of local authorities to collectivism. The campaign against municipal trading which was launched at the end of the 1890s had the objective of alerting the public to the dangers of collectivism in municipal form, and the practical aim of stopping the extension of local authority ownership of industry.

III

The interests directly threatened by the growth of municipal trading were the utility companies. It was the owners and promoters of electrical industry and tramway industry companies who took the initiative to bring the growth of municipal ownership to public attention. The campaign was the brainchild of the group of businessmen who met regularly at the Electrical Trades Section of the London Chamber of Commerce to discuss the state of the industry. The chairman of the Electrical Trades Section, and later of the Municipal Trading Committee of the London Chamber of Commerce formed in March 1899, was Sidney Morse, a solicitor to twenty-nine electrical traction or electricity supply companies including the British Electrical Traction Company.[13] He was succeeded as Chairman of the Electrical Trades Section by Percy Sellon, an eminent electrical engineer. Emile Garcke, an ever present party to the controversy, was the founder and managing director of the British Electrical Traction Company, the foremost tramway firm and an organisation with extensive electrical industry interests. He was chairman of seven BETC subsidiaries, a director of a further nineteen companies and a publisher of *Garcke's Manual*, the industry's trade directory. He made numerous public addresses on municipal trading and in 1907 published a pamphlet on the development of electricity in Britain blaming its backwardness upon municipal interference. Sir Charles Rivers-Wilson, a leading member of the Liberty and Property Defence League, was the Chairman of the BETC and another electrical company. William Madgen was a director of twelve electrical companies and managing director of the Electrical

Power Distribution Company. Morse, Madgen, and Garcke gave evidence to the Select Committee on Municipal Trading on the damaging effects of municipal ownership upon the progress of electricity supply and electrical traction. The involvement of these leaders of the electrical industry in the campaign against municipal trading earned the opponents of local authority ownership of utilities the soubriquet 'the electric light wire pullers'.[14]

The British Electric Traction Company and its managing director were treated with singular hostility by the municipal press and by supporters of municipal trading. The company was repeatedly accused of being the paymaster of the campaign and of the Industrial Freedom League. The Industrial Freedom League, an organisation described contemptuously by the *Municipal Journal* as 'the mouth-piece of Emile Garcke', was established in May 1902 with Lord Avebury as President to promote the formation of local groups, such as Manchester's Anti-Municipal Trading League, to act as grassroots watch-dogs over the trading activities of local authorities.[15] While there is no doubt that Garcke sympathised with the aims of the League, and he may have contributed personally to its funds, the contributions made by the British Electric Traction Company were small, amounting to no more than £375 in total between 1902 and 1904.[16] The company made a further financial contribution to the anti-municipal campaign through its payment of £100 per month to Robert Porter, an anti-municipal journalist, 'in consideration for his services'. The payments were sanctioned by the Board in September 1902 but it is not clear for how long they continued.[17] These subventions fell far short of the scale of funding suggested by the correspondents of the *Municipal Journal*. Contrary to their conspiratorial interpretations, criticism of municipal trading was not confined to clients of the BETC 'octopus'.

The members of the Electrical Trades Section were supported in their stand against municipal trading by individuals and organisations worried by the advance of 'collectivism'. Lord Avebury, a banker and prominent Liberal member of Parliament, and President of the Association of British Chambers of Commerce from 1900, took a leading part in the fight. He was a staunch opponent of public enterprise whether it was state ownership of the telephone or municipal ownership of utilities.[18] The liberal libertarian convictions which prompted his stand against the collective ownership of industry were set forth in his volume *On Municipal and National Trading* published in 1906. Earl Wemyss committed both personal effort and the resources of the Liberty and Property Defence League, of which he was president, to the struggle against municipal trading. Members of the League arranged for the insertion of articles attacking municipal trading in the press and Wemyss himself apparently secured the publication of a series of seventeen hostile articles on the subject in *The Times* in 1902 which caused great offence in town halls.[19] Wemyss was a veteran campaigner against socialism and saw the struggle to stop municipal trading as but another campaign in the wider war.[20] 'What', he demanded, 'is really at the bottom, more or less, of all this aspiration for state and municipal trading? The desire to make the state or municipality omnipotent and to put individuals under the heels of officialism.'[21]

Businessmen critics contributed examples of the inefficiency of municipal enterprise and the alleged abuses of power by local authorities. They also took up the broader themes. Sir Charles Rivers-Wilson, for instance, connected contemporary economic preoccupations, Britain's declining share of world trade and the industrial threat from Germany, with the struggle against municipal trading. On the occasion of the inaugural meeting of the Industrial Freedom League, he told his audience that, 'if we are to hold – I will not say maintain our supremacy – but even to hold our own with other countries, we must battle with this most insidious foe'.[22] Sidney Morse took up another issue, the abolition of private property, towards which he claimed municipal trading was the first step. It would 'do away with private enterprise' he predicted before a London Chamber of Commerce dinner in April 1900.[23]

The identity of private enterprise and progress was a fundamental conviction of the anti-collectivist ideologues. 'The history of arts, inventions, manufacturers, of all ages and all countries', wrote Robert Porter, 'has demonstrated that individual progress has invariably been the work of individual effort, and not of states or municipalities, or of organisations of officials.'[24] The growth of municipal trading thus threatened to undermine the nation's industry and culture. Towler, an extreme exponent of the virtues of individualism, added municipal trading to the list of collectivist influences sapping the national spirit of individual enterprise and contributing, in the fashionable language of eugenics, to the decline of the race.

> The conclusion, therefore, to which we are driven is that the balance between individualism and state action has been upset by the introduction of municipal trade. We are entering upon a barren region of human stagnation, where reigns a steady decay of all the faculties making for the good development of the race . . . Effort is stunted intelligence weakened, and responsibility destroyed.[25]

Supporters of municipal trading spoke up in its favour against the onslaught of criticism. The case for the local authorities was presented in two parts. The first part was defensive; accusations were answered and examples were given to illustrate the achievements of municipal undertakings. The second part was counter-offensive; the benefits of municipal ownership were enumerated and the motives for municipalisation expounded.

Robert Donald, editor of the *Municipal Journal*, was often called upon to put the local authority point of view. Customarily, he dealt first with the objections to municipal trading, 'one by one, and set forth the other case'.[26] He then turned to the positive advantages of municipal trading. Although he asserted that it could be shown that municipal enterprises earned respectable rates of return, this was not the reckoning by which he, or fellow radicals, measured success. 'There is in every city, as the results of municipal work', he wrote, 'a social and moral balance sheet which cannot be represented in figures, but the effect of which is enjoyed by all in the lives saved from disease, in a higher standard of living, and in an amelioration of the social conditions of the whole community.'[27]

Fabian authors also devoted space to dismissing the arguments against the municipal ownership of utilities. Shaw even took the trouble to refute 'new accusations against municipal trading' – that it led to 'irreligion and licentiousness', that it stood in the way of tariff reform, and that it drove capital out of the country.[28] 'Impudence', was his description of these rather desperate charges. The socialist pamphleteers put particular stress upon exposure of the 'evils of private trading' and the 'anti-social' behaviour of commercial companies.[29] Underlying their arguments was the implict, and occasionally explicit, identification of municipal ownership with municipal socialism.

The portrayal of municipal ownership as socialism suited the tendentious purposes of both socialists and anti-socialists. The former cited it as a shining example of socialism in practice; the latter, as a warning against the creeping collectivism which infected the body politic. Many local councillors, however, were distressed by the identity. They protested that the achievement of socialism was not their intention nor would it be the result of their actions. 'These things are not socialism at all', exclaimed Lord Rosebery, a former Progressive councillor, 'they are a vital necessity for a great city'.[30] Radicals such as Robert Donald were also eager to repudiate the term municipal socialism. 'It has none of the characteristics of socialism', he wrote, 'municipal ownership is more correctly described as a corporative undertaking in which all citizens are shareholders and directly or indirectly participate in the benefits'.[31] Donald attacked the use of the term because it provoked a hostile public reaction which hindered the progress of constructive local government. Shaw also arrived at the conclusion that crowing over the impending arrival of socialism was counter-productive, and he accused *The Times* of wilfully applying the label municipal socialism to discredit the policies of the London County Council Progressives.[32]

The reaction of local councillors to the claims of collectivist motives reveals a division in the ranks of businessmen in their attitude to municipal trading. Provincial businessmen, who were well represented on their local authorities, supported the municipal proprietorship of utilities if it promised cheaper and more plentiful supplies. The divergence between their views and those of their metropolitan counterparts who launched the campaign is reflected in the monthly reports of the deliberations of provincial chambers of commerce carried in the *Chamber of Commerce Journal*. While the London Chamber of Commerce was preoccupied by the subject during 1899 and 1900, it was rarely raised in provincial chambers. When Sidney Morse sought the endorsement of the conference of the Association of Chambers of Commerce in April 1900 for his motion calling upon the government 'to define the limits to municipal trading . . . and pending the contemplated inquiry no enlarged powers for trading purposes be conferred on municipalities' several provincial representatives spoke against it and a delegate from Warrington described it as 'a retrograde proposal'.[33] The conference declined to approve Morse's motion as it stood and instead passed an amended version which he described as 'amounting to nothing'.

Nevertheless, the campaign did enjoy some success. The opponents of municipal trading achieved the objective of drawing public attention to the issue and provoked a vigorous controversy among metropolitan politicians, businessmen, and journalists. Moreover, they managed to get the subject raised in the forum which mattered most if action was to result from their initiative, the House of Commons.

IV

The incident which prompted the members of the Electrical Trades Section to action was the rejection of a private Bill promoted by an electrical company, the General Power Distribution Company, in 1898.[34] The Bill, the first bulk power measure to come before Parliament, proposed the establishment of a company to supply power to the district around Chesterfield, an area of over a million inhabitants, most of whom were not already consumers despite the acquisition of electricity provisional orders by the urban local authorities. By production of electricity on a large scale at the pithead and use of the most recent technology for distribution the company was confident of being able to supply a unit of electricity at a fraction of the cost of the small generators appropriate to the requirements of an individual local authority area. The promoters of the power company argued that everyone would benefit from the economies of large-scale production: local authorities would receive bulk power at a cheaper rate than they could produce it themselves; local industry, which was staunchly behind the measure, would get cheap power; households would be able to afford domestic electric lighting; the company would prosper as falling price led to a growth in demand and further economies of scale in production. Bulk generation appeared to promise private promoters the means of wresting control of the industry from local authorities and the bill was regarded as a test case by both parties.

The Chesterfield area's local authorities regarded the scheme with deep suspicion. They saw the company as an alien intruder which threatened to deprive them of control over local affairs. Their alarm was widely shared by local authorities that were not directly affected by the measure but recognised the threat which the spread of bulk power companies might pose to their own parochial scale electrical enterprises. They mobilised opposition through the Association of Municipal Corporations which led to the rejection of the Bill at its second reading.

Parliament's decision dismayed not only the electrical interests but many people, both inside and outside the House, who were astonished at the ability of the local authority lobby to mobilise members against a seemingly sensible scheme. The government recognised that the episode raised important issues and established a Joint Select Committee under Lord Cross to examine the development of electricity supply and make recommendations about the principles that should govern the granting of franchises. The Cross Committee's report, published towards the end of 1898, recognised the advantages of bulk power supply and recommended measures which would encourage the establishment of power companies. The rejection of the General Power Company's re-submitted Bill in 1899, despite the Cross Committee's report, seemed to confirm suspicions that local authorities were more concerned to protect their vested interests than to promote the public good and reinforced the calls for an inquiry into the whole vexed question of municipal trading.[35]

Private enterprise's counter-offensive against municipal trading was launched in early 1899. In January the Electrical Trades Section passed a resolution, 'that the scope and scale of municipal enterprise in opposition to and exclusion of private enterprise should be defined'.[36] The cause was taken up by the Council of the London Chamber of Commerce with the ultimate objective of securing legislation, or at least a change in administrative practice, to halt the spread of the municipal ownership of utility enterprises and, if possible, to reverse the trend. The preliminary to action was the establishment of a consensus as to the legitimate spheres of private and municipal enterprise. To this end the establishment of an official inquiry into the question of municipal trading was urged as a first step. In the meantime, pending the results of the inquiry, the Chamber of Commerce demanded a moratorium upon further municipalisation of private enterprises and the suspension of the issuing of provisional orders to local authorities for the establishment of undertakings in competition with private firms.

On 1 February 1899 a paper was read to the Society of Arts, a meeting place of politicians and industrialists of anti-collectivist persuasion, bringing to their attention the recent rapid increase in municipal trading.[37] Sir Henry Fowler raised the issue in the Commons and asked for the publication of a statistical paper to show the extent of the municipal ownership of utilities.[38] The London Chamber of Commerce and the Liberty and Property Defence League mobilised provincial support and between 21 February and 3 March 293 petitions from chambers of commerce, employers' federations, companies and ratepayers' associations were presented to Parliament asking for an inquiry into municipal trading.[39] On 2 March 1899, in response to requests by several members, Arthur Balfour, Leader of the House, promised 'to proceed at once to appoint the committee'.[40]

Although Balfour was often reminded of his words it was not until a year later that the Joint Select Committee on Municipal Trading was appointed. The delay was a reflection of the contentiousness of the issue. While it was by no means an issue of universal interest among members, the partisans of the opposing camps had strong feelings.[41] Municipal sympathisers saw the call for an inquiry as an attack upon local authorities and argued forcefully against the establishment of the select committee. Balfour himself apparently had misgivings though he justified his repeated refusals to name a date for the appointment of a committee on the grounds of inadequate time for debate that session. His procrastination was to no avail and the persistent reminders of members eventually obliged him to act.

The parliamentary debate on municipal trading opened on 29 March 1900 on the government's motion for the appointment of a committee 'to consider and report as to the principles which should govern the powers given by Bills and Provisional Orders to municipal and other local authorities for industrial enterprise'.[42] Members in favour of the establishment of a committee expressed hopes that 'the result of the inquiry will be that certain rules will be laid down under which municipal enterprises will be properly regulated in the future'.[43] The President of the Board of Trade supported the proposal because it offered the prospect of relieving the confusion of the Board's officials who 'require to have some kind of direction, such as that suggested to enable us to deal properly with the constant applications that are being made to us by corporations'.[44]

Opponents of the inquiry waged a vigorous resistance in Parliament. The demands for the appointment of the committee were attacked by John Burns as 'deferring to that body of company promoters *in excelsis*, the Liberty and Property Defence League', and 'pandering to the ignorant prejudices of Lord Wemyss and the gang of company promoters who met at the Society of Arts three months ago'.[45] The inquiry was portrayed as an insult to the integrity and responsibility of local authorities in the conduct not only of trading enterprises but of every local government function. 'Let me ask the House', appealed Sir Albert Rollitt, President of the Association of Municipal Corporations, 'to seriously consider how the municipalities work for the health and strength of the people, and whether these have been built up by being limited within hard-and-fast bounds?'[46] Despite his plea the motion to appoint the Joint Select Committee on Municipal Trading was approved by 141 votes to 67 on 5 April 1900.

The select committee's terms of reference stated that it was to gather evidence with the objective of establishing 'the principles which should govern powers given . . . to . . . local authorities for industrial enterprise'. It sat for sixteen days between 18 May and 27 July 1900 taking evidence from senior civil servants, industrialists, local councillors and local government officers. The session drew to a close with the committee feeling that its investigations were by no means through. Its proceedings had not elicited self-evident principles defining the legitimate limits to municipal trading, and the members were unable to draw the requested guidelines. Their report consisted of a recommendation that the committee should be reappointed in the next session further to consider the question.

The failure of the select committee to offer a definition of the limits to the municipal ownership of industry was a disappointment to the opponents of municipal trading. It was a tactical reverse since it was plain that their initial strategy to establish a clear boundary to municipal activity had not succeeded. The leaders of the attack pressed for the re-establishment of the select committee but they also called for other anti-municipal measures which included pressure for tighter administrative constraints upon the behaviour of local authorities, private member initiatives to restrict the economic activities of local government, and an intensification of the extra-parliamentary propaganda campaign against municipal trading.

The reappointment of the select committee was raised regularly in the House but action was deferred on account of the problem of finding parliamentary time. By the time that the re-establishment of the committee was moved, in June 1903, the public controversy had produced a plethora of contradictory evidence on the advantages and disadvantages of municipal ownership. The focus of the public debate had shifted from the issues of broad principle to arguments about the respective performances of undertakings under the alternative forms of ownership. The committee made no fresh attempt to establish general guidelines governing the scope of municipal trading but restricted its inquiries to the accounting practices of local authorities. Critics alleged that dubious accounting disguised the true performance of municipal trading enterprises, misleading the public and confusing the debate on the merits of municipal trading. The demand for an investigation into accounting practices was also a tactical move on the part of the opponents of municipal ownership who believed that any tightening of procedures could only make life more difficult for local authorities. Although the committee's report made several specific proposals for the improvement of municipal accounts, it offered no support for the contention that they were grossly misleading.[47]

The first hope of the opponents of municipal trading, for a parliamentary inquiry which would lead to government action, brought them no satisfaction. Frustrated by the Government's indifference, back-benchers promoted private members' measures to achieve their objectives. An Electricity Supply Bill was introduced in 1904 which sought to remove the local authority veto upon the granting of electrical provisional orders and a Municipal Borrowing Bill in 1905, which had the purpose of imposing a statutory ceiling to local authority borrowing.[48] Both Bills failed. A further reverse to the interests of private enterprise in the utility industries was the non-renewal of the Light Railways Act of 1896 upon its expiry in December 1902 since the measure was much more favourable to companies than the Tramways Act of 1870.

There was no majority in Parliament for the motions of the staunch opponents of municipal trading. Although the anti-municipal lobby blamed the sinister influence of the Association of Municipal Corporations the defeats were really victories for moderate opinion. Most members found the fervour of the anti-municipal zealots as disturbing as that of municipal socialists. *The Economist*'s leader writer spoke for them in 1903 when he wrote,

> For our part, without at all ignoring the dangers which may attend municipal trading in some of the forms which it now takes, and while recognising the need for some greater safeguards than now exist against abuse and mismanagement, we look upon municipal institutions as providing, to a large extent, the very salt of English life.[49]

While the campaigns in Parliament and the press to restrict municipal trading failed to secure legislation they enjoyed a limited success in Whitehall and in town halls. The borrowing terms allowed by select committees on local bills became more stringent following the prompting of the Local Government Board and the recommendations of the 1902 Select Committee on the Repayment of Loans by Local Authorities.[50] The select committees that examined local bills became increasingly reluctant to accept pleas of local circumstances as the justification for allowing 'novel powers'. Only clauses with precise precedent or statutory sanction were allowed. The campaign led to a stricter exercise of the discretionary powers of the Local Government Board and the Board of Trade respecting the repayment terms of loans raised by provisional orders under general statutes. The Treasury added its weight to the growing administrative hostility to increases in local authority borrowing. The climax of Whitehall's antagonism to local government was the outburst by the Chancellor, Austen Chamberlain, in his Budget speech of March 1904 when he accused the municipalities of having 'spoiled the money market by their own large demands' and threatened that restrictions might be necessary.[51]

The campaign also set local opponents of municipal expenditure on the offensive against municipal trading. It provided new evidence of municipal extravagance to the ratepayers' associations which proliferated in the late 1890s and 1900s as a result of the increases in municipal expenditure and consequent rates rises. 'With accumulating municipal indebtedness and increasing local taxation the plain everyday ratepayer who has no axe to grind is beginning to ask for an accounting', wrote Robert Porter in the American journal *Municipal Affairs* in 1902. 'From now on', he concluded, 'it may fairly be assumed that both municipal trading and municipal socialism in Great Britain have been compelled to assume the defensive.'[52]

Contrary to Porter's expectations the local authorities conducted a successful defence of their gains until the danger passed. The failure of the select committees to recommend general reforms had made the prospect of action remote but the election of the Liberal administration in December 1905 put paid finally to any chance of a restrictive measure. The Prime Minister, Sir Henry Campbell Bannerman, told the members of the Association of Municipal Corporations as much at their annual conference in 1906. 'Parliament is bound', he said, 'to see that in their higher efforts, in their perhaps more adventurous experiments, and in all the directions to which the genius of their rulers can be turned [municipalities shall] at least not be hampered and hindered by obsolete, or unnecessary or galling restrictions.'[53]

V

The business interests that initiated the controversy over municipal trading lost the argument. Despite the vociferous support of anti-socialist allies they were unable to persuade a Conservative administration to take action to halt the municipal takeover of their industries.

The allegations of an ideologically based collectivist purpose on the part of local authorities were never convincing except to those searching for a conspiracy. After all, although Labour representation was increasing on local authorities, the number of councils with an avowedly socialist majority prior to the First World War was no more than a handful of London boroughs. As for the predictions of the dire social and economic consequences of municipal trading, most local councillors were prepared to live dangerously and ignored the warnings. Even the counsel of *The Times* against credulous good intentions fell on deaf ears; 'whether they realise the fact or not, and whatever their motives may be, the local authorities in question are undoubtedly playing the socialist game'.[54]

'Whatever their motives may be', asked *The Times*. To the majority of local representatives the real reasons for the municipal ownership of utilities were not in doubt. They were a combination of concern for the welfare of the local community, dissatisfaction with the services provided by companies, dislike of outside control of basic local services, a desire to put the profits of trading undertakings to public purposes, and perhaps an element of calculated self-interest on the part of local businessmen. These locally determined and thoroughly utilitarian objectives of municipal supply account for the provincial acceptance of this form of public ownership of industry at the turn of the century and explain the fund of public and parliamentary good will towards the municipal trading undertakings.

But if ideology was not the answer, why else did so many local authorities commence utility supply in the decade from the mid-1890s to the mid-1900s? Several economic factors have been identified that affected all local authorities at the time, notably, the level of interest rates, the boom in residential building, demographic changes which produced an acceleration in the rate of population and family formation, and a spate of private utility company promotions.[55] The rapid growth in municipal trading appears to have been a result of stimuli to demand for utility services and calls for public ownership given by these factors in conjunction with expanded expectations of local authority services.

In a perspective spanning the last century, the controversy over municipal trading may be seen as a significant episode in the progress of the public sector of the British economy. The legitimacy and expediency of the collective ownership of industrial undertakings was forthrightly challenged and vigorously debated in public. The failure of the campaign to stop the spread of municipal ownership resulted in the establishment of a sizeable municipal public sector before 1914.

3 The Politics of 'Organised Business' in the First World War

John Turner

I

The appearance of two 'peak organisations' for British industry – the Federation of British Industries and the National Confederation of Employers' Organisations – was among the more durable political consequences of the First World War. The FBI was founded in 1916 by a number of leading industrialists who hoped that it would be able to speak with authority as the representative of British industry to government. The NCEO was created in 1919 to give coherence to the employers' position in negotiations with the government and the trade union movement. Although the occasion for its birth was the National Industrial Conference of February 1919, its conception was rooted in wartime conditions. Relations between the two bodies were never easy, but between the wars they embodied the political views of big business and tried, with varying success, to influence government policy towards industry, the labour movement, and economic affairs in general. Their emergence during the war owed much to the ebb and flow of state intervention in the economy, but was also in part a response to labour militancy and in part a reflection of the new acceptability, in wartime political conditions, of a xenophobic commercial nationalism. Post-war economic and labour conditions ensured that the FBI and the NCEO did not follow the National Confederation of Associated Employers of Labour and the Employers' Parliamentary Council into oblivion; but the two organisations were conceived in circumstances very different from those which allowed them to survive, and this study emphasises the explanation of their wartime conception.[1]

II

Disquiet in the munitions industries was the catalyst for the development of both the major peak organisations. In March 1915 the Chancellor of the Exchequer, David Lloyd George, initiated the 'Treasury Agreements' with trade unions in the armaments industries in an attempt to increase production. In return for the abrogation of the right to strike and the abandonment of restrictive practices, especially over the employment of women and unapprenticed men, trade union representatives were promised post-war restoration of working practices and a guarantee of control of profits. In a less publicised encounter the President of the Board of Trade, Walter Runciman, impressed on leading engineering employers the need for higher output, fair dealing over wage levels, and the control of profits.[2] These 'agreements' were given statutory form in the Munitions of War Act of June 1915, which established the Ministry of Munitions with powers to organise industrial production.[3]

The Ministry of Munitions was the incarnation of a policy of greater involvement with the details of industrial production, costs and labour policies. The major premise of this policy was that the government would subordinate both the industrial relations strategy of particular industries and the commercial interest of firms to wartime exigencies. When this meant the rapid ending of strikes by readiness to compromise with strikers' demands, as in July 1915 when an illegal strike by miners in South Wales was settled by Lloyd George's action in conceding almost everything the miners asked, employers in general became unsettled.[4] Even though businessmen in large numbers joined the Ministry of Munitions as temporary officials, the possibilities for conflict between the ministry and the firms it controlled were very great; the major employers responded by forming the Association of Controlled Establishments under the leadership of Lionel Hichens of the shipbuilders Cammell Laird.

Disquiet soon led to considerations of common action. Allan Smith, the powerful Secretary of the Engineering Employers' Federation, floated a scheme for a confederation of employers in heavy industry, but at first received little support.[5] More enthusiasm greeted a 'Central Association of Employers' Organisations' launched in Manchester at the end of the year by a small group of businessmen and politicians. The 'conveners' were mostly drawn from the heavy engineering, steelmaking and textile trades: the most prominent was Sir Charles Macara, who had taken the lead in 1911 in the Employers' Parliamentary Association and was president of the Master Cotton Spinners' Federation, but the leading spirit seems to have been W.P. Rylands, an ironmaster who was a vice-president of the EPA and president of the Iron and Steel Wire Manufacturers' Association. The two EPA figures were joined by Sir John Harmood Banner, MP (Con), an accountant who sat with Rylands on the boards of Pearson and Knowles Coal and Iron Co. and Rylands Brothers; F.R. Davenport, president of the British Electrical and Allied Manufacturers Association; Sir Edward Evans of the chemical manufacturers Lascher and Webb, who was also chairman of the National Liberal Federation; and Sir John Randles,

MP (Con) of the Workington Iron Company, a former member of the Tariff Commission, chairman of the House of Commons Commercial Committee, and, like Harmood Banner, a member both of the Unionist Business Committee in the House of Commons and the Parliamentary Committee of the Associated British Chambers of Commerce.[6]

On 3 December 1915 Macara and his associates circulated a letter to a number of businessmen and employers' associations, urging that

> Labour is organising along broad lines; Capital has no corresponding Organisation, and it is essential that such an organisation should be formed now, so that Capital and Labour may confer with the Government on equal terms, and in some cases co-operate.

Despite this rubric, and despite the chosen title of the new organisation, this was not to be a federation of employers' associations to deal with labour. The programme made it clear that 'the main object of the Central Association is to afford a means for bringing the industrial interests of the country as a whole into close relation with the government'; the methods suggested included the establishment of a 'Ministry of Commerce' and 'the appointment upon [its] board . . . of elected representatives from the Central Association of Employers' Organisations and from the Central Association of Trade Unions'. The first of the organisation's formal objects was 'to safeguard the interests of employers in legislation, actual or proposed, affecting industry', and its appeal included the promise that it would be run by 'elected businessmen not politicians'.[7] The document forms an interesting bridge between the immediate discontents of employers grappling with the extension of state activity and the new found influence of the trade unions, and grievances and aspirations of longer standing. Distrust of politicians was an old theme; the demand for a Ministry of Commerce reflected discontent with the Board of Trade and the desire for a more forceful commercial policy; and the very title was a direct imitation of the German *Zentralverband*, revealing the respect felt by the organisers for German commercial organisation. About fifty businessmen, most representing trade or employers' associations, attended a meeting called on 16 December. Fibre and clothing manufacturers predominated, but representatives were also sent by associations in the metal and engineering trades; regionally, Lancashire was best represented but participants came also from London, Scotland, the Midlands and the North-East. In structure and leadership the new movement seemed to be a conflation of three established tendencies: fear of hostile legislation, manifest in the pre-war Empire Parliamentary Association, a willingness to co-operate with employers in different trades to combat trade union organisation, exemplified in the presence of many members of the Midlands Employers' Federation which had been set up in

1913 to resist the Workers' Union, and a fierce commercial nationalism, associated particularly with the British Electrical and Allied Manufacturers' Association.[8]

As the Central Association scheme gathered momentum, other groups caught the fever of political organisation. The Associated British Chambers of Commerce had tried in the early months of war to lobby the government about import prohibitions and the registration of foreign companies.[9] In early 1915 it had tried to act as a clearing house for smaller engineering firms, with no success.[10] In late 1915 the Executive Committee espoused a post-war anti-dumping policy directed against Germany, which foreshadowed a move into more active politics.[11] A dozen MPs, active back-benchers rather than decorative statesmen, were elected honorary members in January 1916, and in February a special meeting adopted a 'programme' which was to represent the interests of the 'trading community'. Its major elements were imperial economic development, a tariff reform to favour the empire and Entente countries to the detriment of Germany and neutrals, navigation laws, prevention of the foreign control of British companies, a government supported credit bank for industry, improved consular services and better technical education.[12] In May the ABCC reconstructed its leadership to give the General Purposes Committee, in contact with a committee of sympathetic MPs, greater control over the making and promotion of policy; and plans were laid to circulate test questions to parliamentary candidates.[13]

Another aspiring organisation was the British Engineer's Association, founded before the war to encourage the engineering trade with China. In late 1915 it adopted the cause of a 'Ministry of Industry', and in March issued an extended policy statement, remarking that

> Several attempts are being made in other directions to associate existing associations to cope with after-the-war conditions. If these attempts succeed it is all the more important that the engineering trade should possess an association which can, with authority, voice its interests and impose upon the Government demands which are for the common good.

The BEA wanted a Ministry of Industry, better consular services and technical education, discrimination against 'enemy' firms in Great Britain, a rapid abandonment of government controls over the economy after the war, and 'to obtain from bankers a change of policy which will place British engineers on an equal footing with their continental competitors'. The question of a tariff was omitted from the 'immediate programme', but mentioned favourably in the preamble.[14] Like the ABCC, whose secretary spoke darkly of 'organisations [which] have been promoted by gentlemen who desire to start an organisation of their own',[15] the BEA was suspicious of rivals, in particular the Central

Association. 'It is no good the Engineers coupling up with Macara's or any other scheme which proposes to take all trading interests', wrote a leading member, 'they must look after their own.'[16]

But the Central Association's most formidable competitor was the British Manufacturers' Association, set up in Birmingham somewhat earlier in the war. Its leading figure was Frank Dudley Docker of the Metropolitan Carriage, Wagon and Finance Co. A brilliant financier and company promoter, Docker had been before the war an active supporter of Tariff Reform and a generous contributor to the Unionist party. Disappointed by the party's lack of protectionist resolve he bought the *Globe* newspaper in 1914 to be the organ of a 'non-political' business protectionist interest, threw himself into the organisation of a 'Business League' which he had helped to form before the war, and began to organise the British Manufacturers' Association, whose support came almost exclusively from the Birmingham metal and engineering trades. Docker was also an active member of the British Electrical and Allied Manufacturers' Association and a founder member of the Midlands Employers' Federation.[17] The BMA under his leadership was not intended, like the Central Association, to be the 'association of associations'; it was simply to be a new and better lobby for a protective tariff. But Docker was a determined organiser, and in April 1916 he called at a BEAMA meeting for the formation of a powerful association to represent British manufacturers, ostensibly to be based on the BMA.[18]

There could hardly be room for two such organisations, and within weeks Docker had resolved the potential conflict by joining forces with the conveners of the Central Association to form a 'United British Industries Association' which was to be 'a strong and influential body on which all other proposals would be urged to crystallise'. Docker had made as successful a use of the merger technique in political association as he had already done in business. The organisers of the UBIA circulated an appeal to leading businessmen asking for one hundred founder members, contributing £1000 each, to form a Grand Council. The Grand Council was summoned in July and invitations were sent out at large to firms and trade and employers' associations to join the now re-named Federation of British Industries.[19]

The FBI's early path was not smooth. Its greatest asset was sheer wealth: the endowment of about £100,000 from its Grand Council subscribers enabled it to buy a considerable staff and engage in a large public relations exercise directed both at government and at potential members in industry. The chief salaried official was R.T. Nugent, a Foreign Office clerk with commercial training who left the newly formed Commercial Department to become Director of the FBI at £1500 a year, the same salary as was then being paid to the *de facto* secretary of the Cabinet and more than was received by the permanent secretaries of many government departments. No other representative organisation could match this financial strength – the ABCC was unable to pay its only salaried official his full agreed salary in 1915[20] – but money alone could not guarantee success for the FBI. The *amour propre* of other organisations was a major obstacle. The British Manufacturers' Association, despite Docker's efforts, would not subsume itself in the FBI, and at a large meeting in June 1916 elected George Terrell, MP as its president.[21] The British Engineers' Association president, Percy Reid, complained of the 'philanthropists who are going to do everything for everybody. . . . The deluge of Docker literature is a great nuisance to our organisers because it unsettles and confuses the eligible firms whom we are trying to induce to join the BEA.'[22] The BEAMA also made difficulties, despite the presence of its president, Davenport, on the FBI's Executive Council, and much of the effort of FBI organisers in 1917 and 1918 was to be devoted to overcoming the resistance of members and branch organisations of the BMA, BEA, and BEAMA to recruiting drives.

The absorption of the Employers' Parliamentary Association in early 1917 consoled the FBI's leaders for these setbacks. Negotiations began in September 1916, and by 8 November a joint meeting agreed to recommend to both Executive Councils that the FBI should take over the organisation, funds and membership of the EPA, with large firms in the EPA joining the FBI as individual members.[23] The decision caused a split in the EPA: Rylands and T.H. Spencer, who as Secretary of the Midlands Employers' Federation was closely associated with Docker, favoured merger against the resistance of Macara, who regarded the FBI as the creature of big business. Protesting against the subscription rate of £100 a year for three years, and calling for a representative organisation which was 'more democratic', Macara resigned at the moment of fusion in January 1917.[24] In 1917 he led the Master Cotton Spinners' Federation in refusing to allow the FBI to canvass its members.[25] This alone would have been a small price to pay for the EPA organisation. Nugent noted that the merger

> practically doubles our membership at one blow and gives us a ready-made organisation in four principal industrial centres; we shall thus become far the largest organisation in the country, and there can no longer be any question in any body's [sic] mind as to whether the FBI or any other body is the right one to join.[26]

The real cost of the EPA merger was not the hostility of Macara but the infusion of Free Traders into the FBI. The original Executive Council included Herbert Dixon, of the Fine Cotton Spinners and Doublers' Association;[27] after the EPA merger he was joined by Sir Edward

Evans, the former National Liberal Federation chairman. Together they were able to prevent the adoption of a protectionist policy by the FBI, by threatening to lead most of the EPA members out of the Federation. It was an effective lever, but its use set up damaging tensions. A questionnaire circulated to member firms in December 1916 indicated a clear division between the protectionist majority and a solid Free Trade minority. With the British Manufacturers' Association, dedicated to protection, preserving its identity but taking part in FBI discussions as an affiliated association, the FBI leadership could do nothing without offending one or other important section of their membership. Committed to expansion, and to the establishment of the FBI as 'a Central Authority in Industry which could be consulted and would be ready to advise on all matters affecting the general interests of all those connected with Commerce and Production',[28] the organisers of the FBI were divided over tactics.

III

The fledgling FBI had to make its way in a world inhabited by powerful employers' organisations with vested interests which they were willing and able to defend. The formal relationship between the FBI and other organisations, envisaged in the original constitution, posed special problems in dealings with the major employers' bodies. The FBI's founders had an eye to rapid growth and financial security. There were two classes of membership, for individual subscribers and for trade associations whose members received the benefits of joining the FBI through their association. The Grand Council, formally the supreme governing body of the Federation, consisted of the original subscribing firms with co-opted representatives of affiliated trade and employers' associations. The distribution of power was skewed towards the individual large firms who had provided the early finance of the FBI, at the expense of smaller firms and the affiliated associations. Since the FBI expressed large aspirations to co-ordinate the representation of industry to government and the public, this maldistribution of influence alarmed the leaders of the employers' associations, particularly Allan Smith of the Engineering Employers' Federation. Smith's determined campaign against the pretensions of the FBI greatly modified its aims in the last two years of war, and led directly to the creation of the National Confederation of Employers' Organisations in 1919.

Members of the EEF had suffered particularly from the development of labour politics since the outbreak of war. The Treasury Agreements of March 1915 had cut across their procedural agreements with engineering unions. Inspectors from the Ministry of Munitions had curtailed their control of work practices, restricted their ability to hire and dismiss workers, and laid conditions on their wage negotiations. Engineering establishments had borne the brunt of the shop stewards movement, from the first strike organised by the Clyde Workers' Committee in October 1915 to the outbreaks of unrest in Sheffield in May 1916.[29] By making reluctant concessions the employers had been able to limit the threat of strikes during the summer of 1916, but this limited success in keeping the industrial peace by their own efforts had only increased their impatience with the Government's handling of industrial disputes; in particular, EEF members did not like to see trade union officials and Labour politicians taken in as advisers and confidants of government departments. On 25 August 1916 the Emergency Committee of the EEF, its chief policy-making body, received a letter of resignation from J.R. Richmond, a Glasgow employer

> referring to the probable creation by the Government of a Labour Advisory Department with Mr Arthur Henderson at its head; to the supine and inactive policy of the Federation during the past two years; to its failure to educate Government and public opinion in order to counteract the activities of Trades Unions and to the fact that the first intimation of the new departure had been received through the Press.

Richmond also demanded that Allan Smith should withdraw from all the many government committees on which he sat.[30] Soon afterwards the Birmingham Association of Engineering Employers supported this call, and proposed that 'the Federation should endeavour to have a representative in the House of Commons'.[31]

These moves precipitated a radical change in the aims and methods of the EEF. The Emergency Committee was replaced by a smaller Management Committee under the chairmanship of Allan Smith. Sectional committees were established, which soon made effective links with other employers' associations. Though a parliamentary committee was envisaged in the new structure, political initiative was in practice reserved to the Management Committee.[32] The effect of the reforms was to give Smith greater power in the Federation and greater authority in his dealings with government and other associations. Smith immediately confronted the FBI's attempts to set up a single 'peak organisation' for industry.

The EEF's Emergency Committee had earlier greeted the propaganda for the United British Industries Association with little enthusiasm.

> As regards . . . associations whose activities are confined to commercial questions, it is felt that there is room for such organisations which must of necessity however be somewhat limited in their scope owing to the varying and in many cases opposing interests of the different sections of employers.[33]

Learning about the FBI's constitution in October the Emergency

Committee had deemed it 'unworkable', declined to affiliate, and advised EEF members not to join.[34] Sir Vincent Caillard of Vickers Ltd, a prominent member of the FBI Council, opened negotiations with Smith, who demanded that the FBI should abandon both its interest in labour questions and its self-description as a trade union. 'This apparently stuck very badly in the gizzards of his Council', Caillard reported.[35] The FBI's organising committee proposed to set up a separate labour section, open only to employers' associations with no 'trade' functions, 'which should be a separate entity, but in which the Federation [of BI] itself should be a member and have a considerable share in the control'.[36] The EEF Management Committee accepted this *démarche*, on condition that 'there should be inserted a substantial provision that the Federation of British Industries shall not deal with questions affecting the relations between employers and employed', and lifted its proscription against its members joining the FBI.[37]

Smith's continued pressure ensured that the new body, named the Employers' Advisory Council, was 'purely advisory'.[38] While FBI officials continued to proselytise for it, Smith convened informal meetings of the larger employers' associations, including the Steel Ingot Makers, the Shipbuilding Employers' Federation and the textile federations, to settle a joint attitude to government departments.[39] When the Ministry of Munitions appointed an Employers' Advisory Committee, Smith ensured that it was monopolised by his Federation.[40] In April 1917 he agreed to join an advisory committee of trade associations summoned by the Ministry and led by the FBI; he withdrew from it in June, complaining that it had accepted the Ministry's proposals for concessions to the trade unions which could be used 'as a springboard for further concessions [sc. after the war] simply because we had agreed, under stress, to the amendments that they propose'.[41] He then won the support of his Management Committee for a *putsch* which forced the Ministry to accept advice on labour matters from a committee consisting of six representatives from the EEF, three from the Shipbuilding Employers' Federation, and two from the National Employers' Federation (the renamed Midlands Employers' Federation).[42] Then, enlisting the support of the textile employers, the Ingot Makers, and the National Federation of Building Trades Employers, he rounded on the FBI officials who were trying to transform the Employers' Advisory Council into the sole channel for giving employers' labour advice to government, forced the FBI to withdraw, and extracted a re-affirmation of the policy of abstinence from labour questions, first proclaimed in January.[43]

The exclusion of the FBI from day-to-day discussions with the Ministry of Munitions was not enough for Smith's purpose. The Ministry had to be persuaded to listen to the advice given by its advisory committee of employers' associations. Smith challenged Addison, the Minister of Munitions, when the Ministry abolished the 'leaving certificate' for munitions workers against the advice of the old advisory committee.[44] The new committee was scarcely more successful, despite the initial encouragement of the new Minister, Winston Churchill: in November 1917 the Ministry proposed, against the employers' objections, a scheme for works committees, and in January 1918 announced a general 12½% wage increase.[45] Frustrated by this lack of leverage, Smith pressed forward with a scheme for a national confederation of employers' associations, entirely independent of the FBI, to be built around the three member organisations of the Ministry of Munitions Consultative Committee. The idea had first been raised by the Birmingham Engineering Employers' Association, which wanted to co-operate with the National Employers' Federation.[46] By November the NEF had begun to abate the hostility it had expressed towards the EEF in the first meetings of the Consultative Committee.[47] Meanwhile the SEF proposed discussions on post-war problems; and in February 1918 joint meetings between the three organisations had begun.[48]

By the time the employers' associations had begun their discussions, relations between the EEF and the FBI had further declined. Leaders of the FBI had interpreted their self-denying ordinance on industrial relations somewhat narrowly, and had set up a Labour Sub-Committee to discuss general questions about the relations of labour and capital. In December 1917 the Sub-Committee, under W.P. Rylands, issued a report on 'Industrial and Commercial Efficiency' which discussed the effects on the labour force of the rationalisation and reorganisation of industry which would be necessary in post-war conditions. Arguing that 'one effect of the War has been to cause an almost universal dislike and distrust of State interference, which is always cumbersome, expensive, and irritating', it went on to propose a scheme of social insurance, paid for and jointly run by employers and trade unions, which would provide superannuation, sickness and unemployment pay, and thus create the conditions in which labour would consent to rationalisation. The Sub-Committee had taken a rather apocalyptic view of industrial relations on the eve of war, and the report urged a new departure in the relations of employers and employed so that disaster could be averted.[49] Circulation of the report deeply angered an EEF committee which was preparing its own report on post-war labour relations, based on the opinions of local associations. Pouring scorn on the apocalyptic premises of the FBI report, the EEF committee urged with the confidence of a veteran organisation that 'in labour questions there is no finality' and concluded that the important aim was not to change society but to establish a permanent machinery for resolving disputes. The proposed social security measures it dismissed as an attempt to 'pauperise the workforce at the hands of the employer', remarking shrewdly that only large companies would be able to afford them; instead, it took the view that such activities were for the state to perform.[50] Smith made a further demarche to the FBI and secured the withdrawal of the offending document and yet another promise that the FBI would eschew labour questions.[51] In April 1918 he was able to obtain the FBI's support for the establishment of a new employers' confederation in which the employers' associations, rather than the FBI, would play the leading part.[52]

Having eliminated the competition of the FBI, Smith had now to rally support among his allies in the employers' associations. He believed that an employers' association should confine itself strictly to labour matters. The Shipbuilding Employers' Federation had never taken this view, and negotiations for the establishment of a confederation were obstructed when Smith and the EEF insisted that only 'pure' employers' associations should be allowed to join.[53] During the hiatus the NEF, apparently under the influence of its secretary, T.H. Spencer, and Dudley Docker, proposed a merger with the EEF, which was formally consummated in August.[54] This gave the new combined federation much wider support in engineering and related trades, but deflected the earlier movement towards a larger confederation in which existing associations would keep their identities and organisations. Even *ad hoc* arrangements proved difficult to operate: the EEF and SEF agreed to negotiate jointly with the trade unions over a claim for shorter hours in late 1918, but at a special conference at the Caxton Hall on 26 November Smith and Sir George Carter, the SEF president, openly disagreed about the trade union demands. The result was an angry exchange of letters and a further cooling of the relationship.[55] Relations were somewhat restored in early 1919, and the National Confederation of Employers' Organisations was finally set up in response to the poor showing made by employers at the National Industrial Conference summoned by the prime minister in late February.

The sudden re-discovery by Smith, Carter and the leaders of other employers' associations that common action was vital in the face of a trade union movement 'organised up to the hilt' is well known. After the first session of the conference an invitation was circulated to more than thirty employers' organisations, suggesting a Confederation which would settle policy for just such occasions, but not interfere in the industrial relations policies of its affiliated organisations. The NCEO was fully active by the summer of 1919. The National Industrial Conference had been the spur to action, but, as the above account makes clear it is a mistake to suggest that the NIC alone explains the establishment of the NCEO.[56] Instead, the emergence of the second major peak association should be seen as the natural outcome of Smith's policy of containing the FBI.

IV

The two peak associations were set up to defend business interests in a political climate which all agreed was hostile; even so, there was constant disagreement about the nature of the threat and the best way of dealing with it. In addition to its arguments with the EEF, the FBI stumbled into disunity in 1917 over its political methods. In early 1917 the staff of the FBI had concentrated their attention on departmental officials and ministers, stressing the virtues of the FBI as an authoritative spokesman for 'business views'. The method was not a success.[57] In May 1917 Nugent advised Sir Robert Hadfield, a member of the Executive Council, that

> recent events have shown that unless the Federation can obtain some form of political influence at once it will not obtain sufficient consideration from the Government. This has been particularly noticeable in regard to the Munition Bill and the recent Labour Unrest, in connection with which the Advisory Committee set up by the Federation at the request of the Ministry of Munitions, has given advice which has been totally disregarded.[58]

The political influence question brought into the open latent differences between former members of the EPA and the 'Docker group'. In May, E.F. Oldham, an Executive Council member who had been an elected officer of the EPA, circulated a memorandum proposing the establishment of a Parliamentary Committee to review legislative questions of interest to the Federation and to lobby sympathetic MPs. Against this proposal Caillard urged that the FBI set up a formal alliance with the London Imperialists, a small group of industrialists and financiers which he had helped to form in December 1916. At this stage the London Imperialists were especially concerned to press the government to embark on planning for a post-war trade policy which would discriminate against Germany in accordance with the resolutions of the Paris Economic Conference of April 1916. In March 1917 Caillard had persuaded a number of leading FBI members to join the Imperialists, including Docker, Godfrey Isaacs (Marconi), Edward Manville (Daimler), and Lincoln Chandler (Metropolitan Carriage, Wagon and Finance Co.).[59] The entry of the United States into the war in April intensified the need for concerted pressure, because President Wilson refused to countenance the Paris Resolutions; so when Oldham's proposals for political action by the FBI were circulated, Caillard and his allies were all the more determined to construct an explicitly protectionist movement with FBI support.

Resistance to Caillard's proposals was led by Rylands and Herbert Dixon, both former EPA members, who opposed both the protectionist strand in the London Imperialists' thought and the suggestion that an attempt should be made to get pledged candidates elected to

Parliament as the core of a separate 'business party'. The FBI staff, led by Nugent, shared their reservations and lobbied the Executive Council accordingly; and even the fiercely protectionist George Terrell MP, who had led the British Manufacturers' Association into affiliation with the FBI and who now spoke in Parliament on behalf of both bodies, warned that

> a false move could do more harm than good . . . and I am not at all sure that to work privately will not be more effective than any public move, which might excite jealousy and hostility in the House.[60]

In anxious meetings the EPA faction prevailed, and a 'Parliamentary Influence Committee' was set up under Oldham's chairmanship, which discussed technical legislative questions and reported to the Executive Council, a body which in any case included a number of MPs. To defuse controversy in the FBI at large, Docker announced in the FBI *Bulletin*

> that it is the declared policy of the Federation to take no action in any purely political question which does not affect industry. It cannot be too clearly understood that the Federation is not taking, and does not desire to take, any part in any political party or organisation.[61]

During 1917 and early 1918 the Parliamentary Influence Committee continued to feed detailed information to sympathetic MPs, concentrating on the Excess Profits Duty and the implications of H.A.L. Fisher's Education Bill for juvenile employment and technical education. In March 1918 MPs who were members of the FBI were assembled into a committee, itself part of a larger scheme, never completed, 'to bring Parliamentary influence to bear on behalf of the Federation through Local Committees formed in the various constituencies of members of the [FBI]'. The Tariff Reform bogey lurked even here: Cecil Cochrane MP, a Liberal and a coal-owner, had previously warned that 'local interests' might on 'certain subjects' diverge from the position adopted by the FBI on behalf of industry as a whole.[62] A new Parliamentary Committee was set up in the 1919 House, consisting of the predominantly Conservative members of the FBI brought in by the Coupon Election. Ironically, its first act was to combine with the parliamentary committee of the British Commonwealth Union, the successor of the London Imperialists, to form the Parliamentary Industrial Group.[63]

The emergence of the British Commonwealth Union as a political force in 1918 owed much to the conflicts within and between the developing peak organisations. The extreme Tariff Reform faction in the FBI renewed its pressure in August 1917, calling for a new questionnaire, on the grounds that members who had joined since December had the right to be consulted about FBI policy. The Manchester sections took fright, but Rylands once again prevailed. Nugent reported to the Manchester organiser that 'everything went through like clockwork . . . we have scotched the Tariff Reform Resolution', only to find the Tariff Reformers raising the question a few days later.[64] On that occasion, Docker persuaded Caillard and Isaacs to desist, but by the autumn the energies of Caillard and his allies were increasingly transferred to the British Commonwealth Union,[65] a renamed and reorganised successor to the London Imperialists. In late 1917 the BCU opened negotiations with the EEF and the Shipbuilding Employers' Federation, which enabled it to solicit members and funds, and prepare a list of candidates for the next parliamentary election. One of its most active members was Allan Smith, who saw it as an integral part of his scheme for a confederation of employers' organisations. In February 1918 he explained to his Management Committee

that various commercial, financial and parliamentary interests were moving in regard to the formation of an organisation to link up for the purpose of parliamentary action bodies of employers dealing with labour questions, manufacturers' organisations dealing with commercial questions, 'city interests' and a Parliamentary party which would have for its object the development and maintenance of British industrial and commercial interests. . . . The political developments which are taking place and the probable large increase in the strength of the Labour party in the House of Commons makes such action appear to be a necessary development of the proposed confederation of British Employers.[66]

The depth of feeling among businessmen about the threat of socialism and the Labour party enabled the British Commonwealth Union to flourish despite latent divisions over economic policy. Smith took the key position in the newly reformed organisation, as chairman of the General Purposes Committee, with the support of Sir George Carter of the SEF. It was apparently the leaders of the employers' organisations who persuaded Dudley Docker, still an active member of the BCU despite being prominent in the FBI, to restrain his enthusiasm for a separate industrial party; instead the BCU supported candidates of other parties (18 Conservative, 2 British Workers' League, one Liberal, one National, one 'Lower Deck', and one 'Women's'), so long as they were biddable in industrial matters. On economic questions the prominence of tariff reformers among the active membership of the BCU outweighed the influence of Smith and Carter, who were both committed to Free Trade, and the involvement of Conservative politicians brought party-political considerations to the forefront. In preparation for the election of 1918 the BCU drew up a 'White List' and a 'Black List' of parliamentary candidates. Criteria for membership of the 'White List' included full commitment to the Paris Resolutions; while any MP who had identified himself with the Asquithian opposition to the Lloyd George–Conservative coalition by voting against the Government in the Maurice Debate in May 1918 was automatically included in the 'Black List'.[67] But these diversions of effort from a strictly industrial endeavour were apparently of little account to the firms that subscribed generously to the BCU's funds, so long as it kept up an active campaign against Labour candidates and a propaganda effort in favour of 'patriotic' labour and against industrial unrest. During 1918 the BCU sponsored articles on industrial subjects in W.H. Mallock's organ, *New Outlook*, and organised a team of speakers who addressed factory-gate meetings – a practice which was to be revived during 1919. In 1919 the BCU co-operated, covertly, with the Coalition Whips to set up a well-funded organisation for 'Anti-Bolshevik' propaganda; this was re-formed in January 1920 as National Propaganda, without direct participation by Coalition politicians.[68]

These lavish propaganda efforts – National Propaganda had a notional budget of £250,000, though it probably never spent that sum – were prefigured in the development of FBI attitudes during the war. Attitudes to the trade union movement shifted from tentative co-operation to active aggression during 1917 and 1918. At the moment of fusion with the FBI, leading members of the Employers' Parliamentary Association were about to open secret negotiations with the TUC; these were scotched because the 'Docker Group' took a sterner line.[69] A less direct relationship was set up through the National Alliance of Employers and Employed, established in December 1916. The Alliance, organised jointly by a committee of trade unionists and employers (mostly FBI members), preached the abandonment of restrictive practices and the common interests of employer and employee. In May 1917 it issued a joint statement with the FBI calling for full implementation of the Paris Resolutions.[70] In this period the FBI tried to accommodate 'responsible' trade union leaders: an unsuccessful attempt was made to persuade W.A. Appleton, the secretary of the General Federation of Trade Unions, to join the FBI as an official to 'ginger up' the National Alliance.[71] Later in the year, responding to the extension of shop steward activity, the FBI set up a propaganda campaign and 'clearing-house' for information on the 'Rank and File Movement and associated Pacifist and Revolutionary bodies'.[72] From this, after discussions with the EEF, grew the National Stability League. The League's agents were particularly active in the first half of 1918. In April, after the initial success of the German Spring Offensive, a League report from Sheffield urged that the opportune moment had arrived for the extension of conscription by the government and that

> Employers need not be afraid of the Shop Stewards' power as hitherto. Now is the time for any firm to get rid of men who are agitators or undesirable in the shop.[73]

Funds for these efforts, as for the BCU, came in part from the EEF corporately and also from armament and aircraft manufacturers who were members of the FBI; and although the FBI did not subscribe corporately to the BCU, Docker and his supporters all subscribed on behalf of their companies.[74]

Thus by 1919 the FBI and the newly formed NCEO were in practice co-operating in politics, albeit at arm's length, through the British Commonwealth Union, in which leading members of both bodies participated. A common desire to inhibit revolutionary activity in industry by propaganda overcame doubts about the 'soundness' of the FBI on the part of employers' leaders such as Allan Smith, while FBI leaders such as Rylands seemed to accept an outspoken protectionist commitment so long as it was not directly associated with the FBI. The existence of two peak organisations and a semi-secret political organisation, concerned with propaganda and parliamentary work, allowed for the reconciliation in practice of some of the more important political differences within industry; a reconciliation which might have been much more difficult to attain if the attempt had been made to create a single multi-purpose peak organisation.

V

The two peak organisations signally failed to transform British politics in a 'corporatist' direction during and after the First World War. FBI leaders called for a ministry of industry, responsible to organised business, and lost no opportunity of urging a policy of state-backed export combines.[75] Their efforts to enlist state support were constantly undercut by their members' hostility to state intervention, based on the wartime experiences which had first driven them into the FBI. Unable to control their members, they could not hope to strike bargains with the government, and their corporatist aspirations flowed into the sands of 'decontrol' and the apparent collapse of German commercial competition in the immediate post-war period. The NCEO, specifically prevented by its constitution from prescribing a strategy for its member associations, was a bystander even during the strained industrial relations of 1919 to 1921. Measured against early aspirations, this inability to change the system was a major setback for the leaders of the FBI and NCEO. Left-wing critics charged that 'the capitalist class, behind the shadow of Parliamentary government, [was] building up a new political authority based not on citizenship . . . but on the ownership of legal claims to the product of human labour'.[76] On the contrary, parliamentary government remained solid, while the new political authority was no more than a shadow. The multiplication of overt and covert political groups such as the BCU and the National Stability League was not the sign of a rampant corporatism, but the symptom of its failure. Unable to beat the party-political system, British 'organised business' was obliged to join it.

4 Tariffs and Steel, 1916–1934: The Politics of Industrial Decline

Steven Tolliday

The 'riddle of the tariff' in twentieth century British history has been discussed in two main ways. Firstly it has received attention as an issue of party politics, particularly in so far as it shaped the evolution of the Conservative party's policy and leadership.[1] Secondly it has been discussed as an issue of economic calculus, an assessment of the costs and benefits of Protection versus Free Trade.[2] But consideration of the ways in which these two spheres intersect has been limited. The implication of tariff policy for broader questions of the evolution of government intervention in industry and of the shifting attitudes and practices of industrialists towards government, in short what might be termed 'business politics', have been neglected. It is these issues which form the subject of this essay.

I

It was around the question of tariff protection that the issues of the extension of government involvement in the steel industry were fought out between the wars. In contrast to prior government involvement in optical glass, cellulose, dyestuffs or naval fuel oil, steel did not command attention as an issue of national security.[3] Nor did the government have to protect its special interests as a monopsonist customer with rigid quality and supply needs in a non-competitive market which had forced it to extend its activities in the armaments and fuel oil sectors.[4] And steel was quite free of the intensely politicised industrial relations which had forced intervention in coal on successive unwilling governments.[5] As we shall see, some of the problems of steel – particularly those of combination, efficiency, monopoly power and the relationship between supplying and consuming industries – had been raised in rather different political and institutional contexts in the railway and electricity supply industries.[6] But, broadly speaking, government relations with steel opened up new issues of both principle and practice at all turns and they provide a useful optic for considering the shifting boundaries of government/industry relations in the 1920s and early 1930s.

The steel industry in the 1920s faced inescapable problems of reorganisation. A century of world dominance had been followed by fifty years of piecemeal improvements. The legacy of this, in a period of chronic depression, was an industry with too many firms and too many plants. Ownership was fragmented, equipment was a motley assembly of new and old units poorly integrated with each other and below optimum capacity.[7] In particular, blast furnaces fell well below American and European scale and the average size of steelworks was only a fifth of what contemporary experts reckoned to be the minimum efficient scale. Above all iron and steel-making were rarely integrated adequately in hot metal practice with consequent diseconomies in speed, organisation and fuel economy. Where there were new modern units, particularly in steelmaking and rolling mills, low capacity utilisation pushed overhead costs up punitively.[8] The location of the industry was based on locational choices made fifty years or more earlier to suit a very different configuration of raw material costs, notably of domestic coal and ore resources that were now nearing exhaustion.[9] The results were high costs and collapsed profits, and, during the 1920s, an increasing flow of imported cheap continental semi-finished steel.

The structural reorganisation that was required in these circumstances was considerable. It had to involve simultaneous contraction and modernisation, processes which rarely go easily together under competitive conditions. Diagnosis of the ills of the industry was far easier than cure. It was not difficult to draw up blueprints of a desirable reorganised structure for the industry centred on compact regional amalgamations using the best existing plant in combination with new modern units so as to eliminate overlapping and sub-optimal production. But it was harder to persuade businessmen that the risks involved would pay off, even if the necessary capital could be raised.[10] For instance, there was general agreement among Scottish steelmasters that a scheme drawn up by the American consultants H.A. Brassert & Co. in 1929 could result in the production of cheaper steel at a new integrated tidewater plant on a green-field site on the Clyde. The scheme was enthusiastically endorsed in both government and banking circles. Yet few managers were convinced that the scheme could bring sufficient profits in the medium term to enable them to justify the sacrifices that shareholders, bankers and owners would have to make. Without such guarantees the force of parochial jealousies and antagonisms exercised a fatal influence on the prospects of the scheme.[11] No one could guess with any great confidence about likely future returns on giant investments in an industry in such a depressed state.

Moreover the steel firms themselves were not organised to take such risks. Financial interests, debenture holders, creditors, owners, customers and managers all had varying interests in the patchwork of firms and too widely varying views of their immediate best interests. Thus on the North-East coast, debenture holders who wanted to preserve the security of their loan capital combined with Hartlepool shipbuilding interests who wanted to preserve their local steel supply to undermine a comprehensive amalgamation scheme. The major banks, notably Barclays, were caught between trying to promote the merger and preserving their extensive industrial loans and their relations with their industrial clients who had antagonistic interests in any merger. The whole prolonged venture finally came to grief after court actions by the various parties in the early 1930s.[12] Bold and concerted action from such internally divided business units was hard to achieve. The tendency, therefore, for most firms was to look towards piecemeal cost-reducing improvements in the interim until broader changes in the conditions of trade should make wider reorganisation more feasible. The flow of these modifications was continuous and their effects could be very significant so that a 'patching' policy had much to recommend it. But by continuing to commit fresh resources to the old locations and plants they tended to make thoroughgoing reorganisation more difficult.[13]

What most firms wanted from their bankers or from the government was not large-scale plans but practical amelioration of their immediate distress so that they could retrench and keep their businesses together through the depression. Amalgamations and new investment were, they agreed, desirable and would be pursued whenever the way was clear. But in the conditions of the 1920s and early 1930s the way seldom was clear. Thus the heavy steelmakers told the Government in 1929 that despite their general support for a programme of regional amalgamations 'they would not undertake it unless assured of the home market'.[14] And John Craig of the biggest Scottish firm, Colvilles, told the same inquiry that even if the necessary capital could be raised on the market, he would 'not take the responsibility for accepting it for investment in the present conditions'.[15]

These internal divisions and lack of a coherent idea of how to carry through reorganisation among the industrialists was reflected in their indecisive relationship to government in the 1920s. If the industry had been able to speak with a fairly unified voice it might conceivably have been able to exert sufficient pressures on the government to make it possible to give some form of tariff protection to steel as a special case in the mid-1920s. As we shall see below, broader political considerations finally ruled this out, but there was considerable sympathy for the industry within government circles and a plan for reorganisation in the context of a tariff from within the industry would have carried considerable weight. But as John Turner has noted, the divided and backward structure of the British economy tended to prevent the emergence of united political leadership among industrialists. 'The political backwardness of British industry . . . was closely related to the much better known phenomenon of British industrial retardation.'[16] This on the one hand prevented the emergence of politically coherent demands from employers, and on the other meant that the government risked embroilment in a complex set of rival vested interests if it once began to involve itself with established industries. This sort of complex inter-capitalist conflict had been one of the main reasons for the government opting out of railway reorganisation before the First World War and for keeping clear of the oil industry as far as possible after it.[17] The industries where governments had been most ready to intervene had been those such as cellulose, dyestuffs or fuel oil where a compact body of employers with a clear plan had been able to win the support of a government department for a specific course of action for a specific purpose.[18]

The steel lobby, however, was a muted and somewhat internally divided affair. During the war and the preparation of the Scoby-Smith report on the industry's future for the Board of Trade in 1917, nearly all steelmakers had anticipated a post-war era of intense economic nationalism, tougher international competition and a general breakdown of the old economic order. All but a small minority of the report's highly influential signatories from the industry had accepted this and called for protection to resist it.[19] But the pessimism of 1917, and the unity of the industry, did not last. It was put into the shadow by the defeat of Germany and the prospects for a new buoyancy for British heavy industry in a period of European reconstruction with German industry disabled by defeat. These prospects resulted in a sudden swing back against protectionism at the end of the War with Free Trade as an acceptable corollary to speedy decontrol of the industry.

The earlier prognosis was to prove more accurate than the later one. But the erratic fluctuations of the immediate post-war years, and notably the impact of the Ruhr crisis in 1923, masked for a while the extent to which European industry had come through the war with its competitive power only briefly impaired. As a result, the wholehearted shift of the major firms behind political support for a tariff was somewhat delayed. The National Federation of Iron and Steel Manufacturers (NFISM), the principal trade association, for instance, was significantly silent in the 'tariff election' of 1923, and took a position of formal neutrality in regard to an application from the industry for protection under the Safeguarding Acts in 1925.[20] It was only as the pattern of international trade became clearer that protectionism became dominant. The North-East coast steelmakers came over to protection almost unanimously from 1924 to 1925.[21] GKN, the largest importer of foreign semi-finished steel in the country, opposed protection in 1925, but soon realised that 'trade was not going to right itself' and shifted their position in the next three years.[22]

For many other employers it was the General Strike which scotched the lingering hope that cheap imports would teach British workers the 'facts of life', demonstrate the 'unreality' of British wage levels and force workers to accept lower wages and living standards.[23] Only in Scotland, where Colvilles depended largely on imported pig iron, was the conversion of a major firm delayed much beyond this. There, though several leading managers favoured protection much earlier, the Board as a whole was not convinced until 1930.[24]

Protracted opposition came only from a few small firms such as the Steel Company of Scotland and Dunlops in Scotland who feared that removal of cheap imported steel would increase their dependence on bigger firms,[25] and from the re-rollers who had carved themselves a niche by using cheap imported semi-finished steel to undercut their big rivals. The latter formed an active lobby who were able to exploit the broad political problems raised by the tariff issue to exercise an influence in the debate out of all proportion to their economic weight, particularly through the columns of the trade press and their evidence at the major government inquiries.[26]

These divisions and uncertainties took a lot of pressure off successive governments which themselves had rather ambiguous and divided attitudes to the merits and implications of tariff policy. The final advent of tariffs in 1932 was claimed by some of its partisans as the culmination of a thirty-year campaign for Joseph Chamberlain's 'Great Policy' of tariff reform.[27] But in fact by the 1920s the policy was the same in name only. Over the years, the tariff had been transformed from a cornerstone of Tory policy, embodying a comprehensive strategy of Empire and social reform to a fairly restricted tactic.[28] By the end of the First World War a majority in the Conservative party probably supported tariffs as *a* policy, but few were prepared to commit the party to it wholesale when to do so might jeopardise a wide range of interests of the traditional order – the Union and the House of Lords before the war, a possible Labour government afterwards. When Baldwin revived the tariff issue in 1923 he hoped to avoid making it a central political issue. But bad political miscalculations landed the party in fighting an election on an issue which few supported wholeheartedly.[29] In the aftermath of the electoral defeat the Free Trade minority in the Party were able to keep the protectionists on the defensive. Baldwin, the Prime Minister, Philip Cunliffe-Lister, the President of the Board of Trade and Arthur Steel-Maitland, the Minister of Labour, were all personally committed to protection and in particular sympathetic to the claims of the steel industry. But from 1923 they accepted that they would have to manage as best they could without a general tariff. Baldwin clearly stated that the Party could not put the issue to the country again unless there was clear evidence that they would get a different result.[30] He was convinced that safeguarding was the most that the electorate would accept and he embodied this in his appointment of the strongly Free Trade Churchill to the Exchequer as a guarantee that the pledge against protection would be honoured. But at the same time he counterbalanced this by putting in Cunliffe-Lister at the Board of Trade to push the existing safeguarding against 'unfair' competition, as far as it would go *within* the general framework of a pledge against a general tariff. Some hoped that this process could be extended until there was a general tariff in all but name. The case of steel which was investigated by the Committee of Civil Research in 1925 was the testing case for the extent to which this could be pushed. The application was defeated by a combination of Churchill's vigorous opposition at the Treasury, the weakness of the steelmakers' lobby and Baldwin's electoral prudence.[31] But beyond this, what ruled out any possibility of steel slipping through as some sort of special case was that the inquiry brought to the fore issues which would loom large in the next six years of the relationship between a tariff and a wider government industrial policy for reorganisation.

While, as we have seen, the eyes of industry turned to government for protection to create a breathing space, such a proposition was not likely to be welcome to government. The role of bolstering ailing industrialists was not an attractive precedent when so many declining sectors could make similar cases for aid. The government was only likely to look favourably on intervention when, as in the case of the electricity supply industry their involvement could be linked fairly directly to a programme of active reconstruction – in the case of electricity through the establishment of the National Grid.[32] Thus while a majority of steel industrialists wanted an essentially defensive tariff, government ministries looked towards the promotion of rationalisation. The question that bridged these two positions was whether or not tariff protection could provide a trigger to industrial regeneration by rationalisation.

The case that there was such a link did not emerge convincingly in the 1925 inquiry. It became clear that there was no clear understanding even among the steelmakers who advocated tariffs as to what exactly the linkages were between a tariff and the revival of the industry. Churchill, in several telling memoranda produced in the Treasury, was able justifiably to characterise the whole issue as clouded by 'confusion and looseness of thought'.[33] One view was that the current downturn in the steel trade was merely cyclical, and that the need was for temporary action 'during the transitional stage in the revival of world trade'.[34] Tariffs would boost profits and investment and thus lower prices, paving the way for a new export-led assault by the rejuvenated industry.

But there was no very clear attempt to specify why tariffs should produce competitive reinvigoration rather than monopoly effects. The main argument put to the Committee of Civil Research, and to the Balfour Committee on Industry and Trade which ran in parallel to it though with a rather wider brief, was that the exclusion of imports would give a new impetus to the industry by giving it a full load on its most modern equipment.[35] The steelmakers suggested that an import prohibition would bring a further two million tons of steel to be made in Britain which would in itself result in a cost reduction of 10*s*. per ton or something like 10%. Amalgamation and the elimination of small makers alone, they argued, could not achieve such economies. As Sir William Larke, the President of the NFISM, put it, 'the small orders which are economically transferable to the big plants are not nearly enough . . . it is the orders for imported steel that can alone give the big plants what they need'.[36] As an argument for tariffs, this merged into arguments for the impossibility of reorganising *before* tariffs. Reorganisation required increased loads and these could only come from a monopolised home market.[37]

There was some substance in this argument, though Churchill was rightly critical of the notion that the exclusion of two million tons of imports would simply mean the transfer of that amount to home production. Moreover he felt that the 'violent deflection and derangement' of the world steel trade would probably result in intensification of foreign competition in British export markets and in more finished products.[38] This was a danger, but it should be noted that by the mid-1920s only 40% of British steel exports were going to 'neutral' markets where Britain did not enjoy some preference, and of these over 60% were of highly finished steel sheets or tinplate which Britain's main source of imports, Belgium, did not export and where Britain's superiority was most marked.[39] Hence there was some reason for optimism that a steel tariff could have a strategic impact in international competition.

What could not be guaranteed was that this advantage would not be used to bolster inefficient production by reducing competition, raising prices and profits and promoting malinvestment within the existing structure of the industry. Anti-monopoly regulation had long been a significant theme in government–industry relations in Britain, particularly in relation to the railways and electricity supply where firms enjoyed considerable potential quasi-monopoly powers over a wide variety of industrial customers. In general nineteenth century governments had leaned towards 'competitive' solutions and in the case of railways, parliamentary legislation had made considerable inroads on the ability of the companies to set their freight rates so as to maximise profits.[40] Yet from the turn of the century governments had come to appreciate the possible advantages of combination to eliminate unnecessary and wasteful competition. The Board of Trade had espoused this point of view in relation to railway combination before the War and in relation to electricity supply after it, though in both cases their desire simultaneously to regulate such amalgamations brought them into conflict with the companies.[41] Similar problems arose in the case of steel. The government wanted to see the elimination of excessive competition but it feared the responsibility of creating monopoly conditions for an industry with such a wide variety of industrial customers.

As a result, the aim of both Conservative and Labour governments between 1925 and 1931 was to foster private rationalisation through merger with the aim of creating a slimmed down, more efficient industry which could justify protection once it had set its own house in order. But the idea of rationalisation remained more an article of faith than a precise, informed strategy. In its abstract form, the theorem of rationalisation was that mergers would eliminate excess capacity and concentrate production. This would lower costs and lead to increased capacity utilisation and output leading to new investment and a renewal of a cycle of virtue. Amalgamations were often simply equated with reorganisation. The government never looked at, nor were allowed by the industry to look at, problems of plants and firms. The firms only produced the information they chose to give and the government never challenged this. Hence discussions of costs, for instance, almost always dealt with the average costs of British producers rather than analysing differences in costs *between* various producers. Judgements had to be based almost entirely on the informed opinions of leaders of the industry. When the Committee of Civil Research in 1925 and its successor the Sankey Committee under a Labour government in 1929 recommended regional amalgamations, they were in no position to make any assessment at all as to the impact on costs of such mergers or to do more than guess at the sort of capital needed to make such an amalgamation effective.[42] Such questions were not tackled until the Bank of England began to turn privately to the American consulting engineers H.A. Brassert & Co. from the late 1920s for authoritative figures based on an analysis of actual works practice. It was these investigations which provided the basis for the report on the reorganisation of the industry drawn up by the Bank's senior industrial adviser Charles Bruce Gardner in 1930.[43] Until this time, however, neither government had an authoritative idea of *how* steel should be reorganised other than that amalgamations should in general be encouraged.

Moreover, despite the priority that the government accorded to amalgamation, it had no means in practice to induce such measures. In

1925 Cunliffe-Lister had concluded that the chances of amalgamation by persuasion in the British steel industry were very limited,[44] and Hugo Hirst, the head of GEC and one of the major 'rationalisers' with the ear of government, warned Baldwin that 'The atmosphere is not congenial for amalgamation [in the steel industry] and I am afraid that government pressure would be futile.'[45]

What options did the government have to induce amalgamations short of direct intervention or compulsion? Broadly speaking there were two main avenues which were explored. The first was to use the prospect of a tariff in some way as a bargaining counter. But here both Conservative and Labour Governments ran into the contradictions of their own positions. The two inquiries held by them into the affairs of the industry (the Committee of Civil Research and the Sankey Committee) had both concluded that there was actually an inverse relationship between protection and reorganisation, contrary to the arguments of the industry. As Sankey had noted, 'Protection at the present time would, we believe, actually delay the reforms that are urgently required, as it would lead to the maintenance of a number of plants not designed for efficient production or suitable for amalgamation, which in the interests of the country as a whole should not be encouraged to continue.'[46] Both parties had come to accept this. Steel-Maitland, the Conservative Minister of Labour, despite his general pro-tariff outlook believed that protection 'would awake the old reactionary individualism of the industry'.[47] As a result if protection were introduced 'at the present juncture . . . reorganisation would be indefinitely postponed'.[48] The two Labour Governments of the 1920s held this view even more firmly. Tariffs, according to Ramsay MacDonald, were 'a remedy that was no remedy at all',[49] and Philip Snowden, his Chancellor, was consistently adamant that, come what may, reorganisation must precede any state aid to the steel industry.[50]

Since both parties feared that their only lever over the industry would not be compelling, they were inhibited in using it. In particular it made the Tory government in the late 1920s shy away from putting forward any sort of authoritative blueprint to the industry. This method of promoting rationalisation was discussed in 1928 when they considered establishing a carefully chosen committee to produce an authoritative report which could then be used to pressurise the industry. Such a committee would take as its model the recent Weir Committee on Electricity Supply rather than the Samuel Commission on Coal; in other words, it would be a committee of practical businessmen to devise a plan rather than an exercise in political balance. Weir was proposed as Chairman, with a financier (either Peacock of the Bank of England or Vivian Smith or Catto of Morgan Grenfell, the merchant bankers) and the leading accountant Sir William McLintock plus Brassert as technical adviser.[51] But it was scotched after controversy in the Cabinet, for, as Cunliffe-Lister noted, a truly authoritative report would actually put the Government in an invidious position.

Your committee would say: 'You shan't have a duty considered unless you carry out the recommendations of an amalgamation committee.' This may be sound economically, but you have not said it to other industries. . . . Moreover, the moment you make such a pronouncement, the Steel industry will certainly say to you: 'If we carry out the amalgamation will you then give us a duty?' Your reply must be: 'We cannot tell.' The Steel industry would reply: 'You cannot get the result from an amalgamation alone, but only from amalgamation plus the duty.' I do not see what your answer is to this, unless you are prepared to go back on the pledge that steel will be treated like any other industry.[52]

Thus direct bargaining was ruled out both by the uncertain impact of tariff protection on reorganisation and by the wider political implications of such moves. In its absence, the Conservative government's conception of its role remained broadly that of Baldwin's classic dictum that government should confine itself to 'holding the scales'. In industrial reorganisation as in labour relations, the Government sought some sort of neutral enforcement role, bringing together industrialists to decide policy and managing a resultant consensus. But in steel they were managing not a consensus but a series of conflicts of interest while broader political considerations ruled out more direct intervention. In an industry internally divided at all levels by rival interests any government intervention was bound to discriminate between rival firms, and it appeared that a tariff, in so far as it interfered with the mechanism of the market would actually institutionalise and sanction certain non-competitive deformations to the advantage of some businesses at the expense of others within the industry and to the advantage of the supplying industry at the expense of its customers. The Government did not want direct responsibility for such a state of affairs.

Since the ability of government to manage the conduct of the industrialists in the industry taken as a whole was so limited, one alternative was to attempt to influence the conduct of the industry at the level of the firm. We have already noted the complexity of interests operating within the various steel firms and this presented a complex arena within which to attempt behind the scenes persuasion and the exercise of influence. Both Labour and Conservative governments felt that their best prospects of inducing firms to reorganise was through the intermediary of the banks. Their most important potential ally here was the Bank of England. Montagu Norman, the Governor, had a clear shared interest with the government in industrial regeneration since it was felt by many in the Bank that continuing industrial decline imperilled the stability of the Gold Standard and Britain's world financial power.[53] Beyond this, the Bank of England itself had come to take a rather special interest in the fortunes of the steel industry because it was itself involved in the affairs of particular steel companies, notably Vickers-Armstrong, Beardmores and the Lancashire Steel Corporation.[54] Norman and the Treasury enjoyed a close similarity of outlook on these matters. In particular they held firmly to the view that reorganisation had to come from within the industry itself and that tariff protection would only delay the necessary moves.[55] But except in those companies with which the Bank of England was directly involved, Norman could only exert pressure on steel firms at one remove – through the agency of the clearing banks which held the companies' accounts. Hence for most of the 1920s his activity was largely confined to occasionally prodding a bank in the direction of a receivership for their clients or informally encouraging them to take action in the 'national interest'.[56]

Mostly, however, the clearing banks had their own interests to defend. Many had built up a banking position among industrial clients which they did not want to jeopardise by throwing their weight around. Others were intent on nursing frozen loans through a period of depression in the hope of recovering their money when trade improved. Many of these had well entrenched positions in terms of priority of claims in the event of liquidation which they were unwilling to exchange for holdings with less rights in the course of an amalgamation, and such holdings could be very awkward barriers to reorganisation. Moreover local managers made their own individual and conflicting assessments of the prospects of particular amalgamation schemes. These factors undercut the prospects for systematic bank action at the level of the firm.[57]

Moreover, at a wider level, though the Bank of England was sympathetic to the Government's desire for rationalisation it rejected a role as a catspaw for government in industry. When the Balfour Committee, at the time of the Committee of Civil Research Safeguarding inquiry in 1925, floated the idea of a systematic application of bank pressure in reorganisation through a Bank Trust, Norman bluntly told the Chancellor that he had no intention of doing *anything* 'until the inquiry into subsidies (i.e. tariffs) is ended and forgotten'.[58] The Bank's fiscal priorities came first and beyond that they and the clearing banks refused to get involved in any 'parental responsibility' for the industry. As Norman put it, their fear 'was too great of the charge of domineering over industry through money trusts'.[59] By December 1928 Steel-Maitland recognised the weakness of the strategy of indirect pressure through the banks. 'I had hoped at one time . . . to get them [the banks] to join in pressing the industry to reconstruct. . . . But on further inquiry it seems hopeless to expect them to take this course.'[60]

Under the Conservative government of 1925–9 the banking establishment was prepared to work autonomously along lines broadly similar to government thinking. They too saw the reorganisation of industry as an alternative to state intervention and a way of bolstering free enterprise and maintaining free trade. During the 1929–31 Labour government, however, Bank of England suspicions of what they saw as the Labour party's interventionist designs caused them to step up their efforts to encourage reorganisation while at the same time making it clear that they were not prepared to tolerate any moves towards direct intervention. Thus, when in 1930 Norman heard that the Labour Cabinet was considering a public utility corporation to take over the steel industry, he at once dispatched an emissary round to the Board of Trade to warn that if such talk went any further 'everything was stopped' as far as the provision of bank finance for the reorganisation of industry was concerned. The threat was immediately effective in getting the scheme dropped.[61] But though the Bank continued under Labour to maintain a consistent position of resistance to protection and pressure on firms to reorganise, it became increasing clear as the depression deepened that the Tories were wobbling on these principles. In the summer of 1930 Norman's industrial advisers held secret talks with the Conservative party to encourage them to take a hard line in refusing to give the steel industry any promises about future protection since these would put back reorganisation, 'if not for many years, at least for a considerable time'. The result was disappointing. Cunliffe-Lister would go no further than undertaking to stress to his steel friends that the *amount* of protection they would get would depend on their efforts to reorganise.[62] As the trough of the depression neared, both parties began to soften on the principle that reorganisation must precede assistance and the Bank took on more and more the role of the sole consistent guardian of this orthodoxy, now no longer hand in hand with government but increasingly in opposition to it.

The institutional framework which the Bank developed for this purpose was centred on building up a formidable pool of industrial experts and advisers. As we have already noted, it was Norman who first turned to the leading American engineering consultants, Brasserts, for detailed technical analysis of the industry and the formulation of detailed plans for regional reorganisation. During 1928–9 he recruited a collection of distinguished industrial experts to the Securities Management Trust (SMT), the body that handled the Bank's industrial holdings; and in 1930 the same group formed the core of the Bankers Industrial Development Co. (BIDCo.) which Norman formed as an alliance between the Bank and the leading merchant houses to provide capital for schemes of reorganisation approved by the Bank along the lines of a series of regional amalgamations outlined by Charles Bruce Gardner on the basis of Brassert's recommendations.[63] The latter body, which was to take the Bank deeply into industrial affairs in due course, was in its conception largely a political response to the perceived threat to private industry posed by the Labour government. Norman was quite explicit to his city friends that the BID was formed to 'keep the government out of industry' and the steel industry was seen as one of the most vulnerable points.[64]

The Bank tended to overestimate the interventionist aims of the Labour party. The issue of compulsion was fought out and rejected early in the life of the Labour government around the Mosley Memorandum. Mosley wanted a comprehensive government scheme for industrial reorganisation and the provision of finance through an industrial bank.[65] But his scheme was speedily defeated in the Cabinet and though echoes were to be heard later from individuals such as Attlee, Henderson, Hartshorn and Graham in the Cabinet the orthodoxies of evolutionary socialism as expounded by MacDonald and Snowden remained dominant.[66] Snowden believed that intervention was 'contrary to all I have ever heard you [MacDonald] say about the steps to be taken in the direction of socialism'.[67] The political framework of the Labour leaders disarmed them before the prospect of a conflict with powerful vested interests involved in such a strategy. As Snowden and J.H. Thomas noted, moves towards compulsion would bring private sector efforts to a halt. Shareholders and creditors 'would at once stiffen and you would be left to choose between extravagant claims and compulsion which would be called confiscation'.[68] It would be 'practically impossible for any government' to enforce 'the essential sacrifices' from industry in terms of writing off losses.[69] In this situation, the Labour government resigned itself to the same role that the Tory government had filled before it: 'The best service which the government can render . . . is to continue to act as a bridge between industry and finance. . . . At the same time, the great weight attaching to the public utterances of ministers affords a valuable opportunity of impressing on the industrial world the need for rationalisation.'[70]

Thus on the eve of tariff legislation majority thinking in both parties remained the traditional one that the role of government was to do no more than oil the wheels of private industry. The failure of traditional market mechanisms to bring about structural reorganisation had as yet produced little new thinking about the role of government, nor any significant attempts to formulate an industrial policy. Steel did not raise the sort of issues of national security or political stability that had forced governments to develop a more positive relationship with other industries. Instead in confronting the problems of the steel industry successive governments were aware that they would face a whole range of new problems. The structure of the steel industry was fragmented: divisions between and within firms and conflicting and overlapping interests prevented the emergence of positive programmes from within the industry itself. Reorganisation may have been favoured generally, but in any particular case the conditions of depression made the immediate advantages to be gained by owners, managers or creditors fairly marginal and often risky. If reorganisation by amalgamation were to proceed speedily some stimulus other than the invisible hand of the market would be needed. But the steel industrialists themselves had neither a coherent programme nor the political unity to lobby effectively for a solution of their own and in the absence of such pressure internal divisions within the Conservative party and the pledge against a general tariff ruled out protection for steel as a 'special case' in the late 1920s. The steelmakers could not demonstrate any clear link between protection and reorganisation and Government circles more and more took the view that far from encouraging reorganisation, protection would be one more barrier to it. Hence both Conservative and Labour governments turned to rationalisation as an *alternative* to protection, though they lacked any means to induce firms to reorganise and did not themselves have any clear plan as to *how* reorganisation should take place.

The tariff was not a credible bargaining counter to promote reorganisation and both Conservative and Labour governments came to look towards the banks as their most valuable ally in promoting amalgamation schemes. The clearing banks, however, had their own interests to defend and the Bank of England itself, though sympathetic to government aims in regard to reorganisation, did not want to be used as a catspaw for government in industry. The main thrust of Bank of England activity in industrial reorganisation under the Labour government was, in fact, directed to keeping government out of industry. Both ideologically and organisationally, the Government was unprepared for the power over and responsibility for the steel industry that the establishment of a tariff would thrust on them. All the issues that had been avoided through the 1920s would have to be resolved after the Government had committed itself to assisting the industry rather than before. The Government knew that protection was no guarantee of the reorganisation they wanted to see. Either the Government would develop an industrial policy and find ways of using it for that purpose or industrialists would, as the politicians of the late 1920s feared, use their newly strengthened position to seek their own salvation. The next few years would show who would be using who.

II

When import duties finally did come with the legislation of April 1932,[71] they were no longer a part of any conscious strategy for reorganisation. They were a simple recognition that the old world economic order of free international trade was defunct and that Britain had willy-nilly to come into line with this fact. It was openly admitted that although the tariffs were necessary for 'economic progress' and 'national security' they were in themselves inadequate to regenerate industry without thoroughgoing industrial reorganisation. The Government, and more particularly the Import Duties Advisory Committee (IDAC), the small specialist advisory committee of civil servants which was set up under Sir George May, a former director of the Prudential and a leading government financial adviser, to advise the Treasury and the Board of Trade on the progress of protected industries, hoped that reorganisation would be eased by protection. Neville Chamberlain, the Chancellor of the Exchequer, shared their hopes. But other Treasury officials and the Bank of England, in contrast, took a more pessimistic view that unless the duties were explicitly temporary and conditional, they would hinder reorganisation.[72]

The next three years showed that the Bank's pessimism was justified. Their broad strategy of regional amalgamations depended on resolving conflicts of interest within the industry in favour of the most efficient producers. But by dealing with the industry *as a whole* they saw that a solution conciliating all interests became more likely and overall reorganisation less likely. May and IDAC disagreed with this view. But they had no clear alternative strategy except to rely on the 'good sense' of the industry. But, as we have seen, what was good sense for particular firms or particular interests within those firms did not necessarily correspond to the thoroughgoing reorganisation of the industry. The starting point for May and IDAC was the need for central representational machinery for the steel industry which could take an overall view of policy for the industry. This would have made sense if there were a workable consensus among industrialists. But if a consensus did not emerge the government would find themselves in a position of responsibility without power.

From the start, leading figures at the Bank of England foresaw the difficulties of pushing reorganisation under tariffs. The most critical were Charles Bruce Gardner, the Bank's senior industrial adviser and himself a former director of the Shelton Iron and Steel Co., and Andrew Duncan, the Chairman of the Central Electricity Board and one of the most prominent of the industrialists involved in the SMT and BID, who was to play a leading part in the history of the steel industry in the next two decades. They feared that IDAC's opening move, which was to approach the principal steel trade association directly, would shift attention from the development of practical amalgamation schemes on to questions of the formal organisation of the industry. They wanted instead to 'get straight on to the people who were actually negotiating' and thus 'keep Sir William Larke [the President of the NFISM] out', since he would tend to push to the fore the conciliation of the wide array of particular interests represented in the NFISM. It was believed in the Bank that the first meeting between IDAC and the NFISM had been 'engineered' by Larke who 'had a very close friend in Mr Ashley, the Secretary of IDAC', and that as a result discussion would at once be channelled into 'going over the ground again' with minority interests in the industry 'who had refused to play'.[73]

Contrary to the worst fears of the Bank, however, it seems that May and IDAC did intend at first to insist on coupling the production of reorganisation schemes with the establishment of representative machinery for the industry. Bruce Gardner thought that the steelmakers had expected to be able to 'pat Sir George May on the back' and then get on with electing their own committee, and he was surprised that May acted to circumvent Larke by appointing Charles Mitchell of Dorman Long, who Montagu Norman respected and wanted to recruit to BID, as Chairman of the new National Committee which was set up to produce reorganisation proposals.[74] This, Bruce Gardner felt, was 'a bombshell' which 'told the steelmakers where to get off' and left the industry 'scratching its head'.[75] But though May's appointee was more dynamic then Larke, IDAC still had no real power in its hands and in the next few months May's conciliatory speeches to the various trades associations within the industry amounted to an absolute guarantee of the autonomy of the makers in working out their own salvation. As he put it to the sheet-makers, 'The whole thing rests with you. . . . I want you to do it all for yourselves. . . . Why do you not all have a meeting and decide what you are going to do yourselves. . . . It is your affair, it is not mine; honestly it is not. After all you are all reasonably minded men. If you get together you will surely find a solution.'[76]

The scheme agreed on at the June meeting of the NFISM envisaged a national plan being built up on the basis of district schemes formulated by regional and sectional committees based on the existing trades associations in the industry which the National Committee would then fuse together. But, once set up, despite the urgings of May and Alfred Hurst, the leading Treasury official with special responsibility for IDAC, the committees relegated reorganisation and concentrated on their own arrangements of association and lobbying for higher tariffs.[77] By July the SMT felt 'the whole thing seems to be wrapped in fog' and May was unable to make any positive demands of the steelmakers.[78] By October he was ready to concede that he had no objection to schemes being made *conditional* on Protection as long as there *were* schemes.[79]

This was exactly what a strong body of opinion in the Bank and a section of the government had feared. Duncan at the Bank for instance had argued for a tough line of making tariffs conditional on real action on physical amalgamations. In September 1932, seeing the drift of things, SMT even discussed pushing this position by getting Norman to see May personally to 'lodge a protest before it was too late' against his soft line.[80]

Civil servants in IDAC committed to reorganisation were acutely dissatisfied with the National Committee's lack of progress too. Nevertheless, they felt it impossible and undesirable not to renew the tariff for a further two years in October 1932. But they recognised that the devolved method of preparing schemes through Regional and Sectional Committees had produced nothing and it was abandoned. In its place, a three-man sub-committee of Mitchell, Larke and the Treasury official Hurst was set up to draft proposals. It was hoped that the intimate involvement of Hurst would ensure serious pursuit of reorganisation.[81]

The Government's agreement to renew the tariff for steel in October 1932 was publicly declared to be based on 'most definite assurances' on reorganisation.[82] In fact, the Government was quite well aware that these assurances were meaningless. Runciman, the President of the Board of Trade, had already written to Neville Chamberlain at the Exchequer to tell him that: 'May could not tell me anything that I could say in the House to demonstrate that the iron and steel industry had in fact begun to reorganise itself. . . . He is as convinced as I of the recalcitrant and procrastinatory nature of many people concerned.' Steel had, in effect, 'received protection which was beyond all its hopes a year ago and has come nothing'.[83] Snowden meanwhile underlined the point to the Prime Minister, MacDonald: The 'assurances' that May had got

> are vague and not really worth much. It looks as if the Iron and Steel Committee are simply playing with him [May], and the difficulty is that a great deal of ammunition will be given to those who said that you must make protection conditional on reorganisation and that if you gave protection first you would never see reorganisation. In fact, it is difficult to avoid the conclusion that May and Hurst have mishandled the business and been bamboozled and May continues to be bamboozled and the brunt of criticism and trouble will fall on you.[84]

The new three-man sub-committee of the National Committee which followed tariff renewal prepared its scheme between October 1932 and March 1933. It did not even consider amalgamation of firms or concentration of production. Such moves, they stated, could only have local or sectional impact. Instead they sought to develop 'national co-operation' in the form of industry-wide price associations grouped around existing trades associations to stabilise the industry.[85] Hurst made some efforts to raise the issue of production and of a strong central body funded from a levy and with statutory support, but as Bruce Gardner noted, the plan the Committee drew up concentrated instead on 'the much more seductive path of trying to placate the majority by means of making the price association more comprehensive and powerful'. Its references to reorganisation were spurious. It just listed 'a number of desirable functions of the Association, all of which are permissive' and never went further than 'pious words'.[86]

The SMT saw the scheme as an actual 'obstacle' to regional amalgamations, and the Treasury agreed that it 'relaxed' pressure to regroup.[87] Amalgamations would eliminate redundant plant and concentrate decision-making and planning. But this scheme would have the opposite effect. By 'placing every manufacturer within a Confederation of Associations' it would institutionalise the conflicts within the industry as conflicts between a number of elected representatives, all in competition with each other. Such a body could not promote rationalisation, but would be 'a dead hand on outstanding initiative and enterprise'. High cost enterprises would resist investment by competitors to establish low-cost plant.[88]

The Bank of England, therefore, lamented that 'the worst fears of six months ago had been realised',[89] but politically, they, like the government, accepted that the tariff had to stay. The very absence of reorganisation meant that if the tariff were to be removed, the industry and its employment would be even more vulnerable than they were before.[90] Both Bank and government were confined to coaxing and criticising the recalcitrant industry. The BID, in fact, refused to co-operate with IDAC to provide finance for the development of the iron and steel industry within the framework of this confederation of Associations.[91] But, as they predicted, the Government rejected any recourse to compulsion and Runciman admitted that if the industry were agreed on what they wanted, the Government had no alternative but to go along with that.[92] Meanwhile, despite the rancour and disillusionment in many government departments, the Government continued to profess in public that the new scheme embodied in a White Paper in February 1933 was a 'real step forward' in reorganisation.[93]

Why was the steel industry so unwilling to move towards the sort of national reorganisation that bankers and politicians were so convinced was necessary? The main answer is to be found in the variety of views taken by different firms and sections of the industry of the impact on their particular interests of a powerful central authority sponsored by government to promote reorganisation. These clashes of interest can be traced in the debates inside the two sub-committees of the National Committee which were set up to translate the White Paper into final proposals, and which sat between July 1933 and April 1934.[94]

Three main currents existed. In the first stood the large relatively prosperous and expanding firms, United Steel, Richard Thomas, and Stewarts and Lloyds. With their lower costs and favourable market positions, they wanted to strengthen their ability to expand at the expense of others, particularly since each saw the prospect of achieving either a regional or product monopoly. They saw themselves as the main beneficiaries of a particular type of increased legislative or government involvement. Hilton of United Steel, for example, was a vigorous advocate of a powerful central organisation with large funds, and of a flexible quota system which would enable low-cost firms to increase their share of trade. Firth of Richard Thomas, facing problems of a growing firm needing a whip hand against tenacious small enterprises, went further and wanted a body with statutory powers to enforce regional reorganisation. He was a severe critic of IDAC for not raising duties high enough to drive out the small re-rolling firms which relied on cheap imported semi-finished steel to undercut large integrated British concerns such as Richard Thomas which had higher overheads. These firms were sitting tight and waiting for imports to revive. Hence Firth wanted a body with some coercive power.[95] A.C. MacDiarmid of Stewarts and Lloyds who enjoyed a near monopoly position in the expanding tube sector also favoured an Enabling Act to coerce small awkward rivals.[96]

The second and most powerful grouping included the big heavy steelmakers who were still backward and depressed, represented by Dorman (Dorman Long), Talbot (South Durham and Cargo Fleet), Beale (Guest, Keen, Baldwin), and Craig (Colvilles), and who had the influential support of Larke of the NFISM. It was their view which largely shaped the final scheme. Their main concerns were to revive profitability within existing company structures and current levels of demand. To do so, industry had to 'discipline itself and restrict developments here and there'. Even under tariffs, internal competition could destroy profitability and so it must be restrained. Even if profits revived, they feared that this would generate 'a new spate of competition in the more profitable parts of the industry and this competition must be regulated'.[97] Hence they wanted increased tariffs which would ensure their position of monopoly suppliers to home finishing trades[98] by making possible long-term price fixing arrangements with the finishers.[99] Amalgamations had to be left to natural market forces.[100] At the same time, they resisted any strong central body, and they stubbornly resisted the proposal for a substantial central levy.[101] For them, the advantages of having some scheme were primarily in stability, as a guarantee of government favour and as clearing the way for them to strengthen their own position.

The third groups, numerically important but economically lightweight, were the finishers, smaller firms and re-rollers such as Whiteheads, Bairds, Skinningrove and the Steel Company of Scotland. They feared that a central organisation would 'put all the various sections under the domination of the heavy steel industry' (McCosh of

Bairds).[102] They resisted all apparatuses of control or quota schemes, loyalty rebates and penalties because they saw the whole question of control implied there. As Hutchinson of Skinningrove noted, it raised 'the grave question of where the control of each association is to be, especially if questions of efficiency and redundancy are to be raised'.[103] Hence the latter two groups were prepared to make common cause to reject the quota proposals that Hurst and S.C.E. Lloyd of Stewarts and Lloyds pushed through one of the National Committee's sub-committees. These allowed for an 'auction' of a proportion of proposed annual quotas to enable progressive firms to expand at the expense of backward ones. This implied 'an automatically diminishing quota on the part of many firms and involve(d) their ultimate extinction'.[104]

The only consensus within the industry was on the need to maintain the tariff, to maintain prices and to develop a more effective national voice to bargain over tariff levels and negotiate with government. When it came to programmes of reorganisation all the latent conflicts of interest came to the fore and brought progress to a halt. Thus when in February 1934 a constitution for a new central organisation was passed 76–28 by the NFISM it had only the most limited powers.[105] May assured the National Committee that this was the best way of keeping control of the industry in their own hands and warned that public criticism would be aroused if the powers of the central body appeared too meagre.[106] Nevertheless the Revision Committee which drew up the final constitution of the new central body, the British Iron and Steel Federation (BISF), still further safeguarded the autonomy of the Associations, and IDAC's original concept of a central supervisory body exerting control through a general policy of binding agreements on prices, quotas and rebates, was reduced to a shadow. The final scheme was not one of reorganisation but solely one of price maintenance.[107]

IDAC accepted these developments more or less unhappily. Ideologically they rejected central planning and direction of the industry both as undesirable and as unenforceable and politically dangerous. They saw their role as 'breaking down individualism and educating businessmen in many industries to work together'.[108] Their intellectual rationale was that free competition was the only effective long-term way to reorganise the industry, but that in the short term this would only result in the industry 'bleeding to death'. Hence the position they were left with was that the industry had to be kept alive through the depression by maintaining its profits at a reasonable level through price maintenance so that when recovery came, reorganisation could then follow in more favourable conditions. Hence the development of central machinery was primarily a way of developing channels to co-ordinate voluntary reorganisation at a later stage.[109] Therefore, they were prepared to accept 'toned down' central structures and let it 'play itself in' for the future.[110] Leading figures in the Treasury, however, did not like it. The situation left them 'with an uncomfortable feeling that a defence is being made for being content with something rather ineffective'.[111]

What of the other Government departments? Runciman, the President of the Board of Trade, and his officials saw the adoption of these proposals as putting the industry 'into a straitjacket'. The price maintenance and quota scheme was no more than 'a seductive selling scheme'. Yet, they concluded, if the industry were agreed on this policy 'it is difficult to see what can be done to induce them to change their opinion'. In this situation, the government might well have preferred to step back and leave the industry alone. But they could not. Whatever the new structures of the industry were, IDAC consent gave them the legitimation of government backing. Pragmatically, the National Government were prepared to make considerable departures from *laissez-faire*. Circumstances pushed them into a more active relation to industry, yet, at the same time, ministers and departments, like Runciman at the Board of Trade, wanted to maintain definite limits on such moves. Runciman feared the implications of getting involved in any scheme that had powers of central direction or that would make possible interference with the management of individual firms to such an extent as to cast into doubt the controlling role of shareholders. This would 'lead pretty directly to the late Government's Public Utility Corporation'.[112] The result of this attitude was a pervasive unwillingness to take any governmental initiative.

The BISF came into existence with a constitution but, because of the reluctance to define the terms of affiliation, without any members. Its very existence depended on its getting the goodwill of the industry and persuading the various trades associations to affiliate. Both IDAC and steelmakers such as Hilton who saw a role for a central body saw the credibility of the new BISF and its potential for evolving into something more positive as depending largely on the choice of a chairman. He had to be a 'man of eminence' who could not simply be labelled a tool of the heavy steelmakers.[113] The process of the choice of chairman reflected something of a government–industry convergence. Both accepted the limitations of BISF as an arena whereby they could exert mutual influence and conciliate conflicting interests.

Meanwhile, as a result of a considerable shift within the SMT during 1933–4, the Bank of England also came to accept this as inevitable.

The SMT majority, and especially Bruce Gardner and Norman, had originally wanted to 'have nothing to do' with the National Committee Report of February 1933,[114] or with the final report a year later which was a 'poor affair'.[115] But during this period, discussion was opening up within SMT as Duncan began to shift away from his earlier highly critical position.[116] By March 1933, he was arguing 'the report might not be what we wanted, but there it was, and in his view we should consider whether we could not turn it to good account'. Though it did not contain a plan, it did contain 'machinery for a plan' and 'this was the only way the sanction of the industry could be obtained'.[117] By the time of the final draft he could see no alternative to the scheme except 'Government control'.[118] Hence the best way of working within the existing constraints was 'to involve the right people' in the running of the machine,[119] which boiled down by April 1934 to the need to get the right chairman.[120]

If the SMT were to follow Duncan's reasoning it would involve the recognition by SMT that its whole regional amalgamation strategy was defunct. The other members of the SMT accepted this rather more slowly and unwillingly. But, once the option of using tariff changes as a bargaining counter disappeared, their options narrowed rapidly. During the summer of 1933, Sir William Larke at the NFISM had got wind of 'a very strong movement in Bank of England circles to force Bruce Gardner into the position of Chairman of our Corporation' and he suspected that the Bank might be prepared to exert financial pressure to get him in. MacDiarmid of Stewarts and Lloyds was arranging a dinner party in the following week at which the Bank were intending to float the idea. Larke felt that the whole prospect of co-operative organisation among the producers might be jeopardised by such a 'false step' and he circularised his friends to organise opposition. He told John Craig the head of the largest Scottish steel firm that: 'the best thing to do is to categorically show that it is *impossible* and *unthinkable* at the outset *now* before anyone is publicly committed to it. Just say, if asked, impossible no one would seriously entertain it.' His own solution would be for himself to be chairman at first with Hurst as his deputy. In the meantime he would not 'surrender my self-respect and reputation by succumbing to this horrible log-rolling pressure'.[121]

Both this suggestion and a subsequent one to put in a hardliner like Sir Robert Horne as Chairman of the Federation to bring governmental pressure to bear on the industry[122] got a cold reception and were not persisted with. By 1934, the Bank had to recognise that the alternatives were either an unacceptable degree of far-ranging intervention, or a compromise Chairman who would have the goodwill of the industry and who would attempt to promote reorganisation by voluntary methods.

Horace Wilson the leading industrial adviser at the Treasury, outlined what such an alternative strategy would involve. At the very least, the Government would have to create legislative powers to enable them to buy up minorities in the industry at a fair valuation and re-sell them at the same price to merged interests. But, if they did this, the demand to extend the legislation to coal – and beyond? – 'would be powerful'. Moreover, debenture holders might stick out for better terms if they saw that the Government intended to ensure mergers. Moreover, compulsory buying and scrapping would create politically difficult redundancies – which had been one of the main reasons for the reluctance to create compulsory amalgamations through the Coal Act. Or else, if a bought-up firm then re-started new plant with its cash, the Government might then have to block this too and end up being drawn further and further in.[123] In the cotton industry, where there was clear majority support for proposals formulated within the industry, the Government was prepared to undertake a limited legislative intervention in the 1936 Spindles Act,[124] but in steel, where there was no such clarity within the industry over what was required, such an undertaking was too hazardous. The Treasury doubted the Government's ability to deal effectively with the complex internal problems of firms that an attempt to force reorganisation would throw up.

The Bank and the Treasury, therefore, came to recognise that they had to make the most of a bad job and pursue conciliation and suasion. Andrew Duncan of SMT was clearly the best candidate for this. Norman had sounded him out in January 1934, and when the BISF Committee selected him, Norman intervened behind the scenes to overcome the unwillingness of the Minister of Transport, Hore Belisha, to release him from his post as Chairman of the Central Electricity Board. Duncan took office in January 1935 with Larke as his deputy. The choice of Duncan with his background in the CEB was highly significant. The CEB had been developed as a state-backed co-ordinator of existing private undertakings; it was conceived of by the Government as a commercially-minded and efficient executive body 'managed by practical men in close touch with industry' (Baldwin); under Duncan it maintained rigorous independence from the Government and was subject to only minimal Treasury or ministerial control; and during the period of Duncan's leadership it had concentrated on an extensive round of conciliating private interests within the electricity industry, employing personal contact and confidence as one of its main methods.[125] In all of these features it set up precedents that marked governmental thinking about the possible evolution of the BISF. In practice, as we shall see, Duncan was not able to simply repeat the successes of his CEB period in steel where he was faced with more powerfully entrenched interests and lacked the centralising weapon of the Grid. Nevertheless the CEB background was a powerful formative influence on his approach and strategy at the BISF.

III

In the late 1920s most government departments had taken the view that tariff protection would hinder rather than promote the rationalisation of the steel industry. The early 1930s showed this view to be correct. Montagu Norman and his industrial advisers at the Bank of England who shared this view argued after 1932 that the logical course for the government now to follow was to manage the protected industry in such a way as to support the most efficient producers and facilitate their expansion at the expense of weaker firms. Yet IDAC, the Board of Trade and the leading figures in the National Government rejected such an approach. Like the Bank they still believed in reorganisation via amalgamations, but unlike the Bank, which both directly and indirectly had a certain amount of experience of direct managerial involvement at the level of the enterprise, they were not prepared to back particular firms at the expense of others. The traditional reluctance of governments to promote monopoly proved stronger than the desire to maximise efficiency as they saw it. Instead, the National Government opted for a strategy of industrial self-government. In effect this was an attempt to foster an effective central body for the industry with which the government could deal and negotiate to develop reorganisation without taking the responsibility for such reorganisation out of the hands of industrialists. The strategy foundered, however, on the extensive internal rifts within the industry and the absence of a workable consensus among the steelmakers. While many firms saw much that was desirable in amalgamation and rationalisation, industrialists also had a number of other goals which were seen as equally important and often in conflict with reorganisation, such as the defence of particular vested interests within the firms (debenture holders, owners, local customers, creditors, etc.) or the avoidance of risk; most reorganisation schemes were complex and their results not easily predictable. There was a sound material basis for the 'recalcitrance' of the steelmakers and it required consistent and positive pressure if it was to be overcome.

This was not to be forthcoming. The government did not develop more precise mechanisms for intervention such as a system of incentives and penalties. Partly this was a result of the National Government's moral and ideological resistance to the notion of compulsion. Partly it was a fear of the consequences of confronting vested interests in the industry. But more than this the government had neither a bureaucratic apparatus nor the expertise to tackle the problems of the industry and government departments profoundly doubted their own competence to intervene and deal with the complexities that would arise. The Bank of England with its rather more developed corps of industrial experts was more prepared to contemplate a strategy of direct intervention in firms – though its own experiences in attempting this were singularly unhappy – but the National Government ruled this out. There were no significant advocates in government circles of the view that the government could run industry better than the industrialists. Far from the state acting 'in the true interests of capital as a whole' at all times, the National Government were quite clear to themselves that they did not know what the 'true interests' of capital were.[125]

Politicians were acutely aware that government protection of the steel industry in the early 1930s was being used by the industry for its own private ends, but they fairly soon resigned themselves to accepting the position. The Bank of England did not concur until 1933–4 but they too came to accept the strength of the position of the industry in relation to government as an accomplished fact. The appointment of Duncan as Chairman of BISF in 1934 marked the acceptance by both Bank and government that industrialists in steel could not be pushed along against their will. The task now became one of creating an effective central organisation with a certain authority in the industry which in the long term they could hope to influence in terms of overall policy and guidelines. In the years before the Second World War this policy was a weak one. In effect the state sponsored a cartel over which it had little control.[126] In the longer term, however, the foundation was being laid for the close familiarity of government and industrialist circles which characterised the relations between the Conservative party and government and the industry during the post-war battle against nationalisation.[127] The National Government built up the BISF as the recognised intermediary between government and the industry; it fostered its prestige and authority; it won its confidence as a friend of the industry and it developed a close mutual understanding between Conservative politicians and the leading industrialists. These slowly developing underlying changes were laying the basis for a new relationship between government and industrialists during and after the war. Government was slowly permeating and being permeated by the industrial milieu with which it had for so long been unfamiliar.

In most European and Japanese industrialisation, governments were usually involved in the process from an early stage, often via tariff manipulation. But in Britain the unquestioned primacy of British industry in the world economy in the nineteenth century had been accompanied by a unique degree of government abstention from economic intervention. The British state was not by any means a non-interventionist one, but it developed its active functions in this period primarily in imperial, legal and financial matters. Above all it traditionally sought to provide a stable framework within which industrialists could carry on their own affairs. When the crisis of the inter-war years undermined this simple position, government had to develop a new relationship with a set of industries already well established and representing powerful entrenched vested interests. The case of the tariff and the vested interests in the steel industry shows how this new relationship of mutual reliance began to develop initially with the government lacking any clear industrial policy or any organised interventionist apparatus. Having conceded tariff protection it had no alternative but to back the existing interests in the industry and hope over a period of time to build up a role of influence through prolonged co-operation. In the short run, however, the government and its agencies were quite conscious that they had surrendered the initiative and were being rather pushed around by the steelmakers. The tariff had long since ceased to be an active policy for social and economic reorganisation; the experience of its early years in practice underlined its inadequacy as an instrument in the restructuring of depressed industries.

5 The Politics of Producers' Co-operation: the FBI–TUC–NCEO Talks, 1929–1933

Michael Dintenfass

To critics of the liberal, individualistic social order which characterised Britain between 1832 and 1939 the ideal of co-operation between the owners of capital and the owners of labour offered an attractive alternative to the marketplace clash of individuals seeking to maximise their own self-interest. For Carlyle and Arnold, the common devotion of employers and their workers – indeed, of all British citizens – to national ends above and beyond their own immediate needs promised society a moral tone superior to that arising from innumerable 'cash-nexus' transactions.[1] Observers of the industrial scene as different as Col H.C.S. Dyer, manager of Armstrong's Elswick works during the 1897–98 engineering strike and a major figure in the creation of the Engineering Employers' Federation, and Sidney and Beatrice Webb endorsed an alliance between producers on economic grounds. Co-operation between masters and men, they held, would make possible the elimination of irrationalities and inefficiencies which competition had introduced into productive processes.[2]

Contemporary analysts of inter-war Britain valued a producers' alliance primarily for the political possibilities that it seemed to hold open. The mutual interest of industrialists and their workers in the prosperity of trade appeared to provide the basis for political alignments which would serve as vehicles for economic strategies alternative to those pursued by the governments of the day. Keynes, for example, spoke of the community of interest between manufacturing employers and employees and their common opposition to the banker and the rentier.[3] Oswald Mosley consistently organised his plans for the regeneration of the British economy around Keynes's distinction between the active, or productive, and passive participants in the economy.[4]

Recently, a number of historians of the inter-war period have found the concept of a producers' alliance illuminating. Sidney Pollard and John Foster have seen in the peculiarly British divorce of finance from industry a fleeting glimpse of what might have been: a unified producers' front against the slump.[5] Keith Middlemas has located an alliance of employers and trade unionists at the very heart of the twentieth-century constitution. In *Politics in Industrial Society*, he has argued that 'a peculiarly subtle and pervasive form' of collaboration between organised management and organised labour formed the basis of the corporatist triangle which defined inter-war politics in Britain.[6]

Certainly, the historical record provides ample evidence of attempts at industrial co-operation during the 1920s and 1930s: the National Industrial Conference of 1919, the Mond–Turner talks and the joint talks held among the Trades Union Congress, the Federation of British Industries, and the National Confederation of Employers' Organisations in the period 1929–33. Whether these instances highlight an emerging 'corporatist bias' or represent a series of unsuccessful variations on an attractive but difficult theme is an open question.[7] Both the National Industrial Conference and the Mond–Turner talks have been judged routinely as failures.[8] Consequently, it is upon the discussions among the TUC, the FBI and the NCEO that arguments about inter-war industrial politics have turned.

The purpose of this paper is to provide an account of the FBI–TUC–NCEO talks of 1929–33. By outlining the achievements as well as the limits of this experiment in co-operative decision-making, the author hopes to define the extent to which organised management and labour were able to align behind a programme aimed at conquering the slump. In the process, he attempts to highlight the factors that were conducive to co-operation as well as those that militated against it. Finally, through a discussion of governmental responses to these forays into the arena of economic policy formulation, he suggests a rough measure of the degree to which the FBI, the TUC and the NCEO were incorporated into the decision-making networks of inter-war Britain.

Of course, formal co-operation in matters of economic policy at the national level does not exhaust the possible forms of a producers' alliance or the functions that such an alliance may perform. Middlemas has suggested that the FBI, the TUC and the NCEO played important roles in maintaining the consent of their constituents to governments presiding haplessly over massive economic dislocation.[9] It is equally plausible that co-operation between masters and men at the local level or in particular industries helped to mitigate the worst social and economic consequences of chronic, large-scale unemployment, at least for those party to the bargains.[10]

Neither the putative social control nor social welfare functions of producers' alliances find any place in this paper.[11] This silence ought not to be regarded as a judgement upon the existence of alliances of this sort. Indeed, if it can be shown that employers and employees frequently proceeded jointly in social and economic matters at the local level, then it will be necessary to reassess prevailing opinions about local politics and popular opinions during the 1920s and 1930s. It is doubtful, however, whether local alliances will prove to be of decisive import for the analysis of central government. If the national organisations of management and labour did no more than to compel their constituents to obey policies in whose formulation these organisations played no part and to succour them against the harsh consequences of these policies, then these organisations did not occupy a central place in the inter-war constitution.

I

The joint talks held among the FBI, the TUC and the NCEO were the culmination of the several attempts to bring together leading industrialists and trade unionists which followed the General Strike. At first, the Government, in the person of Sir Arthur Steel-Maitland, Baldwin's Minister of Labour, provided the initiative. Already in October 1926, while the coal dispute which had precipitated the nine-day stoppage in May smouldered, Steel-Maitland was working to win organised management and labour for an 'Industrial Concordat'. His efforts foundered, however, when the Prime Minister insisted upon pushing ahead with the Trade Disputes Bill. To trade unionists this measure, which banned sympathy strikes (or so the ambiguous language of the Act seemed to suggest), substituted 'contracting in' to the trade union political levy for 'contracting out' and forbade civil servants from joining unions affiliated to the TUC, was deeply offensive. Following its publication in March 1927, the delegation of trade unionists led by Ernest Bevin, General Secretary of the Transport and General Workers' Union, withdrew from the informal talks with an employers' group led by Lord Weir which Steel-Maitland had sponsored.[12]

By September 1927 the trade unionists were again favourably inclined towards co-operation with employers. In his presidential address to the TUC Annual Conference, George Hicks (Amalgamated Union of Building Trade Workers) called upon the representative organisations of management and labour to create effective machinery for exchanges on views relating to efficiency and standards of living. When the FBI and the NCEO responded coolly to the TUC's overture, Sir Alfred Mond stepped in. Allied with a group of thirty-nine leading industrialists, Mond invited the TUC to discussions covering 'the entire field of [industrial] reorganisation and industrial relations'.[13] The TUC accepted, and in January 1928 talks began. Seven months later the Conference on Industrial Reorganisation and Industrial Relations, as the talks were formally titled, bore fruit in the shape of a joint Interim Report which embodied the following provisions: recognition by the employers of the TUC and its affiliated organisations 'as the most effective and appropriate representatives of the workers in matters of industrial relations and industrial policy'; a pledge by the employers not to victimise workers on account of trade union activity; the recommendation that a National Industrial Council empowered to create machinery for the peaceful resolution of industrial disputes be established; joint approval of rationalisation provided that due allowance were made for trade union consultation and the welfare of workers displaced; and a call for a review of the nation's monetary policy.

The efforts of Mond and his associates to win the support of the FBI and the NCEO for these proposals led directly to the FBI–TUC–NCEO conferences. In neither of the employers' organisations was a majority prepared to approve the Interim Report which the TUC had endorsed at its 1928 Annual Conference. The climate of expectation aroused 'by the very success of the Mond–Turner talks in framing a joint report', however, made outright rejection a delicate matter politically. Therefore, the FBI and the NCEO included in their letter of rejection of February 1929 an invitation to the TUC to meet with them to explore the possibility of further talks.[14]

Ten months of meetings, letters and manoeuvring resulted, in December 1929, in an agreement upon a procedure for talks and a list of topics. Each organisation was to enjoy the right to propose for discussion subjects which fell within its competence but which did not violate such autonomy as the constituents of the three organisations retained. Since 1919 the FBI and the NCEO had maintained a rough division of labour whereby the former took responsibility for economic and commercial questions and the latter for labour questions. An Allocation Committee now was to be set up to distribute topics between the two organisations accordingly.[15] Each organisation was to be entitled to refuse talks on any subject provided that a reason was given for the refusal. Among the topics tentatively scheduled for consideration were: unemployment, industry and finance, inter-Empire trade, social service co-ordination by departments, taxation of industry, and general international labour questions.

While the FBI, the TUC and the NCEO were negotiating, the political and economic climate was changing. In June 1929 Labour entered Downing Street after five years of Conservative government. Shortly thereafter, the financial situation began to deteriorate. The flight of capital from London to New York and Paris almost pushed Britain off the gold standard in August. The Hatry scandal in September renewed fears about the vulnerability of sterling which were calmed only when the crash on Wall Street sent funds back across the Atlantic.[16] Trade, meanwhile, remained depressed. Unemployment, though lower in the summer and autumn of 1929 than it had been a year before, showed no sign of dropping below one million.[17] Dismayed by this dismal picture, Philip Snowden, the new Chancellor of the Exchequer, set up the Macmillan Committee on Finance and Industry to investigate the connection between domestic and international banking, finance and credit and the state of British trade.[18]

The appointment of the Macmillan Committee prompted the Federation of British Industries to make use of the new consultative machinery. In February 1930 the Federation, after the Allocation Committee had granted permission, invited the TUC to discuss the submissions that the two organisations were scheduled to make to the Macmillan Committee. The TUC's General Council accepted the invitation subject to the provisions that its acceptance 'not imply giving joint evidence' and that meetings be postponed until its Economic Committee, then preparing the TUC's submission, had more fully developed its policy.[19] Consequently, representatives of the FBI and the TUC met to discuss the relationship between finance and industry only after both organisations had made appearances before the Macmillan Committee.

Though prepared independently, the first submissions that the FBI and the TUC made to the committee covered similar ground and reached similar conclusions. The TUC testified that the policy of deflation 'deliberately pursued' since 1920 had occasioned increased unemployment, a decline in wage rates and industrial unrest. As a means to the elimination of these evils, the TUC suggested the stabilisation of the general price level. How this stabilisation was to be achieved was not specified.[20]

The FBI likewise concentrated on the harmful effects of post-war monetary developments. The root cause of the contraction of British trade, the Federation argued, was the failure to restore the international gold standard to its pre-war operation. The British monetary authorities had tried gamely to re-establish the old arrangements. Unfortunately, in an economically nationalistic environment their efforts had proved harmful to British traders. Though foreign governments and merchants had manifestly failed to play by the rules in the 1920s, the FBI insisted that Britain's industrial salvation depended on international cooperation. Collective action by the central banks of the leading industrial nations to set in motion a slow, steady rise of wholesale prices, the FBI contended, was 'an essential condition for the restoration of prosperity'.[21]

Prior to the first meeting of their representatives the FBI and the TUC had exchanged copies of their submissions to the Macmillan Committee. Not surprisingly, the first joint discussion of substantive matters by representatives of the two bodies produced the agreeable impression that 'the views of the two organisations as to the underlying circumstances of the present situation very largely coincide'.[22] In fact, this impression was illusory. Beneath the similarities discernible in the initial submissions which the FBI and the TUC made to the Macmillan Committee lay profound differences – differences deriving from the diametrically opposed ways in which the two organisations interpreted Britain's economic difficulties. With their second statements to the Macmillan Committee the TUC and the FBI laid bare these differences.

The FBI, in its second statement, confined itself to two observations about banking and industry. Firstly, the Federation argued that the absence of credit facilities of an intermediate character made it extremely difficult for British traders to compete with their rivals 'in financial facilities needed to adapt plant and organisation to present day conditions and to enable marketing terms as good as theirs to be offered to overseas buyers'. Secondly, the FBI noted that the ignorance of ordinary commercial bankers about industry had produced an unsatisfactory distribution of the available credit. Dubious enterprises in industries already suffering from over-capacity were obtaining finance without difficulty while deserving projects went short of funds. To remedy this situation, the FBI recommended that 'the banks should be adequately informed in regard to such matters as the general productive capacity, market prospects and other relevant statistics in connection with the major industries'.[23] That the banks could be adequately informed without directly involving themselves in industry was a point upon which the Federation placed great emphasis.[24]

The FBI's testimony was fully consistent with the organisation's other assessments of Britain's inter-war economic problems in that primary responsibility for the nation's ills was placed upon institutions and individuals outside British industry.[25] Here, the stress was placed upon the contributions of commercial banks to the contraction of British trade. In part I of its Macmillan Committee testimony, the FBI had shown how foreign industrialists, often in collusion with their governments, and British monetary authorities had destabilised the environment in which British manufacturers had to work. Elsewhere, reproach was heaped upon successive British governments for their profligate habits.[26] Various members of the FBI also held that the rigidities and frictions which trade unions introduced into the labour market bore an important share of the responsibility for Britain's economic difficulties. These sentiments, of course, could not be expressed by the Federation itself because of the exclusion of labour issues from its field of responsibility.[27]

Industry itself, the Federation steadfastly maintained, could shoulder only a small share of the blame. Of course, some manufacturers had made mistaken judgements for which they paid with losses, even bankruptcies. Their example, however, should have educated others whom the market then would have rewarded for their perspicacity.

That all British entrepreneurs – the wise and the not so wise alike – were having difficulties showed that the market's normal distribution of prizes and penalties was being obstructed from outside.[28]

The TUC, as we have seen, shared the FBI's view that the monetary policy operated by the Treasury and the Bank of England since the war had been harmful to the British economy. The trade unionists, however, had little sympathy for the Federation's tolerant appraisal of the performance of British industrialists. Indeed, in part II of its testimony to the Macmillan Committee, the TUC argued that British capitalists, when judged by their own chosen criterion of efficiency, were miserable failures.[29]

British industry, the TUC charged, had fallen behind in international competition because it was badly organised and poorly equipped. It was in such a rundown state precisely because ownership had remained in private hands. The pursuit of profits had promoted a thoroughly anarchic pattern of industrial development that was ill-attuned not just to the needs of the community but also to the imperatives of the long-term development of world capitalism. By seeking immediate and secure profits British capitalists had subverted their own ability to continue to accumulate capital.[30]

According to the TUC, the restoration of British manufacturing to a competitive position was contingent upon its reorganisation and re-equipment. And reorganisation and re-equipment were contingent upon the replacement of private enterprise by public ownership and control of production and distribution. Only when reconstituted as public service corporations would the nation's basic industries be able to regain their share of the world's markets.[31]

Thus, on questions of economic policy a wide gulf separated the FBI and the TUC. Whereas the former sought the restoration of an environment conducive to private enterprise, the latter was eager to eliminate private enterprise in favour of public ownership of industry. By reviving trade, international action to raise wholesale price levels might have papered over this abyss. In an economically nationalistic world, however, there could be no meaningful détente between the proponents of nationalised industry and the guardians of private industrial property. The failure of the TUC and the FBI to issue a single joint statement on financial policy or to send even one joint delegation to the government confirms that collaboration in this sphere came to nothing.

II

In May 1930, as the FBI–TUC talks on finance and industry were getting started, the TUC invited the National Confederation of Employers' Organisations to discuss ways of minimising the human costs of reorganisation and re-equipment. The brief round of talks which ensued, like the parallel discussions between the FBI and the TUC, produced no agreement whatsoever. Indeed, these talks merely provided organised management and organised labour with yet another opportunity to broadcast the utter incompatibility of their approaches to Britain's economic ills.

The first meeting between representatives of the NCEO and the TUC, held on 4 November 1930, allowed an open if not especially fruitful exchange of views. Spokesmen for the TUC emphasised the necessity of managements consulting with the trade unions in the course of drawing up their rationalisation schemes. They also underlined the desirability of keeping displaced men attached to their industries lest a regrettable loss of morale and skill take place. The NCEO's representatives explained that 'it was their experience that every possible effort was made to consider the welfare of employees when these difficulties arose'. The employers also suggested a 'review of the unemployment insurance scheme in order to see whether it could not be better adapted to keeping people in employment'. Walter Citrine, General Secretary of the TUC, proposed that a small joint committee be appointed 'to go into the subject in detail and make a thorough investigation of the positions'. The Confederation promised to consider this suggestion, and the meeting adjourned.[32]

Meeting on 11 February 1931, the NCEO's Council approved the formation of a joint committee. On the same day, the Confederation released a pamphlet entitled *The Industrial Situation* in which it gave its version of Britain's economic problems. The root cause of the nation's problem, the NCEO argued, was uncompetitive costs, pushed up by the high level of unemployment benefit, excessive expenditure on social services and legislative restrictions on industry. What was needed, if British industry were to become competitive again, was a one-third reduction in the rate of unemployment benefit, cuts in the wages of public servants and the reduction of public expenditure to a maximum somewhat below the 1929 level.[33] In its reply to this diatribe, the TUC denied that deflation offered a remedy to the nation's ills, arguing that 'action of this kind on our part would be inevitably followed by similar action on the part of other countries'.[34]

The NCEO conceded in *The Industrial Situation* that industrial reorganisation was necessary but minimised the contribution it could make to the solution of Britain's economic problems on the grounds that the same strategies were available to foreign competitors. At the second meeting with representatives of the TUC, on 19 May 1931, the NCEO's spokesmen handled unemployment caused by rationalisation in a similarly dismissive fashion.

Mr Dorman said the matter had been raised by the Confederation side and considerable doubts were felt as to what was really meant by rationalisation. If, as he thought, efficiency was the principal feature of the process, was not the whole aim to lower costs and thereby increase trade. If this was so the Confederation felt that there could not be any real displacement of labour as a result of rationalisation and they thought that everyone would agree in holding that the level of efficiency ought to be raised.

The TUC's representatives found this attitude unsatisfactory and put two specific questions to the Confederation: (i) Did the Confederation agree that safeguards against displacement by rationalisation were necessary? (ii) Were they prepared to collaborate with the General Council of the Trades Union Congress in arranging such safeguards? The NCEO was to reply at a further meeting.[35] That meeting never took place.

III

By comparison with the TUC–NCEO discussions of rationalisation and the FBI–TUC talks on finance and industry, the FBI–TUC discussions of imperial economic policy present a striking example of enduring, productive cooperation between organised management and organised labour. The efforts of the TUC and the FBI to articulate a common programme for the development of imperial trade lasted over three years and survived two lengthy interruptions and a change of government. Nor were these talks barren of tangible results. Three joint policy statements were published, and at least one joint delegation was dispatched to the Secretary of State for Dominion Affairs.

Unfortunately, all this activity was largely for naught. Britain's ability to prescribe an economic policy for the empire depended upon the consent of the Dominions; and, as we shall note below, the Dominions were extremely reluctant to sanction any formal imperial economic arrangements. Consequently, successive British governments were unable to implement the schemes that the TUC and the FBI jointly devised. Agreement between producers on questions of national economic policy, therefore, advanced furthest in the area over which British governments exercised the least influence. Indeed, the very fact that imperial economic development placed great demands upon the Dominions but virtually none upon Britain in large part explains why the TUC and the FBI were able to lay aside their differences for the sake of joint activity only in this area.

In February 1930, when the FBI invited the TUC to discuss their submissions to the Macmillan Committee, the Federation also suggested that the approach of the Imperial Conference, scheduled for October, made joint talks on imperial economic policy desirable. The

General Council responded positively to this overture but again deferred meetings until its Economic Committee had proceeded further in its formulation of TUC policy.

When the two sides did meet, in May 1930, the discussion indicated that the TUC and the FBI, independently of one another, were moving towards two identical conclusions: that Britain's economic interests required the development of the Empire as an economic unit and that the creation of machinery similar to the Economic Secretariat of the League of Nations was a necessary first step in that direction.[36]

In the weeks that followed the May meeting the FBI and the TUC each prepared formal statements of the opinions expressed on that occasion. At the end of May the TUC's Economic Committee completed a report on commercial policy which the General Council, after some controversy, approved at the end of June and which the Annual Conference, after more controversy, accepted in September.[37] In this document, the TUC argued that Britain's prosperity required the development of the Commonwealth as an economic bloc offering regulated markets, internal free trade and a tariff wall.[38] The FBI, meanwhile, had joined with the Association of British Chambers of Commerce and the Chamber of Shipping of the United Kingdom to form the British Preparatory Committee for the Imperial Conference. The Federation, whose views were contained in an appendix to the report which the Preparatory Committee forwarded to the Board of Trade in July 1930, favoured a system of imperial preference as a preliminary to free trade within the Empire. Like the TUC, the FBI advocated the establishment of an inter-imperial economic secretariat and regularly scheduled economic conferences.[39]

At the second meeting of the FBI and the TUC's spokesmen on imperial economic policy, held on 16 July, the two sides decided to limit their joint initiative to convincing the Government to include the inter-imperial secretariat and the regularly scheduled economic conferences on the agenda of the Imperial Conference.[40] The Government proved quite accommodating. Upon receipt of the *Memorandum by the Federation of British Industries and the General Council of the Trades Union Congress on Commonwealth Trade, Economic Secretariat, etc.*, Ramsay MacDonald assured the FBI and the TUC that 'the ideas we have in mind are everything you suggest and have been worked out in great detail'.[41] Indeed, a week earlier the Cabinet had instructed the President of the Board of Trade to prepare proposals for an 'Imperial Secretariat analagous to the economic side of the League of Nations Secretariat'.[42]

In the event, the Imperial Conference realised the joint hopes of the TUC and the FBI only imperfectly. The Conference did resolve that its Economic Section ought to meet within twelve months to examine 'the means and methods most likely to achieve the common aim [of] the further development of inter-Imperial markets', but a regular schedule of such meetings was not drawn up. The fear of the Dominions, especially Canada, South Africa and the Irish Free State, that imperial economic institutions would threaten their independence in economic affairs precluded the establishment of an inter-imperial economic secretariat.[43]

The TUC suspected that governmental inattention to the joint memorandum was to blame for the outcome of the Conference.[44] Similar feelings may have been present within the FBI, for its representatives joined those of the TUC at a meeting on 17 April 1931 with J.H. Thomas, Secretary of State for the Dominions, who endeavoured to defend the Government's behaviour. It was the Government's intention, Thomas explained, to press for the recommendations contained in the memorandum at the Imperial Economic Conference due to be held in Ottawa in August.[45] By this time, however, the government's enthusiasm for the FBI–TUC proposals was beginning to wane. On 22 April Thomas reported to the Cabinet committee responsible for the preparations for the Ottawa Conference that 'neither of the two bodies in question had any real idea of the political difficulties which are involved in discussing these matters with the Dominions'. To educate the FBI and the TUC, and through them the public at large, about the complexities of Commonwealth affairs, Thomas proposed that representatives of the two organisations be appointed to a standing sub-committee of the Economic Advisory Council. His Cabinet colleagues rejected this suggestion.[46]

The fall of MacDonald's Labour government in August 1931 and the postponement of the Ottawa Conference till July 1932 brought TUC–FBI activity on imperial questions to a temporary halt. Their joint position was already on record, and there was reason to think that the National Government was favourably inclined to the development of the Commonwealth as an economic bloc. Until Commonwealth meetings were in sight once more, there was little purpose in pursuing their common imperial aims. Moreover, both the FBI and the TUC had more pressing concerns at this time. The Federation had recently received a mandate from its constituents to lead a campaign for protection, and the TUC was busy trying to repair the damage of August 1931.[47]

Early in 1932, with the approach of the Ottawa Conference, the FBI and the TUC, proceeding independently of one another, once more took up the problem of imperial economic relations. In March a TUC delegation to the Dominions Office expressed support for the proposals submitted in the joint memorandum of September 1930.[48] At about the same time the FBI, through the reconvened British Preparatory Committee (renamed the British Committee on Empire Trade), pressed the Government to win the Dominion's approval of machinery for studying economic problems of interest to the Empire. The Committee also urged the Government to appoint business advisers to the Ottawa delegation.[49]

The Government responded favourably to this last suggestion, and in March the Cabinet invited the FBI, the TUC, the Association of British Chambers of Commerce and the Council of Shipping to nominate advisers to the Ottawa delegation.[50] These invitations were in line with the standard procedure long followed by British governments, not new departures in governmental practice. FBI representatives had been attending international conferences, either as advisers or deputy delegates, since 1923; TUC leaders had been regular participants since 1927. Usually invitations were extended to organisations from which assistance of a practical sort could be expected. The service that the FBI and the ABCC had rendered the Board of Trade in drawing up lists of commodities 'in respect of which new or increased tariff preferences in the Dominions would assist UK exports' justified the invitations to send representatives to Ottawa.[51] Political considerations account for those invitations which seem to defy the logic of technical competence. The TUC, for example, owed its invitations to Ottowa and to the 1933 World Monetary and Economic Conference to the Government's fear of the consequences of excluding it.[52]

The Government's inclusion of the representatives of organised labour in its panel of advisers moved the FBI to seek a resumption of talks with the TUC. Discussions held early in June 1932 revealed that the FBI and the TUC now entertained very different conceptions of the ultimate goal of imperial economic development. The Federation believed that the Empire, through the reduction of imperial tariffs and the co-ordination of imperial industrial development, could serve as a haven for British industrialists in an economically nationalistic world. The TUC, by contrast, was concerned primarily with the revival of world trade and saw in the Commonwealth a limited sphere in which the aims of unrestricted trade and stable prices first could be realised.[53]

Such divergent conceptions proved reconcilable only in a joint statement of exceptional vagueness. The Ottawa Conference, the TUC and the FBI declared, ought to do everything possible 'to facilitate the easy exchange of goods between the different nations of the Commonwealth'. It was also suggested that the Conference establish a 'sterling area in which there could be greater stability of prices'. Neither proposal received much amplification. The document provided no indication of what steps the Conference should take to increase trade aside from 'the wise planning of production throughout the Commonwealth'. Nor did the statement explain how a sterling zone was to be created or how such a zone would stabilise prices. In place of concrete suggestions for the present, optimistic directions for the future were inserted. Once the Commonwealth had succeeded in carving out a prosperous zone of free trade and steady prices, invitations to join were to be extended to non-Commonwealth nations with similar objective – thus, slowly spreading such a zone around the world.[54]

The utopian ring of this statement was a far cry from the pessimism of the employers whose spokesmen had repeatedly warned that little or nothing was to be expected in the short run.[55] The Ottawa Conference brutally justified this lack of optimism. The twelve bilaterally negotiated treaties signed at Ottawa, seven of which were between Britain and the Dominions, honoured the principle of imperial preference only by increasing the charges and restrictions to which non-imperial goods were subject. Duties on inter-imperial trade remained intact.

One year later, in July 1933, the FBI and the TUC made one last joint appeal to the Government on the subject of imperial trade. The occasion was the publication of a report by a special committee set up at Ottawa to study the problem of economic co-operation within the Empire. The committee's recommendations fell short of the consultative machinery long desired by the FBI and the TUC, and in their letter to the Prime Minister the two bodies again called for the creation of a comprehensive inter-imperial economic secretariat. The FBI and the TUC also requested that the Cabinet reconsider its decision to abolish the Empire Marketing Board, an institution which Baldwin's government had created in 1924 for the purpose of promoting a 'non-tariff preference' in Britain for Empire goods by advertising them and subsidising research into their preservation and transport.[56] By this time, the British government had fallen into line with the Dominions. In place of a full-fledged economic secretariat the Cabinet settled for an imperial statistical bureau. The Empire Marketing Board, the Cabinet confirmed, had no future.[57]

IV

Talks between the Federation of British Industries and the Trades Union Congress on British trade with the Soviet Union complete the story of co-operation between organised management and organised labour in the realm of national economic policy in the period 1929–33. Russian trade was the one area of this joint activity in which official developments bore a resemblance to the policy proposals of the FBI and the TUC. The sequence of talks, delegations and treaties, however, makes it doubtful that the producers' co-operative efforts were an important influence upon governmental behaviour.

Throughout the 1920s the TUC championed the establishment of full diplomatic and commercial ties with Soviet Russia. Increased trade with the Soviet Union, the trade unionists felt, would help to counteract the contraction of British exports.[58] The FBI, meanwhile, displayed a distinct lack of enthusiasm about the improvement of Anglo-Soviet relations. In 1924 the Federation denounced a proposed treaty with Russia as unlikely to promote trade.[59] Five years later the FBI was maintaining that the need for new markets for British manufactures was insufficient reason to re-establish relations with Soviet Russia.[60]

Upon its return to office in 1929, Labour, which had worked diligently but unsuccessfully to put Anglo-Soviet relations on a secure basis during its first term in power, once more took up the Russian cause. Diplomatic relations were restored that year, and a new commercial agreement followed in 1930.[61] By 1931 the impact of the worldwide decline in trade led the Government to seek refuge in an expansion of British sales to the Soviet Union. In April 1931, the Cabinet authorised its Export Credits Committee to hold a meeting with representatives of the FBI, the TUC and the Russian Trade Delegation 'in order to ascertain definitely what proposals the latter had to offer for placing Russian orders in the United Kingdom'.[62] The Government's fall four months later thwarted this attempt to bring the specialist knowledge of organised management and labour to bear upon the decision-making process.

The gravity of the economic situation also led the FBI to abandon its anti-Bolshevik stance. In October 1931 the Grand Council resolved that it was 'desirable to try and persuade the National Government . . . to bring about a more even balance of trade' between Britain and the Soviet Union.[63] Joint talks, however, awaited a formal invitation from the TUC and began only in November 1932.[64]

From the start only divergent views of Soviet creditworthiness stood in the way of an FBI–TUC agreement on trade with Russia. The trade unionists took the sanguine view and recommended that the Soviets be granted credit guarantees on all classes of commodities and lengthy repayment schedules. The FBI expressed concern over the Soviet government's failure to settle outstanding Tsarist debts and fear that further falls in the prices of primary products would undermine Russia's ability to meet the proposed obligations. To guard against a Soviet default, the FBI proposed restrictions on the kinds of goods that would be subject to credit guarantees and graduated reductions in the lengths of the offered credits. The Federation also recommended that special marketing arrangements be created in order to insure that sales of Soviet goods in Britain would be large enough to cover Soviet purchases.[65]

By January 1933 further discussions had narrowed disagreement between the two organisations to the point where a joint delegation to

Sir Horace Wilson, the Board of Trade official responsible for commercial negotiations with Russia, seemed warranted.[66] Anti-communism within the Conservative party, however, precluded rapid implementation of the TUC–FBI recommendations. A temporary agreement regulating Anglo-Soviet trade was signed in 1935, but this measure contained no special credit arrangements.[67] Only in late 1936 did Britain extend credit guarantees to the Soviet Union.[68]

After 1937, Russia, which in 1913 had been the ninth largest importer of British goods, just managed to climb back into the list of the twenty largest importers from Britain for the first time in the inter-war period.[69] The late date and the moderate extent of this increase in Anglo-Soviet trade makes it impossible to regard these treaties as a major contribution to Britain's economic recovery. That a period of almost four years separated the TUC–FBI joint initiative from the conclusion of the treaties makes it doubtful whether great importance can be attributed to this essay in producers' co-operation.

V

The experiments in producers' co-operation which the FBI, the TUC and the NCEO conducted between 1929 and 1933 were the result of a rather fortuitous coincidence of circumstances. By the late 1920s the TUC was dominated by two men, Walter Citrine and Ernest Bevin, who believed that the organisation would only be able to bring the full weight of organised labour to bear upon British political life when it had won the right to regular and continuous consultation in questions of economic policy.[70] Collaboration with industrialists was one way of demonstrating the merit of the TUC's claim to consultation. The agreement of the TUC and Mond's group of employers upon a scheme for the improvement of industrial relations aroused in the press and in the public an expectation of co-operation which forced employers, however reluctantly, to initiate talks with labour. The economic blizzard which swept through Britain after 1929, together with Labour's triumph at the polls, gave the FBI, if not the NCEO, a material interest in an alliance with the TUC. If the Federation could win the support of organised labour for its economic policy proposals, then it would stand a better chance of convincing the Labour government of the merits of these proposals.

This combination of public expectation, economic crisis, the political situation and the organisational identities then prevailing within the TUC and the FBI sufficed to bring organised management and organised labour to the conference table, but it did not prove strong enough to make their joint talks productive. Discussions of rationalisation and finance for industry were utterly barren, generating not even a single joint policy statement. Three years of talks on imperial economic policy yielded three impracticable communiqués. Only in the relatively insignificant matter of Anglo-Soviet trade is it possible to claim for the producers' alliance a contribution to the determination of British policy – and a relatively insignificant contribution at that.

Talks between organised management and organised labour foundered on the diametrically opposed ways in which the two sides explained Britain's economic misfortune. For the employers, the slump testified to the unwarranted interference of Britain's monetary authorities, foreign governments and traders, profligate British governments and trade unions with the market mechanism of supply and demand. Labour, by contrast, regarded the depression as a fitting tribute to private property's mismanagement of British resources. The employers wanted to free private property from all of the destablising influences to which it had been subjected. Labour wanted to bring the rational hand of the community to bear upon the direction of production and distribution. Between the two approaches there could be no compromise. In matters of imperial policy no compromise was necessary because no demands needed to be made upon British governments and British industry. Consequently, joint proposals were possible, though the demands they made upon the Dominions rendered them impracticable.

Perhaps the state could have loosened the hold of these ideological fixations by elevating the organisations of management and labour to the position of governing institutions responsible for the formulation of economic policy. Inter-war British governments, however, evinced no inclination to integrate the FBI, the TUC and the NCEO into the networks of decision-making. To be sure, both the Labour government of 1929–31 and the National Government sought the advice and opinions of both sides of industry and included their representatives in advisory and investigative panels such as the Economic Advisory Council and the Macmillan Committee. Yet, this behaviour did not signify a desire to share the responsibilities of governing. Rather, it demonstrated governmental recognition of the facts that the FBI, the TUC and the NCEO were specialist bodies from whom practical assistance could be obtained on matters falling within their limited competences and political bodies to whom a superficial display of deference was due.[71]

Thus, the National Government sought from the FBI in advance of Ottawa advice about tariff schedules, not help in formulating an imperial economic policy. Similarly, MacDonald was eager to sound the FBI and the TUC out about the specifics of export credits for the USSR but not about the principles of the nation's commercial policy. On occasion, as we've seen, organised management and labour gained access to the state only because political expediency required it.

In *Politics in Industrial Society*, Keith Middlemas has suggested that in exchange for their admission to the 'corridors of power' the organisations of management and labour were expected to discipline their constituents and, thereby, to maintain popular consent to the governments of the day.[72] The evidence presented above suggests that no such incorporation took place in the inter-war period. Whether in fact these organisations made an important contribution to the maintenance of public order in these years remains an open question. In order to answer it, we will need to alter our focus in two ways. Firstly, we will need to shift our inquiry away from Transport House and Tothill Street where no significant co-operation took place to the factories and communities where perhaps it did occur. Secondly, and more importantly, we must turn our attention to the relationships between the organisations of management and labour and their respective constituents. Did the TUC, the FBI and the NCEO deliberately attempt to enforce among their members obedience to the second Labour government and the National Government? If such attempts did take place, were they successful? Would such successes, if there were any, constitute a sufficient explanation of the civic peace which Britain enjoyed amidst economic crisis?

6 The Administrative Origins of Industrial Diplomacy: an Aspect of Government–Industry Relations, 1929–1935

Richard Roberts

I

Studies of the relationship between government and industry tend to concentrate on the course of events in the industry or industries under consideration, set within its political, social and economic context. This paper, although accepting the importance of these studies, has a different emphasis. It concentrates on the administrative method by which officials discussed issues with the business community during the years 1929 to 1935. In many areas of discussion a technique was employed which can be called industrial diplomacy. Its central characteristic was the informality of contact established between officials and businessmen. Behind the use of industrial diplomacy lay a desire by officials to impose definite limits on the change in the relationship between the state and industry in this period. An unintended effect of industrial diplomacy was to concentrate discussion of economic and industrial problems on specific industries to the detriment of overall balance in policy.

The relationship between government and business by the mid-1920s had in many respects returned to a situation very similar to that existing during the late nineteenth century. Apart from the temporary expedients needed for the conduct of the First World War, state involvement in business affairs was limited to certain regulatory activities concerning all businesses, mainly the essentials of business law, or similar regulation of specific commercial operations, for example, railways and coal mines to ensure safety. There were exceptions both before and after the war but in most cases the contact between officials and businessmen was concerned with the administration of a specific piece of legislation. Individual special cases led on occasion to more lengthy correspondence; at intervals an amendment or a codification of the legislation would occur, based on the preceding experience of administration and with formal approaches by the government to the principal trade associations concerned. Most businessmen, however, corresponded with junior officials, applying to register a business name, for the appointment of an official receiver or over some other regulatory activity.

One of the few modifications in the role of the state after the War was the Safeguarding of Industry Act of 1921, amended in 1925.[1] Under this legislation the state was able to protect certain home producers from foreign competition. But this new development did not significantly increase or change the type of contact officials had with businessmen. Officials in the Board of Trade had merely to process applications made under the legislation and to establish by preliminary statistical work if the applicant trade had a *prima facie* case for a duty. The criteria used were published, and few serious applicants failed to pass this stage of the process.[2] On occasion an application did not fulfil all the requirements to establish a *prima facie* case but ministers authorised the application to go ahead, along with all others which fulfilled the conditions, to an independent committee. If the committee recommended a duty the matter went to the Cabinet; at this stage representations from interested groups were usually addressed to ministers, not to officials.[3]

By the time rearmament began in 1935, however, the relationship between the state and industry had markedly changed. The regulatory activities continued; but with structural unemployment in the staple industries at a peak by 1929, and the cyclical unemployment in most trades after the Wall Street crash, both Labour and National governments took initiatives in policy to protect business from the slump or to help the long-term recovery of some industries. Commercial policy changed as a general tariff was introduced in 1932 and a programme of bilateral tariff negotiations to help home and export market producers begun. Attempts were made to reorganise and rationalise the basic trades like coal, iron and steel and cotton to ensure longer-term prosperity. Regional policy and the fostering of new industries was begun in a small way in the same period. The contribution of these efforts to the moderate recovery in the economy up to 1937 has been much debated, although a consensus has emerged that other factors such as monetary policy had a larger role to play than this aspect of government policy.[4] Whatever their effect, these activities changed the relationship between the state and businessmen. Ministers, advised by officials, were now more willing to provide help to ailing industries; and the range of issues on which businessmen were in contact with officials had increased. Often, while furthering government policy, senior officials would discuss issues like the reorganisation of private firms with no legislation to provide a framework for discussion. Even under some of the new legislation, for example the Import Duties Act of 1932, businessmen began to press officials as well as ministers to use this legislation to the advantage of a particular industry, although in the case of tariffs the Import Duties Advisory Committee should have taken the issue out of the government's hands. It is with the nature of this new form of contact, the reasons for it, and the implications of its use, that this essay is concerned.

II

One of the main initiatives by governments to help revive the staple industries between 1929 and 1935 was directed to the cotton industry. The nature of industrial diplomacy can be well illustrated by considering the involvement of government with the problems of cotton, especially the discussions between officials and cotton businessmen to help promote reorganisation. The industry faced problems similar to those of many other staple trades in Britain; but, unlike iron and steel, cotton, as an export trade, stood to gain little from tariff protection. Discussions amongst businessmen on various ways to rationalise production and organisation began in 1926.[5] There were a variety of shades of opinion in these discussions but three broad alternative policies for rationalisation had emerged by 1929.

After the formation of the Lancashire Cotton Corporation in 1929, many of the banks favoured further amalgamations, as did many mill owners. Thus larger, more efficient, units of production would be obtained, some damaging price-cutting removed and (so advocates believed) export markets recovered or at least maintained.[6] The Labour government became involved in the problems of the industry by establishing a sub-committee of the Economic Advisory Council in 1929; the sub-committee's report, published in July 1930, supported this broad strategy for the industry.[7]

Another proposal was for the re-equipment of the industry, either with the more efficient ring spinning machinery used by many of Britain's foreign competitors, or with automatic looms. One continual supporter of this proposal between 1929 and 1935 was Sir Walter Preston who was a Member of Parliament but also a director of a leading textile machinery firm and, as a result, his frequent approaches to the government on this matter were only scantily considered.[8] At the same time, others advocated the increased use of electrically powered machines to produce an additional increase of efficiency.[9]

Whilst this second alternative, like the first, aimed to reduce costs and expand exports to recover world markets, the third alternative was less optimistic and favoured the elimination of surplus capacity in the industry, the restriction of supply and the increase of prices and profits. This way a smaller, profitable British industry could be saved and, on the basis of this new prosperity, amalgamation and re-equipment would be possible in the future, but it would come about through normal market forces. Only in the long run, once market forces had made the industry more efficient, was there the chance that some lost export markets could be regained.

Officials became involved in the problems of the cotton industry as part of the attempt under the second Labour government to reorganise the industry voluntarily along the lines of the Economic Advisory Committee report. The task fell to Sir Horace Wilson and his staff, first at the Office of the Lord Privy Seal and, later, at the Office of the Chief Industrial Adviser in the Board of Trade. Wilson himself was appointed Chief Industrial Adviser to the government in November 1930.[10] These officials, and a small group of cotton businessmen, favoured the third alternative, the reduction of surplus capacity. Discussions over reorganisation lasted, on and off, until 1935 and show well the characteristics of industrial diplomacy. The discussions between Wilson and the various groups of businessmen were informal; they were held at London clubs,[11] Manchester hotels,[12] at meetings of an informal committee to discuss the problems of the cotton trade, organised by the Bank of England but held at the Savoy Hotel in London,[13] as well as in Whitehall. Officials talked to individual businessmen and the staff of the Manchester Chamber of Commerce but not all the Chamber's elected leaders nor to the subsidiary body of the Chamber dealing with the problems of the cotton trade, the Joint Committee of Cotton Trade Organisations.

As negotiations proceeded public statements stressed the voluntary nature of the progress that was being made towards the reorganisation of the industry. This was especially so of the public announcement of certain resolutions adopted by the Joint Committee in May 1931, resolutions which for the first time supported a reduction in capacity as the immediate need of the industry.[14] Moreover, ministers' presentation of a Bill to Parliament in 1935 to support with statutory power the collection of a levy on spindles to finance the scrapping of excess capacity, emphasised that this was nothing more than the industry had requested.[15] The result was the Cotton Spinning Industry Act of 1936. Thus the role of Wilson and his colleagues in getting agreement on the strategy they favoured was unrecorded in public. Unsurprisingly, their more negative contribution, in advising against possible amalgamations during 1930 and 1931 in order to help the acceptance of the strategy to reduce capacity, went unrecorded as well.[16] The contrast between public appearances and private reality continued throughout the period. In September 1932 to preserve the public standing of the Joint Committee, the Board of Trade went to great lengths to ensure that the Indian Cotton Inquiry Committee was appointed with the minimum of government involvement and mainly by the Joint Committee, even though some of the main advocates of the use of Indian cotton in Lancashire, which was the subject of the inquiry, expressed dissatisfaction with the Joint Committee's representative nature.[17] A few months later, in the discussions over reorganisation, the Joint Committee was relegated to a minor role when talks resumed between officials and an informally convened group of businessmen led by Lord Colwyn. It was these discussions which finally led to the 1936 Act.[18]

Industrial diplomacy provided the basis of other discussions between officials and businessmen; in the case of government aid to Cunard in 1934, to complete the Queen Mary and build the Queen Elizabeth, the perseverance of Cunard in pressing the plan on the government is often stressed.[19] Closer examination of the evidence suggests a different view. Initial requests by Cunard for aid in February 1932 only asked for financial assistance.[20] It was only when this request was made conditional on the successful acquisition by Cunard of the White Star Lines that the basis of the subsequent deal was established. This was the plan outlined in Cunard's second appeal to the government in March 1932.[21] Rejected then, this plan was revived when discussions with the Treasury began a few months later, resulting in the North Atlantic Shipping Act of 1934. However, the suggestion of this link between financial aid and the merger was made at a private meeting between the chairman of Cunard, Sir Percy Bates, and a senior Board of Trade official, Sir Charles Hipwood, late in February 1932.[22] A few days later Cunard's second request for aid was made to the Government along the lines advocated by Hipwood.

The British shipping industry as a whole in the 1930s faced many problems of overcapacity in international tonnage, due to the decline of world trade and the competition of the heavily subsidised national fleets of other maritime nations.[23] In December 1933 the Chamber of Shipping and the Liverpool Steamship Owners' Association for the first time called for government subsidies to match those given abroad.[24] Hitherto they had opposed any form of government aid. After long negotiations with the Government, including the attendance of representatives of the Chamber and the Association at cabinet committee meetings, agreement was reached and a subsidy was paid by the Government to tramp shipping for the financial years 1935/6 and 1936/7, subsequently extended for a third year. In fact, government officials had pre-empted the public change in policy by the industry. For over a year before they had viewed the threat to the British mercantile marine with growing concern. Privately, they had advised prominent shipowners, like Lord Essendon, of the need for more definite policy proposals from the industry.[25] These were made by the Chamber and the Association in mid 1933 when they tentatively suggested to officials that they favoured flag discrimination and other forms of non-financial help from the government.[26] The officials advised against this in private, suggesting that a subsidy was a better proposal, and this advice provided the basis for the public announcement of the industry's conversion to the need for a subsidy in December 1933.[27] During 1934 senior officials from the Board of Trade's marine department attended the council meetings of the Chamber of Shipping to give detailed advice on how to present the scheme for the administration of a subsidy to the government.[28]

As a last example of industrial diplomacy, Reader, in his history of ICI, has shown how the agreement between the Government and the company over the development of coal hydrogenation came about after discussions between W.H. Coates of ICI and Sir Horace Wilson in later 1932. In June 1933, when ICI went formally to the Chancellor of the Exchequer, the 'bargaining was over and this was a ceremonial occasion'. Two years previously a similar delegation on the same subject to the Labour government, without adequate preparation, had asked for the type of help the government was never going to give – financial assistance with the capital costs – and received a rebuke which 'left the delegation, including even McGowan, speechless'. The eventual agreement in 1933 was for a tariff preference for oil from British coal through a reduction of excise duties, and this was enacted by the British Hydrocarbon Oils Production Act in 1934.[29]

III

The use of industrial diplomacy by officials during the period under study was not a haphazard development. It came about, rather, as a reflection of the anxieties felt by officials about the conflicting demands of economic theory and economic policy and about the need to preserve the role of Parliament in government. For officials dealing with economic and industrial affairs in the inter-war years a major cause of concern was the emerging conflict between classical economic theory and the more immediate needs of economic policy. On the one hand, although few officials were trained economists, most accepted the main tenets of neoclassical economic theory and believed in a very limited role for government in economic affairs. On the other hand, they recognised the need, for political and social reasons, for a more interventionist economic and industrial policy in the inter-war years. The conflict was reconciled in the minds of officials in the 1930s by a careful distinction between the short and the long run. In the long run the limited role of government was accepted, but in the short run, it was thought, intervention was needed by government to put trade and industry on the right course. This *ad hoc* interventionism provided officials with justification for the help given by government to depressed trades in the 1930s.

This did not mean that the government should necessarily be seen to intervene in industry. Although on occasions, such as in the dealings with Cunard, it was politically desirable that government help should ultimately be conspicuous, usually the aim was to maintain the impression that business was not dependent on direct assistance from the state. In the examples we have considered, owing to the use of industrial diplomacy, the apparent initiative for action by the government came solely from businessmen. Only in the case of coal hydrogenation was this entirely the case.

There was also amongst officials during the 1920s and 1930s a much wider concern over the role of the state and of bureaucrats in society. The First World War had shown the potential power of the state in controlling the affairs of the individual, a power to which many people educated in the nineteenth century liberal tradition would object. A minority, even before the war, looked to the state for progressive reform, although mainly to solve social problems.[30] During the war that minority increased in number as the reconstruction period came and went.[31] In the mid-1920s discussion of the proper power and role of the state was still vigorous. Civil servants were not indifferent to this debate. Most of senior and middling rank had been educated well before 1914. Concern about the potential power and the possible good of the state was eventually to be reconciled for many by the link between the 'Keynesian revolution' and the 'welfare state' after 1945. But in the 1920s broad reconstruction plans had failed. At the same time concern about the potential power of the state did not decline; businessmen saw the civil service as inefficient;[32] and many observers saw some bureaucratic developments as undemocratic.[33]

As a result, many officials in the 1920s were wary of developments that could undermine the parliamentary process, and which would be seen as only illustrating the increasing power of the state and of bureaucrats. An example of civil service opposition to such a development can be seen in the deliberations of the Tariff Advisory Committee of 1923. The committee was established by Baldwin to advise on the form of a general tariff which could be introduced if the Conservatives won the general election.[34] The chairman was Lord Milner, but he received advice from an interdepartmental committee of officials chaired by Percy Ashley,[35] later to be the first Secretary of the Import Duties Advisory Committee. The officials advised Lord Milner that any future tariff system in the United Kingdom would have to include a non-parliamentary tariff advisory body to stop Parliament becoming merely a forum for various industrial interests.[36] Another example can be found in the discussions over the proposal to create an 'economic general staff' in 1929. Warren Fisher, the head of the civil service, advised against any innovations which would give the impression that an executive body was being formed by the addition of a small group of economists to the civil service. This, he argued, would only appear to the public as 'a few more bureaucrats'. As an alternative he wanted a research and advisory body which would help the government on selected issues.[37] Earlier in 1929 he had observed of the Liberal public works plans, then being discussed in the run-up to the general election, that to implement them would need the powers of a Mussolini; a view shared by junior officials.[38]

In the 1930s civil servants' concern about the role of the state did not decline. At the same time, the increasing involvement of the state in industrial affairs in the short run, together with the increasing importance of business opinion in the face of mounting economic problems, again put pressure on the constitutional relationships between ministers, officials and Members of Parliament. Such a threat came from national industrial planning, raised within government by Sir Oswald Mosley and Hubert Henderson as early as the spring of 1930.[39] From the viewpoint of officials, this seemed to mean that a broad strategic plan would undermine the authority of ministers and Parliament in determining the extent and direction of state involvement in the affairs of individuals. Even if Parliament voted on a plan, officials were well aware that in working out the details they were far from being adequately equipped for the job, and would therefore have to rely on business advice. Businessmen would be in effect asked to plan their own prosperity. Moreover the only example of planning available for officials to study before 1933 was Russia, an example unlikely to produce emulation.

Industrial diplomacy avoided this direct threat to constitutional relationships but, at the same time, fulfilled the short-term needs of economic and social policy and party politics to help trade and industry, given the economic problems of the early 1930s. Dr Middlemas has suggested that the main employer and employee organisations in Britain were elevated to the status of 'governing institutions' during the post-1911 period, to the detriment of the parliamentary process.[40] In fact, industrial diplomacy aimed to achieve the very opposite, to attach the increasingly important trade and industry pressure groups to the existing parliamentary process, just as the landed interest and the labour interest had been accommodated in previous periods of economic and social change. Dr Middlemas's conclusions may be more relevant to the period after 1935, when the needs of rearmament overrode the normal relationships between government and industry, than for the inter-war years as a whole. Even here, it would be a mistake to ignore the informal links between businessmen like Lord Weir and

Sir Andrew Duncan and officials such as Sir Horace Wilson, links which had been widened and strengthened before 1935 by discussions over employment and industrial issues.

IV

Industrial diplomacy was a reaction by civil servants to the threat they perceived to economic theory and parliamentary democracy. Its use had unfortunate consequences. In particular, it concentrated discussions between government and industry into sectional, industry by industry channels. As well as the cotton industry, governments tried to reorganise the iron and steel industry and the coal industry with varying results.[41] Even in shipping, although a simple subsidy was given during 1935–7, the Government insisted at the same time on a 'scrap and build' scheme, and the reduction of competition to allow the industry to modernise and reorganise.[42] By the mid-1930s Government had not got an industrial policy, but rather had an industrial policy for each industry with which informal discussion had been held. Only general principles, often unclarified, guided the overall policy and the result was tentative and patchy. A logical next step would have been to use the experience gained in sectional discussions with various trades to produce a common approach to the problems of British industry, with the discussion of common solutions where applicable. This did not happen. At no time in the inter-war years did the government go to the Federation of British Industries, or to other employer or trade organisations, or to the Trades Union Congress, and raise the problems of British industry with them, except by the indirect means of the Macmillan Committee. Indeed, such a move would have led to everything which officials were trying to avoid.

Chances for the development within government of a wider common problems approach did occur in the inter-war years. For a variety of reasons they either failed completely or ultimately developed in a different way. The Balfour committee on industry and trade, which sat from 1924 to 1929, produced a multi-volumed report which tackled the problems of trade and industry with a wider scope.[43] However, the reports were written by the Board of Trade with Treasury help and the end result was merely endorsed by the committee.[44] When the final report was published in 1929, not surprisingly, officials concluded that they were already doing everything the report suggested to help trade and industry.[45] The Economic Advisory Council in the first year of its operation provided another chance for the creation of a wider forum for debate. Certainly, some moves were made in this direction and Bevin, for example, raised the possible conflicts between rationalisation and employment for debate.[46] But the Council increasingly moved away from being a wide-ranging forum by relying more on *ad hoc* committees. Later the sub-committee on Economic Information became the focal point for most discussions of the Council in the 1930s.[47]

The Mosley memorandum of 1930, and the subsequent memoranda submitted by Hartshorn and Attlee, raised the issue of greater state involvement in industrial reconstruction and proposed a new central administrative body of trained economists to guide this involvement. The response from officials to Mosley, partly drafted by the Treasury and partly by Sir Horace Wilson and his staff,[48] stressed that to accept these proposals would, in effect, mean the government assuming control over all industry. The administrative proposals of Mosley, according to the report of the Cabinet Committee on Unemployment which accepted the advice of these officials, could

> only be reconciled with the principles of Parliamentary Government if the new organisation confined itself to consideration of questions of policy and its proposals were first submitted to Departmental Ministers for consideration, thereafter brought before the Cabinet, and the decisions of the Cabinet being thus carried out by the Departments.[49]

The alternative policy, of cajoling industry to reorganise, with finance provided by the banks for sound schemes was, in the committee's view, working. This argument was accepted by the Cabinet and the Mosley proposals failed, with the result that Mosley himself left the Government.

The last chance for the emergence from within the Government of some wider debate on the problems of industry came in November 1930 with the formation of the Office of the Chief Industrial Adviser in the Board of Trade. This development itself was a product of the subsequent discussions over unemployment policy following the Attlee memorandum in the summer of 1930. Sir Horace Wilson himself was appointed Chief Industrial Adviser,[50] and although he and his officials had rejected any government control of industry, in the first few months of the Office's life they did begin to discuss the common problems they had discovered whilst discussing reorganisation and rationalisation with individual industries. Comparisons with organisation and equipment trends abroad were made, and moves were made to set up the Economic Advisory Committee's sub-committee on the problems of rationalisation. But these efforts failed in 1931. Even if the officials involved had been prepared to question their own traditional opposition to greater state control of industry, and some evidence suggests that some may have been willing to do so, they were overwhelmed with detailed work in continuing the discussions with individual industries begun during 1930. This was especially so after the formation of the National government, and the subsequent diversion of

Sir Horace Wilson to other areas of policy, notably the discussions with businessmen over the forthcoming Ottawa conference. The separate Office disappeared completely in 1932 and the specialised staff were transferred to the Board of Trade's Industries and Manufactures department.

If a wider approach to the problems of industry failed to appear from within government in the 1930s, could external influences have persuaded the Government to adopt one? Two particularly plausible attempts were made. An Enabling Bill introduced by Lord Melchett in 1935, after a long period of discussion, aimed to allow any industry in which the majority supported a reorganisation scheme to obtain an administrative order to compel the support of the minority. In addition, during 1934–5 and the preparations for the general election of November 1935, the Conservative Research Department considered a definite statement of principles (based on the experience of the past few years) which the government would observe in any cases of industrial intervention in the future.[51] A possibility discussed at the time was for these two initiatives to be combined and an amended Enabling Bill supported by a definite statement of principles was proposed as a central part of Conservative party policy at the forthcoming election. Indeed, largely at the initiative of Neville Chamberlain, the idea was accepted by the Policy committee of the party in 1934 as a natural complement to the Government's agricultural policy, again a policy which had been mainly provided by the Research Department after policy discussions in 1930–1.[52]

But civil servants argued that an Enabling Bill was not needed, nor a set of general principles. The needs of each industry varied; many industries did not need any legislative assistance to implement reorganisation schemes. Rather, they argued, if an industry needed legislative assistance each case should be considered separately by Parliament.[53] Over the summer of 1935 the Cabinet accepted this advice and, much to the annoyance of the Research Department, the plan for a set of clear principles and a revised Enabling Bill was no part of Conservative party policy or National government policy at the election later that year. Indeed, Chamberlain's subsequent attempt when Prime Minister to convert the Board of Trade to a moderate form of planning and enabling legislation through the appointment of Oliver Stanley to the department in preference to the National Liberal, Walter Runciman, failed as well because at the same time the new Permanent Secretary to the Board of Trade, Sir William Brown was an equally ardent supporter of the *ad hoc* and pragmatic approach developed since 1929.

V

Between the wars, and indeed at any time, the relationship between government and industry is an immensely complex issue. The conclusions of this essay can therefore only be tentative, and must be confined to a single aspect of government–industry relations. Nevertheless, most communication between government and business was handled by civil servants, and the methods employed, and assumptions made, by civil servants are therefore an essential concern of economic and political historians. This essay has suggested that, during a period when the relationship between industry and government was rapidly changing, a particular form of relationship emerged as a consequence of strongly held opinions within the civil service. Officials did not wish entirely to prevent change in the relationship between government and industry; but the method to which their assumptions about the proper role of government led them did limit the extent to which change could take place. Protection of the proper role of Parliament, and the constant avoidance of *overt* official manipulation of industrial decisions, ensured that no comprehensive industrial policy emerged in the 1930s. Instead the period saw a series of unco-ordinated and *ad hoc* policies to help individual industries such as coal, cotton and shipping. Officials in the 1930s were often criticised by contemporary businessmen for being inefficient. Some politicians, especially Mosley, saw them as reactionary. Historians may take the more balanced, and as it happens more charitable, view that the underlying philosophy of government action was in turmoil between the wars, and that officials were afflicted by a sincere and conscientious doubt about their own proper role; within the guidelines they set themselves they achieved much, but not enough either to escape criticism or do more than touch the surface of the problems of British industry in the 1930s.

7 Financiers, The Gold Standard and British Politics, 1925–1931

Philip Williamson

Interest in the inter-war British gold standard has naturally concentrated on its monetary and broader economic aspects. Studies by Clay, Sayers, Clarke, Moggridge and Howson have provided excellent accounts of the economic discussions that preceded the return to the gold standard in 1925, of the difficulties encountered by the Bank of England in maintaining it, of its repercussions upon British trade, industry and employment, and of the Bank's ultimately unsuccessful attempts to defend it during the 1931 crisis.[1] Yet the return to the gold standard also had important political implications, which have been noted or discussed in passing but not systematically examined.[2]

Being on the gold standard meant that monetary policy was technically 'outside politics', under the control not of the government but of a private, self-appointed company, the Bank of England. With the outbreak of war in 1914, however, the Government was called upon by the Bank of England to help deal with the consequences of a European liquidity crisis. As a result, the Treasury began issuing its own currency notes, and as the war progressed and the country's financial position deteriorated, the gold standard was in practice set aside and the Treasury increasingly became involved in other parts of the Bank's traditional functions, particularly exchange control and debt management. With the formal suspension of the gold standard in April 1919, the Treasury became the predominant monetary authority. This suspension was, however, forced upon the government; official committees had already, in 1918, advised that an effective gold standard should be restored, and from 1919 this became the policy of successive governments. Decontrol was as much an official objective in monetary affairs as it was in industrial policy, and received still less discussion, even during the parliamentary debates on the return to gold in 1925. Politicians of all parties accepted the gold standard on conventional economic grounds – a belief that British prosperity was dependent upon re-establishing the country's position within the international economy. Churchill, the Conservative Chancellor of the Exchequer responsible for the ultimate decision to resume gold payments, required rather more convincing than most; but Snowden, the Labour party's financial spokesman, publicly supported the gold standard in principle, and had to be pressed by a party committee to criticise even the timing of the decision[3] – an objection so mild that it was indistinguishable from that of some City advocates of the gold standard. The question of political control barely arose; even of those very few MPs who opposed the decision outright, only two members of the Independent Labour Party complained about credit policy being in the hands of private bankers.[4] The effect of the return to gold, indeed, was that the Treasury officials and their political superiors had only limited influence over a vital determinant of domestic economic performance; that ministers rarely, if ever, needed to think about currency and exchange questions, and that consequently when the Bank of England asked again for government assistance, in 1931, some were intimidated and disadvantaged by inadequate knowledge.[5] This position is notoriously expressed in the reported statement of a former Labour cabinet minister when the gold standard was suspended in September 1931: 'they never told us we could do that'.[6] The first part of what follows examines banking and Treasury thinking about the gold standard and the relationship between monetary policy and politics, in order to explain how such a situation developed.

It has been argued that the Bank of England represented the 'extremely narrow section of overseas finance' rather than City financial interests generally, and further that the gold standard policy was promoted essentially for the advantage of that particular section rather than out of concern for industry and trade.[7] Obviously there were differences between the specific interests of merchant bankers, discount houses, clearing banks, finance companies and insurance firms, but there was in fact no significant difference between these groups over the gold standard, either in 1925 or 1931. Moreover, City financiers regarded the gold standard as establishing the essential framework for a sound and permanent revival of trade and industry. They did not forget that ultimately the City's prosperity was dependent upon Britain's industrial strength, and whatever the earlier differences between financiers and industrialists over the advisability of returning to gold, with the onset of deep depression from 1929 most of them came to adopt similar positions on the issues of Empire trade, import restrictions, taxation and economy.

Much has been written in general about the political role of the City between the wars, but apart from Moggridge's examination of the return to gold, little attempt has been made to substantiate these claims by detailed studies. The second part of this essay suggests how such a study might proceed on the gold standard period itself, and particularly on its final two years – when the division between 'banking' and 'politics' was gradually broken down.

In April 1925 Layton, editor of *The Economist*, wrote that he had been 'amazed at the doubts and hesitations which have been current in the City of London for the last three months about the gold standard'.[8] These misgivings were evident in the annual speeches of the chairmen of the clearing banks in January, and were even expressed privately within the Bank of England. The uncertainty was essentially about timing: it was feared that a premature return to parity, before rising American prices had reached British levels, would involve a risk of being forced back off the gold standard, and might require such a high bank rate as protection for the gold reserves that industry would be hampered. However, of the leading City bankers only McKenna, chairman of the Midland Bank, took dislike of the possibility of deflation to the point of joining Keynes in opposing any return to the gold standard – though not in public.[9] All other leading financiers regarded an eventual return to gold at the pre-war parity as essential, and even McKenna ultimately admitted that for psychological and political reasons an early return was inescapable.[10] And once gold parity had been restored in late April, it was universally accepted in the City that abandonment would destroy British credit, and therefore could not be contemplated.

Treasury officials were as committed as City bankers to the gold standard, because it was believed to be of great benefit to the country as a whole, and not merely a means of strengthening London's financial interests. A fixed currency and stable exchanges were considered essential conditions for a permanent revival of trade, industry and employment; and the City's invisible earnings helped to pay for imports, produced a balance of payments surplus, and so generated capital for the foreign investment which stimulated demand for British exports. The interests of finance, trade and industry were therefore regarded as interdependent, and if merchants and manufacturers were less enthusiastic than bankers about the return to gold, it was thought that this was simply because they tended to take a shorter view.[11] Moreover, the gold standard was also considered to be of general benefit because it served as a 'thermometer measuring the economic activity of a country';[12] it provided a warning against trade imbalances, and even more importantly, acted as a check against an undue expansion of credit. The 'spectre of inflation' haunted bankers and Treasury officials, especially after the financial and economic excesses which had followed the suspension of gold payments in 1919, and after the continental hyperinflations of the early 1920s had left 'debris scattered all over Europe'. It was believed that unless inflation were checked, it would inexorably dislocate all economic relationships, provoke industrial unrest, and lead to political disorder. So great was this fear of inflation and its insidious ways that any alternative to having the currency tied to gold was regarded as impracticable and dangerous;

behind every exponent of a 'managed currency' there was thought to lurk an inflationist.[13] However, the greatest threat to currency stability was considered to come not from such economist and banking critics as Keynes and McKenna, but rather from the politicians. Owing to the political temptations of financial and monetary manipulation, politicians of all parties had to be regarded as potentially suspect. Conservative and Liberal ministers in the Coalition government had been responsible for the inflationary developments of 1919, and during the 1920s there seemed to be a particular threat from some sections of the Labour party. For bankers and Treasury officials, therefore, by no means the least advantage of the return to the gold standard was that it was believed to take monetary policy out of politics.

Great emphasis was laid upon the theory that under the gold standard adjustments were 'automatic'. According to Bradbury – a member of all the post-war committees that recommended a return to the gold standard – this meant that it was 'knave-proof. It could not be rigged for political or even more unworthy reasons.'[14] Moreover, it was also regarded as an important reinforcement for that other check upon political manipulation of the financial system, the 'balanced budget convention'.[15] Even McKenna stressed this point: 'the fear of being forced off the gold standard acts as a salutary check on the extravagance of Governments'.[16] However, insistence upon the automatic operation of the gold standard alone was not considered sufficient; in order to guarantee that its rules were properly applied, it was thought necessary that authority in monetary policy should rest exclusively with the Bank of England, as this was conventionally regarded as a non-political institution.

The Bank of England was in fact a private corporation, and some aspects of its composition and work meant that it provided leadership for all the other private financial institutions of the City. Apart from the Governor and Deputy Governor, the most influential members of the Court of Directors and its Committee of Treasury – the 'Inner Cabinet of the Bank' – were usually partners or directors in merchant banks, acceptance houses and overseas banks, although the Court did also include shipowners and merchants, with a sprinkling later in the 1920s of industrialists, ex-civil servants and former Bank officials. Directors of British clearing banks were traditionally excluded from the Court, but in fulfilling the Bank of England's function as the 'bank of the bankers' and superintendent of the financial system generally, the Governor met at least once a week with representatives of the Committee of Clearing Bankers, as well as with those of the Discount Market Committee and the Stock Exchange Committee. Norman established regular contact with chairmen and other members of many individual banks and finance houses, and successfully encouraged the practice by which 'any reputable person in the City [was] at liberty to see him'.[17]

However, Norman also placed the highest emphasis upon the Bank of England's public responsibilities. So on the one hand, the Bank sought to maintain a position of independence within the City and tried to discipline other financial institutions when their activities seemed undesirable from the standpoint of the country's financial welfare;[18] on the other hand, the Bank adhered strongly to the doctrine that its functions also required it to have political independence. This doctrine was best stated by Norman's deputy, Harvey, to the Macmillan Committee in late 1929: because the Bank of England's main duty was

> to conduct its operations in the interests of the community as a whole, . . . we . . . have always considered that it should be free from the control of particular groups and interests. . . . For the same reason I think I may claim that it is an accepted principle that . . . it should be free from being required to submit to political pressure and to subordinate sound finance to the dictates of political expediency.

The Bank necessarily had close relations with the Treasury, but according to Harvey these were 'fundamentally those of banker and client', and the Treasury did 'not seek to dictate any alternative line of financial policy if [the Bank] . . . consider a particular line of policy essential for the protection of the country's main reserves'.[19] For Norman and the Bank such political freedom was, indeed, a general principle of central banking, as was shown in their international activities. Partly under British influence, the international economic conferences at Brussels in 1920 and Genoa in 1922 propounded this principle, while the Bank demanded its adoption when assisting in the monetary reconstruction of European countries, and when fostering central banks in the Dominions and in Latin America.[20] Where central banks were established abroad, Norman insisted upon dealing directly with them, not with foreign governments nor even through British government agencies;[21] with his encouragement, the leading central banks therefore conducted their own financial diplomacy. Norman also took considerable pains to ensure that the Bank for International Settlements, established under the Young Plan in 1930 to deal with reparation payments and promote central bank co-operation, should be 'beyond the reach of Governments'.[22]

In the domestic market political independence was regarded as extending to all aspects of monetary policy. The return to the gold standard restored to the Bank of England, and to the Governor in particular, control over bank rate, credit supply and – after monetary stabilisation had been completed by the 1928 Currency and Bank Notes Act – over note issue. This control was approved in principle by almost all other interested parties, even by Keynes and the 'business world', despite their criticisms of the Bank's specific policies.[23] Hopkins, Controller of Finance at the Treasury, affirmed that 'the control of our currency is exclusively a matter for the Bank of England. It is not a matter in which the Government intervenes.'[24] Even most politicians upheld the principle of the Bank's independence from their control – largely, it seems, out of suspicion of each other's motives. So both Churchill, as Conservative Chancellor of the Exchequer from 1924 to 1929, and Snowden, his Labour successor from 1929 to 1931, asserted that their governments had no responsibility or influence in the determination of bank rate.[25] Officially the Labour party (and the TUC) were committed to the ultimate nationalisation of the Bank of England, but even so their leaders, above all Snowden, insisted that control should continue to be withheld from politicians, and should pass instead to a non-political public corporation.[26]

As the corollary of its own freedom from political pressures, the Bank of England maintained the principle that it did not intervene in politics. Harvey told the Macmillan Committee that

> we never venture to interfere on any question that can be considered a political question, unless we are asked to express an opinion as to what the financial effect of a certain political operation may be. If we are asked, we give our advice, but we never seek to interfere in politics.

Accordingly, Harvey declared, 'the colour of the Government of the moment ha[d] absolutely no influence whatever' on the nature of the Bank's relations with the Chancellor of the Exchequer.[27] In compliance with this principle of non-intervention, the Bank imposed a number of checks upon itself. In order not to embarrass the Treasury, the Bank would only have contacts with other government departments with its knowledge and approval. Norman asserted that there was an unwritten rule that Bank of England directors should not publicly express views on financial matters differing from those of the current Chancellor of the Exchequer. There was also a tradition that no Bank director should be an MP, except for the City of London, whose Members were expected to preserve more independence from their political parties than most other MPs.[28] The position of the Bank director City MP throughout the inter-war gold standard period was indeed unique – for Edward Grenfell, of the merchant bank Morgan, Grenfell & Co, was also a partner of the leading New York international bankers, J.P. Morgan & Co, the British government's financial agents in the United States. In this capacity Grenfell helped arrange American credits for the Government both when the gold standard was restored in 1925, and when it was being defended in 1931.[29] From several directions, therefore, Grenfell felt public responsibilities transcending his membership of the Conservative party. He particularly claimed that because of its national services, the City as a whole occupied a special position, telling the House of Commons in February 1930 that 'the City . . . is not political in any sense', and that City MPs had always maintained that they were 'freer than any other Member to express [their] opinions on any subject and in favour of either side'.[30]

Formally, then, there was a clear division between the concerns of the Bank of England and those of the government and politicians. As Norman told Snowden in September 1929: 'his was the technical and financial side – the Chancellor's was the political and fiscal side'.[31]

Of course, the real position was not so clear cut. Although the gold standard itself was not in question, there could be differences between the government and the Bank of England on subordinate monetary measures and other financial issues, resulting in encroachments by both sides. Even in central banking doctrine, the government's banker had an ultimate duty to the community to use every possible means to prevent its client from destroying its own credit – an obligation which would inevitably draw the central bank directly into political questions. For example, in the early 1920s Norman advised his counterpart at the Reichsbank to 'make a practice of objecting to any unwise economic measures or to any inflationary policy which your Government may wish to adopt. It matters not whether such policy may seem unavoidable or not.'[32] The Bank of England itself had during its immediate post-war struggle to regain monetary control pressed the British government to cease borrowing, reduce expenditure, and balance the budget.[33] Even after sound finance and the formal division of responsibilities had been restored, however, the Bank and the government still continued in practice to exert influence in each other's fields, particularly as the conduct of government financial business required constant communication between them. In the Governor's at least twice-weekly visits to the Treasury, his 'fairly frequent' calls upon the Chancellor of the Exchequer, and his contacts with various other government departments, he naturally affected political decision-making even while simply reporting conditions in the City or advising on financial aspects of specific policies.[34] Conversely, such communications gave the Chancellor and Treasury officials opportunities to apply informal pressure upon the Bank – and despite their public statements both Churchill and Snowden did protest strongly in private against increases in bank rate.[35]

To some degree, therefore, the formal distinction between banking and politics was a facade maintained by both sides in order to protect the Bank from dangerous demands for even more ministerial intervention, and ministers from public responsibility for unpleasant policies. Nevertheless, until 1929 this demarcation was on the whole observed, and apart from intermittent outbursts by Churchill about credit policy no serious differences arose between the government and either the Bank of England or the City generally. One obvious reason for this was that the Government was Conservative, with policies broadly congenial to the City. Its financial policy was ultimately 'sound' – though some of Churchill's unconventional methods of obtaining a budget balance caused Norman to liken him to a juggler.[36] The Conservative party's abandonment of a general tariff policy in 1924, and the government's cautious use of the Safeguarding of Industries legislation, reduced the possibility of conflict with the City's traditional commitment to free trade. There was no friction when a European and American plea for 'economic freedom' was signed in October 1926 by Norman, Goodenough, chairman of Barclays Bank, McKenna, Beaumont Pease (chairman) and Bell (a director) of Lloyds Bank, Schuster of the National Provincial Bank, Currie of Glyn, Mills & Co, Bradbury (now a director of William Deacons Bank), Holland-Martin, secretary of the Bankers' Clearing House, and other leading British bankers, businessmen and industrialists.[37]

A further reason for this relatively trouble-free relationship was the Bank of England's avoidance of increases in bank rate between December 1925 and February 1929, despite the fact that sterling was repeatedly under strain. Churchill's threats when bank rate was raised during 1925, and his occasional bitter complaints against what he considered to be the Bank's policy of 'deflation',[38] may have had some influence upon the Bank's decisions. However, Treasury officials supported the Bank, while Churchill – lacking the technical understanding to prevail against both of these – always backed down, and it seems doubtful that fear of his bluster would have made the Bank hesitate for long if it had considered increases in bank rate really appropriate. In the Bank's view, the strains upon sterling were caused not so much by domestic weaknesses requiring treatment by means of changes in bank rate, as by external pressures arising from the various post-war distortions of the international financial system – Norman complained about 'how greatly the international machine is out of gear'.[39] Believing these strains to be extraneous and temporary, the Bank considered that British industry and trade should be protected from their consequences, and so developed expedients to defend sterling without increasing bank rate.[40] Although the pound remained based upon a gold standard and the Bank still hoped to return to an 'automatic' system, sterling had in practice become, in Norman's words, 'a more or less managed Currency'.[41]

However, this management was not intended to insulate the domestic economy against 'real' forces of world competition in production, nor against permanent changes in the international financial system; after all, the gold standard was supposed to provide the framework for proper adjustment to such conditions. After 1925 the Bank pursued what it regarded as a neutral internal monetary policy, maintaining a roughly stable volume of credit and whenever possible keeping bank rate at a level which in its view 'inflicted no hardship on trade'.[42] So although Norman and others at the Bank later admitted that the return to gold had exacerbated the difficulties of industry, they did not accept that the monetary system was responsible for industrial depression and unemployment.[43] Rather, they believed that since 1918 British industry and trade had suffered from the 'brute facts' of post-war depression, the consequences of 'general currency chaos', and 'tremendous changes' in industrial technology. Compared to such disruptions, any deleterious effects of the return to gold were minor – and even these had been greatly aggravated by a series of subsequent 'mischances', particularly the undervaluations of the French and Belgian currencies. In the Bank's view, British industry would in any event have had to make considerable readjustments, and its main problem was that this process had become 'jammed', partly because of 'stickiness in respect of wages' but mostly because of a general failure to reduce costs, improve methods and switch to more profitable lines of production.[44] For these reasons, and also because the condition of industry ultimately affected the position of sterling, Norman became from 1928 an enthusiastic supporter of 'rationalisation' of the basic industries.

These views on the relationship between monetary policy and industry were shared by most other City bankers. McKenna, however, emphasised monetary factors as a cause of industrial depression and unemployment. In January 1926 he argued that an 'over-valuation' of sterling had 'seriously impaired our export trade', and although he thought this 'impediment' was 'fast disappearing', a year later he complained that the 'rigidity of the Bank of England system' was such that there was an insufficient supply of credit available to allow for any significant trade expansion. Accordingly, he called for an 'exhaustive inquiry' into the credit and currency system.[45] By 1928 these and similar criticisms by Keynes, by prominent businessmen, and by leaders of the TUC, were influencing opposition politicians whose interest in these issues was stimulated by the continuing high level of unemployment, and by the debates surrounding the Currency and Bank Notes Bill. Abandonment of the gold standard was not proposed, but both the report of the Liberal Industry Inquiry, *Britain's Industrial Future*, and the Labour party's *Labour and the Nation* advocated changes in the conduct of monetary policy and took up the call for a banking inquiry.[46] However, it was not until the following year that the Bank was subjected to such an inquiry.

Indeed, during 1929 the relationship between banking and politics began to change generally. There were three reasons for this: criticism of increases in bank rate in February and September, the appointment of a Labour government in June, and the onset of the world depression from October.

The difficulties over bank rate arose because of the attraction of capital from Europe to New York by the Wall Street stock market boom, which threatened to force sterling off the gold standard. During late 1928 and early 1929 the Bank tried all its expedients for avoiding a curtailment of credit and rise in bank rate, but as the position still deteriorated it felt obliged on 7 February to resort to a rate increase of 1% to $5\frac{1}{2}$%.[47] Churchill again protested to the Bank, and this time even raised the matter in Cabinet on the ground that the increase 'would have a chilling effect on trade revival'. In the event, it was emphasised in Cabinet that the Government had 'no responsibility for the movement of the Bank Rate and does not control the policy of the Bank of England', and Churchill followed suit in parliamentary statements;[48] but the Bank had been reminded again of the political sensitivity of bank rate increases, while criticism of credit policy among producer groups and opposition politicians inevitably increased. Bankers' explanations, such as that of Grenfell in Parliament, that the decision was 'no reflection upon British bankers' because it was 'forced on them' by 'gambling in America', had little influence.[49] In such circumstances, Government denials of responsibility which had previously strengthened the Bank, now had the potentially dangerous consequence of isolating it. The Bank of England therefore found itself in a difficult position in the early summer when increased pressures upon sterling were followed by the election of a Labour government.

Although credit policy was not an issue at the general election, the Labour party was pledged to hold an inquiry into the banking system, and the Bank of England felt that it had to be very careful if it were to avoid interference from the new Government, or agitation for early nationalisation. Although Norman and other bankers knew that the new Chancellor, Snowden, had 'always been quite sound on the gold standard'[50] and on financial policy generally – more so than Churchill – and that he could be relied upon to resist extreme demands against the Bank, Snowden had, on the other hand, spoken of 'reforming' monetary policy, he was more certain of his own judgement in financial matters than was Churchill, and if at all possible the Bank did not wish to embarrass him in his relations with its more threatening Labour critics.[51] While Snowden proceeded slowly, gave private assurances to the Bank, and announced in Parliament in July that he had 'no intention of calling [the gold standard] in question', he nevertheless began preparations for an inquiry 'into possible improvements in our existing system of banking and credit'.[52] Later that month, he also publicly told Bank directors and other leading City bankers that he hoped there would be no further increase in bank rate – something Churchill had never done.[53]

Political considerations were therefore the main reason why the Bank tried to avoid a rise in bank rate during July 1929 – and its position became still more difficult during August. Heavy gold losses and a rise in New York rates seemed to require an immediate increase in London rates, and in addition the political controversies and financial disturbances associated with the Hague Conference on reparations caused Norman and senior Bank directors to fear a crisis similar to that which was to arise in 1931. However, since an increase in bank rate during the conference would cause difficulties for Snowden, Norman again employed other expedients, and obtained American assistance.[54] On the other hand, the financial dangers of a breakdown in the conference due to Snowden's insistence on British claims seemed so great that in mid-August Norman feld compelled to intervene in what was strictly a government matter. He and Lamont, an American member of the Young Committee and a partner in J.P. Morgan & Co, interrupted MacDonald's holiday in Scotland in order to persuade him to caution Snowden.[55] Despite this warning, Snowden successfully maintained his stand, the Hague Conference reached a settlement, and the threat of a German crisis subsided. But the American pressures remained, and in early September Snowden again tried to dissuade Norman from raising bank rate, arguing that it 'would harm trade' and be 'bitterly criticised'. In the end, however, he yielded to the arguments of Norman,[56] who at last felt able to increase the rate to 6½% on 26 September.

Snowden was right about the criticism,[57] which was particularly embarrassing for him in a week preceding the Labour party conference; party calls for a banking inquiry could now 'hardly be resisted'.[58] Despite Norman's plea that 'the mere promise of such a Committee would of itself endanger our financial position', and might even threaten the maintenance of the gold standard, Snowden announced during his speech to the party conference on 3 October that one would indeed be appointed soon, though with Norman's warning in mind he also defended the bank rate increase and said that his own decision did 'not arise out of recent events', nor imply any 'reflection whatever upon British banking and financial institutions'.[59] As Snowden remained attentive to the Bank's interests, Norman's influence was shown in the appointment as members of the committee of Bradbury, a gold standard purist, Frater Taylor, one of the Bank's industrial advisers, and Lubbock, a member of its Committee of Treasury, who was especially vigilant as the Bank's watchdog on the inquiry committee.[60] Brand, a director of Lazard Bros & Co, agreed to serve because he felt it 'very important to British financial interests that the Committee's report should be sound as there are a great many anti-City elements in the

Labour Party'.[61] However, Snowden naturally felt obliged to provide proper balance in the committee's membership, with results which worried even his Treasury secretary, who thought there was a 'danger of giving the impression that the Governor is being put on trial', since the committee was to include 'three of his bitterest critics (McKenna, Keynes and Bevin)' of whom, it was claimed, McKenna was 'known to have pursued an intense vendetta against him for years'.[62] Certainly the appointment as chairman of a judge, H.P. Macmillan, who later admitted to being mystified by finance,[63] did nothing to prevent these three – especially Keynes – from dominating the committee's proceedings.

The change of government also affected the attitude of the Bank and the City generally towards industrial rationalisation. Among Norman's original reasons for assisting armaments, iron and steel, and cotton firms was a desire 'to keep the question away from politics', and for political and financial reasons the Conservative government had welcomed the Bank's involvement. Both were well aware that difficulties in key industries could excite Labour demands for nationalisation; so the Bank, assisted by some clearing banks and merchant bankers, promoted rationalisation as an alternative.[64] However, contrary to the Bank's fears, the Labour government actually welcomed its rationalisation work even more than did its Conservative predecessor, since the Labour government was more committed to relieving the unemployment problem, yet had to deal with the consequences of the world depression and was in a parliamentary minority; its senior ministers were in any case mostly sceptical about radical remedies and nationalisation. Snowden, particularly, told Norman in September 1929 that he 'entirely approved' the Bank's plans for a subsidiary rationalisation company (the Securities Management Trust), and 'would himself at all times support it'; for as he wrote six months later, he believed that by rationalisation British industry could 'in substantial measure recapture export trade'.[65]

Thomas, the minister with special responsibility for employment policy, very early on sought the Bank's help in saving a major armaments firm from liquidation;[66] while in late 1929, with unemployment increasing, with his faith in public works programmes collapsing, and with political criticism and his own demoralisation growing, he appealed to Norman for more general assistance. In fact Norman already had under consideration a plan for linking all the major City banks in a new company to finance rationalisation, though he subsequently found it convenient to encourage ministers in the belief that they had taken the initiative; so he was happy to help Thomas reconstruct his policy, and recover his self-confidence.[67] In January 1930 Thomas read a statement prepared at the Bank announcing the City's readiness to receive rationalisation proposals, and also established contact with the clearing bank chairmen.[68] The formation of the Bankers Industrial Development Company followed in April. However, this fairly close liaison between the City and the Labour government on general industrial policy declined after Thomas moved to the Dominions Office in June,[69] while rationalisation schemes proceeded slowly and encountered difficulties within individual industries. As a result, serious differences developed: Graham, President of the Board of Trade, proposed in January 1931 greater government involvement in cotton rationalisation, and in May a public utility company to take control of the iron and steel industry, both of which the Bank strongly opposed. On the second occasion, Norman threatened to stop the work of the SMT and BID Co, and claimed that an 'experiment' in socialism would alarm foreigners and endanger the country's already delicate financial position.[70]

The other major development during 1929 was the onset of the world depression. The immediate effect of the Wall Street collapse in October was relief on the foreign exchanges, allowing reductions of bank rate to $5\frac{1}{2}$% in November, and then by stages to 3% in May 1930. However, as one source of difference between banking and politics receded, others came forward. On the causes of the international collapse of prices, bankers themselves were divided. One very influential view was that advanced particularly by Strakosch, and endorsed by the League of Nations Gold Delegation: that the price collapse was chiefly a result of maldistribution of monetary gold, caused by its accumulation and 'sterilisation' by the USA and France; and that the remedy was international co-operation to stabilise prices by persuading those countries to increase their foreign lending, and by obtaining economy in the use of gold on the lines of the Genoa conference resolutions of 1922.[71] Among those who shared this emphasis on monetary causes were Addis, Blackett and Stamp among Bank of England directors, McKenna and Leith-Ross, Deputy Controller of Finance at the Treasury.[72] During 1930 the gold question was raised with increasing frequency by backbench MPs of all three parties[73] and in December, with the issue now 'very much in the air', a group of Labour MPs formed a parliamentary 'Gold and Currency Group'.[74] Maldistribution of gold was also mentioned in speeches by Graham and Thomas, while MacDonald declared that the depression was due to 'a complete failure of the whole of the mechanism of exchange. Catastrophe has come upon us from finance'.[75] Ministers were also interested in ideas for stabilising the price of silver, which would improve British trade in the East; in March 1931 the Cabinet replied favourably to a Canadian–US proposal for a conference on silver, and MacDonald suggested that this should develop into an international conference on 'general monetary and financial conditions'.[76] Furthermore, during July a movement for bimetallism began to emerge – proposing the remonetisation of silver to compensate for the shortage of monetary gold. Its chief advocates were Darling, a director of the Midland Bank, Hunsdon of Anthony Gibbs & Sons, the Liberal MP Lambert, and the Conservative politicians, Amery and Horne; it was supported by a group of seven other Conservative MPs, and it aroused the interest of, amongst others, Thomas, Beaverbrook, and Baldwin.[77]

However, none of these developments amounted to rejections of the international gold standard – only to a desire to improve or supplement it. Moreover, most bankers, while agreeing that maldistribution of gold was harmful, did not regard it as the main cause of the price collapse. Brand, for example, thought that world overproduction of commodities was at least as important a cause, Goodenough and other clearing bank chairmen that it was more so – and in their view production could only be re-adjusted by market forces.[78] At the Bank of England, Norman and his advisers also attributed most of the blame to overproduction, and to misguided attempts to stabilise commodity prices by stockpiling.[79]

Still, they did not deny that the gold question was important: in the early 1920s Norman had tried to convene a central bank conference to consider the Genoa resolutions, but various distractions had prevented this and he had soon discovered that other leading central banks were opposed to discussions about gold 'scarcity', which they regarded as 'essentially an English problem'. Although Norman was 'entirely contented' with the Gold Delegation's Interim Report, completed in June 1930, it provoked considerable hostility abroad, particularly in the USA and France; as both Keynes and Snowden observed, it was considered to be 'the result of a British intrigue'.[80] So it seemed that any Bank of England proposal for an international conference on the gold problem would fail, and would jeopardise existing central bank co-operation. Nor did it seem that a British government initiative would have any other result, and in any case the Bank was opposed to government involvement in such matters. For all these reasons, Norman and his advisers deprecated the view that the depression was largely due to monetary causes, and that monetary problems could be alleviated by any means other than discreet persuasion through the Bank for International Settlements. This attitude exasperated Leith-Ross, but he acquiesced and took the Bank's line because it was accepted by Snowden; therefore the official Treasury view towards gold questions was that Britain could not act alone, that further reports from the Gold Delegation were awaited, and that it was a matter for the central banks and the BIS.[81] Since MacDonald and other ministers were also advised by such 'monetary cause' advocates as Stamp and

Keynes that owing to foreign hostility it was 'hopeless' to attempt international action, in the end they felt powerless to do anything.[82] They were in any case hindered by ignorance of currency problems; as MacDonald told Norman in June 1931, 'it is a subject which I have never studied and therefore know nothing about'.[83] For similar reasons, the Bank's and Snowden's views prevailed on the silver question, which they regarded as a distraction from the main problem. In May MacDonald told the American ambassador that an international conference on silver would be a 'mistake'.[84]

International monetary questions never developed into a major political issue. City bankers did however become actively involved in the great political controversy over trade policy during 1930. As the world depression resulted in increased 'economic nationalism' abroad, a sharp decline in British exports and intensified competition from foreign imports, the balance of payments position deteriorated and the industrial base for the City's financial strength came under serious threat. Consequently, a growing number of financiers reluctantly abandoned free trade, and began to support economic consolidation of the Empire and some form of protection. So, for example, Goodenough became treasurer of Amery's and Melchett's Empire Economic Union in December 1929, and by March 1930 McKenna was 'favourably disposed' towards Beaverbrook's Empire Free Trade campaign.[85] This shift in City opinion became generally known with the publication in July of a 'bankers' manifesto' declaring that the hopes of the 1926 plea for economic freedom had been frustrated, and calling for 'urgent measures for the promotion of inter-Imperial trade'. Among the signatories were McKenna and the other chairmen of the 'big five' clearing banks; Smith of Morgan, Grenfell & Co, May of the Prudential Insurance Co, and Snagge of the Atlas Assurance Co; Guinness of Standard Trust, the stockbroker Scott, and Jarvie, chairman of the United Dominions Trust; Granet and Wagg, directors of BID Co, and two Bank of England directors, Anderson and Whigham. Norman, however, made it clear that the manifesto did not originate in the Bank.[86] Privately, Beaverbrook claimed to have instigated it through McKenna and Whigham,[87] and it certainly had the political impact he would have intended, strengthening the arguments of 'whole-hog' tariff reformers within the Conservative party. Amery, for instance, wrote that the manifesto 'means that Free Trade is practically dead', and immediately used it to try and persuade Baldwin to replace the party's proposed referendum on food duties with a 'free hand' policy.[88] Grey, Runciman and other prominent Liberals organised a free-trade reply to the manifesto in September, but despite support from Addis, Bradbury, Bell and Currie, it carried a much less impressive list of City names.[89] And conversions to protection continued, including those of Grenfell,

Schuster, Holland-Martin, and Lewis of the National Provincial Bank and the government's Economic Advisory Council.[90] In January 1931 Norman himself was reported to have accepted that 'a tariff is inevitable'.[91]

These changes paralleled a transformation in prevailing industrial opinion, which the Federation of British Industries belatedly accepted in October 1930. Before then, Whigham and Jarvie had assisted Sir William Morris in establishing a 'National Council of Industry and Commerce', the aims of which included the adoption of protection and imperial preference; Guinness, Scott, Snagge and Holland-Martin were other members, along with a large number of industrialists.[92] In fact by late 1930 many financiers – whether or not they were members of protectionist organisations – were part of a general movement in business opinion which underlaid the Conservative party's adoption of a full imperial trade policy, the beginnings of Simon's Liberal protectionist split, and indeed the conversion of MacDonald, Thomas and a minority of Labour Cabinet ministers to import controls. The Cabinet free trade majority was headed by Snowden; here, at least, the City was politically at odds with the Chancellor of the Exchequer.

However, the area of greatest potential difficulty between the City and the Labour government concerned industrial costs and budgetary policy. Whatever their other explanations of Britain's industrial troubles, all bankers – and industrialists – agreed that levels of wages, taxation and social service expenditure did not assist business confidence and international competitiveness. Taxation and social service expenditure seemed especially onerous because they were more within the control of politicians, yet no government had been able to resist their increase. Bankers had complained of an 'excessive burden of taxation' even while the Conservative government was in office;[93] but in late 1929, when the downturn in British exports and a prospective budget deficit seemed to demand financial restraint, the Labour government increased expenditure on pensions and unemployment insurance. In the annual clearing bank meetings in January 1930, several chairmen warned that the country 'could not afford' further extensions of social services, while an advisory group of businessmen–financiers organised by Thomas called for a 'new political note', including a 'holiday from social legislation'.[94] As the depression deepened and industrial costs became heavier to bear, as revenues declined and expenditure on unemployment insurance rose, bankers became still more critical. By October another large deficit was expected, yet in November borrowing for the Unemployment Insurance Fund was increased and a supplementary estimate for transitional benefit was needed. Bankers declared that taxation had become a 'crushing burden', and there were now complaints about the maintenance of 'arbitrarily' high living standards.[95] According to Holland-Martin, an 'un-thought-out wish to build Jerusalem . . . and to make a land fit for heroes' had produced 'a standard of wages, pensions and unemployment pay totally above' the country's 'real means'.[96] It was widely argued by bankers and industrialists that industrial recovery was dependent upon action being taken against 'rigidity of wages', and especially against unemployment insurance 'abuses' and all other 'unproductive' public expenditure. A second objective of the National Council of Industry and Commerce was to insist upon government economy and 'a drastic reduction of taxation', while in October Schuster thought the financial position so serious that he suggested it might need to be dealt with by the formation of a non-party, 'National' government. Brand feared that in the absence of international action to raise prices, 'there is really no alternative . . . to a direct attack on costs', and that if not done voluntarily 'then ultimately economic forces will . . . bring it about, possibly as a result of a really serious economic and financial crisis'.[97]

This possibility seemed all the more threatening because during 1930 sterling had come under renewed pressure. Large French withdrawals of gold from the Bank of England began in mid-May. The Bank and the Treasury still attributed such losses to external causes, particularly to what they regarded as 'defects' in the French monetary system,[98] but some financiers were already beginning to attribute the exchange weaknesses to domestic conditions. Lamont told MacDonald that government policy was 'sending shiploads of British savings to the United States'; shortly afterwards his partner, Grenfell, gave a similar warning to the House of Commons, and Stewart, an American economic adviser to Norman, told the Macmillan Committee in July that one reason for Britain's gold shortage was the uncompetitiveness of its export industries.[99] The losses were halted, artificially, in early June by the Bank's inability to provide further 'fine' gold bars as demanded by the Bank of France, and for several months the Bank of England actually increased its gold reserves.[100] However, sterling remained weak on the major foreign exchanges, while Sprague, Stewart's successor as American adviser, told Norman in October that 'nothing very useful could be done' about Britain's monetary position 'until there had been a general deflation of wages and balancing of the budget'.[101] In early November, the exchanges fell to a point where it became profitable to refine the Bank's 'standard' gold bars into 'fine' gold for export to France, and the Bank's gold losses resumed, at a rate of £300,000 worth a day.[102] Norman obtained exchange support from the Federal Reserve Bank of New York and the Bank of France, but both of these now thought that the weakness was partly due to doubts about sterling itself. The Americans were accordingly prepared to give only limited assistance, a decision which Sprague favoured because he thought that otherwise such support 'would foster the willingness of England to take her difficulties sitting down, instead of standing against them'.[103] At the Treasury, Leith-Ross continued to attribute the gold losses largely to conditions in Paris, and Snowden was persuaded to authorise discussions with French Treasury officials in January 1931 to try and alleviate the problems. Norman, however, was cool towards these talks, as he was in late 1930 towards Bank of France offers of a loan to ease the Bank of England's difficulties.[104] In both cases, part of the reason seems to have been that now he too believed that there were domestic causes of the pound's weakness, and that action should be taken at home.

In early 1931 there was a combination of sterling and budgetary problems which in many respects foreshadowed the crisis of August. Gold losses continued, sterling fell even in the forward exchange markets, and there were clear signs of foreign loss of confidence in the pound. Snowden and the Treasury gave both Cabinet and public warnings that the prospective budget deficit and borrowing for unemployment insurance were jeopardising British financial stability, and the Cabinet discussed proposals for balancing the budget and cutting the rates of unemployment insurance, but were unable to reach agreement.[105] The City as a whole was alarmed. In their annual speeches in January, all the clearing bank chairmen except McKenna called for 'drastic' government economy measures. On the 27th Grenfell chaired the inaugural meeting of the 'Friends of Economy', a so-called 'non-political' organisation comprising financiers, industrialists and leading Liberal and Conservative politicians, and seeking the cessation of all government expenditure which was not 'absolutely necessary'; the meeting was addressed by Grey and Horne, and the platform party included Brand, Goodenough, Beaumont Pease, Schuster, and the Bank of England directors, Addis, Kindersley, Kitson and Peacock.[106] As foreign opinions of sterling became known in London, the money markets became extremely nervous. For example, on 5 February rumours that the Cabinet was about to adopt Lloyd George's plans for a large development loan produced a sharp fall in government funds, and Snowden had to deny the rumour in the House of Commons. There was even 'more or less open talk' that sterling might be forced off the gold standard, though no responsible person in the City proposed this course – even McKenna wrote that 'those who advocated a devaluation before we returned to the Gold Standard . . . are no longer in favour of such action now that we have in fact returned'.[107] Confidence was further weakened by doubts about the willingness of politicians to face the prospect of unpopular measures. As Brand wrote:

I am beginning to regard the situation as a dangerous one . . . and it doesn't seem to me that our political leaders have any idea of it. This is the reason why I . . . am all for economy. . . . The trouble is that democracies seem unable constitutionally to make Budgets balance. . . . In one country after another drastic economies can only be made by suspending the constitution, and I am not at all sure that our time is not coming.[108]

All of these fears were shared within the Bank of England. Sprague spoke of the need for 'radical remedies' to the Treasury in January and, with Norman in attendance, to the Macmillan Committee in February. He too stressed the political difficulties, telling the committee that 'it is a very real question whether the necessary readjustment will take place in this country under the democratic conditions that obtain', though he did propose a 'national treaty' to couple cuts in wages and salaries with increased taxation of rentiers.[109] When a deputation of Manchester businessmen suggested to Norman and his advisers in February that the Bank could ease the economic position by expanding the note issue, they were instead sent away with the idea of a campaign to 'Face the Economic Truths and act accordingly'. Clay, another of the Bank's advisers, agreed with one of these businessmen that unless something were done to correct the disequilibrium between prices and wages, the country 'might well be in a ruinous position' within six months. He suggested that the King be persuaded 'to announce that in view of the grave national emergency' he would ask Parliament for a 10% reduction in the Civil List, which might embarrass Cabinet ministers into taking a similar cut in salary and so stimulate a 'general patriotic movement' of voluntary reductions in income; in March he proposed another programme similar to that of Sprague.[110] Norman's own views probably did not go as far as those of his advisers; nevertheless he told Treasury officials in February that 'the main troubles of this country were due to the defects of our financial policy during the past few years and the consequent lack of confidence in British Government securities and in sterling'.[111]

Norman discussed the threat of a flight from sterling with Snowden certainly in mid-January,[112] and probably on other occasions. His influence may be detected in the references to the exchange position in the warnings of Snowden and the Treasury. However, these warnings arose largely from an independent belief in the necessity for balanced budgets – as indeed did the alarm among opposition politicians. Any advice given by Norman about monetary conditions merely confirmed and reinforced Snowden's views; so, when Granet showed him a letter from an American banker expressing doubts about sterling, Norman seized upon it as 'exactly the ammunition I want for the Chancellor'. Snowden himself welcomed the agitation from the City and elsewhere for expenditure cuts, and endorsed the view that drastic measures were needed when he accepted the Liberal motion for a Committee on

National Expenditure on 11 February.[113] However, the appointment of the May Committee postponed political discussion of emergency budgetary action for the time being, while monetary pressures were reduced by the eventual success of market operations begun by the Bank of England in late January, which halted the gold drain during February.[114]

The pound nevertheless remained weak; in early March Norman was afraid Britain might 'slide off' the gold standard.[115] With confidence in sterling at risk, the Bank was particularly worried about the character of the forthcoming report of the Macmillan Committee. The Committee of Treasury discussed the drafting of the report with Lubbock, so that he might be better equipped to persuade his co-drafters of the 'undesirability' of some of Keynes's proposals – apparently those on the 'objectives of monetary policy' which Lubbock himself thought so half-hearted about the gold standard that he feared they might precipitate a flight from sterling if included in the report.[116] To the Bank and the City generally, however, the maintenance of the gold standard seemed to depend most upon government policy; as Norman said, 'the future here depends more on politics than on finance'.[117] The arguments for radical remedies therefore continued to be stated,[118] and Norman himself sought to educate political opinion by agreeing to be cross-examined on three occasions by the Labour parliamentary 'Currency Group'. Each time he was accompanied by Sprague, who again talked of the need for deflation and thereby added to his reputation as Norman's *eminence grise*.[119] Although Sprague was always careful to say that he was expressing his own views, Norman did not altogether repudiate them when MacDonald complained that Sprague's statements were being interpreted as those of the Bank.[120]

So well before the financial and political crisis of August and September 1931, it was believed at the Bank of England and elsewhere in the City that the responsibility for the weakness of sterling lay in British levels of income and especially in the government's financial policy – and that since it was unthinkable that the gold standard should be abandoned, it was highly desirable that these should be adjusted. The causes and stages of the crisis are familiar: the effects of the central European bank collapses, and of the publication of the Macmillan and May Committee reports; the gold losses, the increases in bank rate, and the American and French central bank credits to the Bank of England; the subsequent flight from sterling and the Bank's appeal to Labour ministers; the ministerial deliberations on expenditure cuts, and discussions with opposition leaders and the General Council of the TUC; the efforts to obtain American and French credits for the government; the Labour Cabinet split on 23 August, and the formation of an all-party National government on the following day; the new Government's success in obtaining foreign credits, and its economy measures; the attacks of the Labour opposition, the Invergordon naval mutiny, the renewed flight from sterling, and the eventual abandonment of the gold standard on 20 September.

During the first part of this crisis, the growing involvement of bankers in political questions during the previous two years reached its culmination, as the Bank of England, supported by other representative City bankers, attempted to fulfil its duty under the gold standard of ensuring that the Government took steps to preserve the nation's credit.[121] In late July Harvey – substituting for Norman, who was ill – told MacDonald and Snowden that the central bank credits would provide only temporary relief while the government formulated its budgetary plans, and a joint committee of the British Bankers' Association and the Accepting Houses Committee warned them of a serious decline in foreign confidence in sterling and urged immediate action to cut expenditure, balance the budget, and improve the trade balance. When a clear flight from sterling developed in early August, the joint committee's letter was also signed by the chairmen of the chief clearing banks – including even McKenna, for whom the crisis of confidence had swept aside earlier doubts about the desirability of drastic budgetary measures.[122] The Bank was now prepared to lose gold 'in order to make the British government understand the seriousness of their position', and Harvey advised Snowden that only immediate government decisions on the budget problem could restore confidence.[123] Consequently MacDonald broke his Scottish holiday and returned to London, where it was impressed upon him and Snowden by Harvey and Peacock that the solution lay 'in the hands of the Government alone'.[124] Bank directors nevertheless maintained their pressure upon the ministers. This was the effect, at least, of Harvey and Peacock keeping them informed of the Bank's technical position and later of its communications with New York bankers, and it was certainly part of their intention in bringing the leaders of the opposition parties into the discussions. Harvey and Peacock, being 'still in serious doubt as to whether any action would be taken' by the Government, asked for ministerial permission to put 'the facts' before the Conservative and Liberal leaders;[125] only subsequently did MacDonald and Snowden themselves arrange consultations with them. Harvey, Peacock and Grenfell between them informed the Conservatives, Baldwin, Chamberlain and Hoare, of the gravity of the exchange position; Harvey, Kindersley, Peacock and Stamp impressed the same upon Samuel, the acting Liberal leader, while his colleague Maclean was briefed by three Bank directors, one of whom was the former Liberal MP, Shaw. During the last days of the Labour government, Harvey and Peacock talked with Chamberlain and Hoare almost as often as they did with MacDonald and Snowden, and Shaw was frequently in touch with Samuel and Maclean. Bank directors also explained the situation to other influential people: Dawson, editor of *The Times*, was seen by Kindersley and later by Peacock, who as the King's private financial adviser was also in direct communication with the Palace.

Clearly, Bank of England directors were very busy making their views known to those who mattered and, indeed, deliberately precipitated government action on the budget. Their attitude was bluntly stated by Norman, before he left to convalesce abroad in mid-August: the country would pull through 'if we can get them (the Government) frightened enough'.[126] However, this pressure was not interpreted as dictation by the politicians involved, in so far as none of them – not even the eventual dissentient Labour ministers – rejected the bankers' analysis of the exchange position, or doubted that the gold standard should be defended; nor did they question the need for a balanced budget. The subsequent controversy about 'bankers' dictation' concerned rather the manner of balancing the budget, specifically the issue of cuts in the rate of unemployment insurance payments. Over the role of the Bank directors and New York bankers in this matter there was some genuine misunderstanding, as well as wilful distortion by resigning Labour ministers. While the bankers recommended in the strongest terms that the budget should be balanced, on the means of doing so they observed at least the principle of political non-intervention, and did not attempt to impose specific measures. Harvey, true to his evidence before the Macmillan Committee, wrote in his original warning letter to Snowden that he was 'most anxious not to step beyond [his] province'. In the first meetings with ministers and opposition leaders Peacock did offer some suggestions about taxation and economies – apparently without direct reference to unemployment insurance[127] – but these were plainly regarded as personal comments, not as instructions from the Bank. In fact, as Bank directors knew, they did not need to insist upon particular economies, owing to the background of discussion about expenditure cuts culminating in the May report proposals for considerable savings on unemployment insurance. The real pressure for cuts in unemployment benefits during August originated from Snowden and MacDonald within the Cabinet, from the Treasury, and especially from the opposition leaders. The Bank directors' role was essentially as Harvey had described to the Macmillan Committee – advising on the financial effects of particular political operations, though with the difference that they were now advising opposition leaders as well as ministers. Their advice was, of course, that the cuts proposed by Snowden, MacDonald and the opposition leaders would have a most beneficial effect upon financial confidence: when these views were reiterated in emphatic terms by two ministers desperately striving for Cabinet agreement, it could indeed have been seen as an attempt at dictation. As for Governor Harrison and the Morgan partners in New York, their initial advice on the feasibility of a government loan simply reinforced that already given by the Bank of England about the need for a balanced budget. Later, when MacDonald asked for their opinion on his own budget scheme, which included a cut in unemployment payments, they did not feel competent to judge its adequacy, and yet were embarrassed by the knowledge that an unhelpful answer might cause the government to resign. So they tried to compromise, by expressing willingness to help but also asking if the proposed scheme would be supported by the Bank and the City generally.[128] The notorious cable which supposedly caused the Labour Cabinet to resign on 23 August was therefore a reply to proposals made by the Prime Minister, and the crucial sentence was a statement not of conditions but of enquiry – in other words, there was no attempt in New York to dictate specific economies. MacDonald's scheme was in fact acceptable to the Bank and to other leading City bankers,[129] but not to a minority of ministers who had already resolved to reject the cut in unemployment payments whatever the reply from New York, and their opposition was sufficient to bring down the government.

The involvement of Bank directors in politics did not cease with the end of the Labour government; indeed for a time they had even greater influence, since their advice was vital for a National government formed specifically to overcome the sterling crisis. A sudden acceleration of the flight from the pound on 24 August, caused by *The Times* revealing that the earlier bank credits were nearly exhausted,[130] meant that MacDonald, Snowden and their new Conservative and Liberal colleagues spent a few days under considerable pressure from Harvey and Peacock to issue definite statements of the government's composition and intentions, and to hasten the negotiations for government credits with French and American bankers.[131] Declarations of the new Government's determination to balance the budget and cut expenditure, followed by the announcement of the credits on 29 August, restored some financial confidence and abated withdrawals of capital from London. But the exchange position remained delicate and, consequently, Bank directors found themselves asked to arbitrate in ministerial discussions. When Chamberlain, Samuel and Lothian, the Liberal under-secretary for India, approached them on the 27th with the latter's scheme for a capital levy – intended to ensure that the budget did not appear to discriminate against the working class – Harvey and other directors were 'much attracted by the political advantages' but deprecated the plan because they feared it would 'immediately induce a flight from the pound and also be taken by the [Socialists] as a precedent to be repeated'.[132] In mid-September, when the drain of funds had resumed despite the announcement of the budget and the economy bill, Harvey also warned of the dangers to confidence in arguing against a prohibition on British capital exports proposed by Reading, the Liberal Foreign Secretary, but opposed by Snowden and the Treasury.[133] By then, however, the chief question on which their advice was sought was the actual future of the Government.

The Bank directors' views on this issue were considered important because the attitude of the Labour opposition and their TUC allies, together with fears that they might win an early general election, were thought to be affecting confidence in sterling. Peacock saw Citrine, the TUC general secretary, on 24 August in an effort to convince him of the seriousness of the exchange position, and of the Bank's innocence of any attempt to influence the Labour Cabinet's policy.[134] Despite this, the TUC General Council joined Labour ex-ministers in accusations that the previous cabinet had been destroyed by a 'bankers' ramp', and in violent attacks upon the National government and its proposed cuts in social services and public employees' wages – even those reductions that the former ministers had earlier been prepared to accept. Although there was no explicit opposition to the gold standard, these declarations were still disturbing to foreign financial opinion since Labour remained the largest single parliamentary party, the new ministers had expressly formed an emergency government for only a short period, and there was considerable doubt about how the electorate would react to the expenditure cuts. The pressure for a general election arose chiefly because many Conservatives wanted a mandate to introduce tariffs; opinions differed over whether the party should fight independently, or in alliance with other groups. Liberal ministers were opposed to tariffs and wished the National government to continue without an election, while MacDonald wanted tariffs but was torn over the election question. As the deteriorating balance of trade was now contributing to the weakness of sterling, most Bank directors as well as other City financiers wanted urgent consideration of tariffs – and Peacock informed senior ministers of this in mid-September. But all Bank directors – their own views reinforced by opinions from New York – believed that just the talk of a general election was weakening confidence, while actually to hold an election on the old three-party lines would have a disastrous effect, and even one fought by a National government alliance would inflict considerable damage. They wanted the National government to stay in office and deal with the trade balance without bothering about its mandate. These views, elicited from Harvey and Peacock at Cabinet and Cabinet Committee meetings, and pressed by more directors upon Conservative ministers and back-benchers on other occasions, were a major consideration in all political discussions about an election.[135]

However, during this second part of the crisis, from the end of

August, the influence of the Bank of England in fact began to decline. One reason for this was that as the second American and French credits were specifically for the government, the Cabinet and the Treasury had a direct responsibility within the Bank's special field. Another was that with the maintenance of the gold standard now a central political problem and with reputations at stake, ministers could not afford to leave exchange questions as matters to be discussed solely at the Bank. The very fact that Harvey and Peacock were summoned before a Cabinet meeting and sessions of the Cabinet Financial Situation Committee, was a significant change. Although ministers were primarily seeking advice, the directors were nevertheless being required to explain the Bank's calculations; while some ministers and Treasury officials were rapidly developing their own views on the Bank's concerns, and offering suggestions. Moreover, Conservatives were so determined to have a tariff election that they refused to be intimidated by the Bank's advice. They did not repudiate the gold standard, but argued that only if the political uncertainty was ended by an election would the weakness of sterling be overcome.[136] In mid-September even the Bank's warnings that the remaining government credits could not last through an election did not deter them, and the directors had to reconcile themselves to the inevitable Cabinet decision. Before it was taken, however, the effects of the Invergordon incident were felt, and the pressure upon sterling seemed irresistible.

In this final crisis of the gold standard, the Bank of England exercised its traditional independence for the last time. On 18 September, it decided that the position was hopeless, and allowed the exchange rate to fall and gold to stream out of the Bank: only subsequently were MacDonald and other ministers informed,[137] even though this decision vitally affected their government. Bank directors had earlier been urged by senior ministers to seek further assistance from New York and Paris, but they now deprecated offers of help and advice from these quarters.[138] However, the National government met the embarrassment of going off gold mid-way through the passage of its economy measures by claiming that a balanced budget would prevent even worse disasters; it thereby survived the ordeal and went on to win the general election. For the Bank of England, the abandonment of the gold standard was the end of its exclusive authority in monetary policy. The decisions on whether to return to gold, or how to manage the sterling exchange if this were not done, were now a matter for the Government, and Treasury officials were soon busily discussing these issues.[139] As there was, in fact, to be no return to the gold standard, the establishment of the Exchange Equalisation Account and the introduction of cheap money in 1932 marked the beginning of a new partnership between the Bank of England and the public authorities – though nationalisation was not to come for another fourteen years.

8 Arms, Government and Businessmen, 1935–1945

George Peden

Interest in relations between business and government has tended to focus on ways in which businessmen have sought to influence government, with success of interest articulation being judged by the degree to which government has acceded to businessmen's wishes. There is, however, another side to the picture. Government has purposes other than economic policy; for example, government is responsible for national defence, and may seek to make use of businessmen to that end. (Other examples, not considered here, would be colonial policy and foreign policy.) Government, in making demands upon business for non-economic reasons, may thereby expose itself more or less willingly to business influence. This essay is a study of government use of, and dependence upon, businessmen in a period when Britain was either preparing for, or conducting, a major war.

In the term 'government' is included not only the Cabinet of the day but also the whole administrative apparatus of Whitehall, civil and military. The extent to which government is an entity separate from, and independent of, the business community is a matter for examination. For Marx 'the executive of the modern state is but a committee for managing the common affairs of the whole bourgeoisie',[1] and certainly there is ample evidence that most ministers and administrators in the period shared with the business community a common stock of economic assumptions and political prejudices. The National government's cabinets from June 1935 to May 1940 were headed by men sympathetic to business – Stanley Baldwin, for example, was an ironmaster's son – and the introduction of Labour ministers to Churchill's coalition government thereafter made less difference than might have been expected, since as Ernest Bevin, the trade union leader who became Minister of Labour, noted, acceptance of the existing economic and social system was a condition of the continuation of the coalition.[2]

It was inevitable, too, that relations between defence departments and their major suppliers should be close; according to the historian of Vickers, members of that firm 'got on very well' with naval officers and civil servants at the Admiralty, 'in an atmosphere of mutual admiration'. There was less mutual admiration between Vickers and the Air Ministry, but, even so, connections could be close: for example, Sir

Charles Craven, who became chairman of both Vickers (Aviation) and Supermarine in 1938, was a personal friend of the Secretary of State for Air, Lord Swinton, with whom he had been at Winchester.[3] Again, at the hub of the Whitehall bureaucratic machine, as Secretary both of the Cabinet and the Committee of Imperial Defence, until his retirement in 1938, was Sir Maurice Hankey, who felt so strongly about the importance of maintaining a commercial arms industry that he decided, apparently on his own initiative, although with tacit ministerial approval, to give evidence in 1936 to the Royal Commission on the Private Manufacture of and Trading in Arms. He put the case against the prohibition of private manufacture so strongly as to give the Chairman the impression that his contribution was analogous to that of counsel rather than that of witness.[4]

The Royal Commission itself drew attention to the fact that 'the very existence of a private trade in arms in this country is . . . the result of a deliberate policy directed by succeeding governments', in that defence departments placed contracts with private industry rather than make exclusive use of the Royal Dockyards, Royal Ordnance Factories or Royal Aircraft Establishment, as might have been done in peace. On the other hand, the Royal Commission noted that modern warfare required mobilisation of the whole of a country's industrial capacity, so that nationalisation of the arms industry would not obviate the need to prepare private industry for the production of arms in war. Moreover, private industry was deemed to have advantages of flexibility, some firms being capable of producing arms or civilian goods, which, it was assumed, a nationalised arms industry would be unable to do, given 'obvious and admitted objections to the entry of the state into the production of commercial goods of a non-armament type'. Apparently drawing heavily upon Hankey's evidence, the Royal Commission concluded that the balance of advantage lay in a system of collaboration between private industry and government, with both providing 'sources of ingenuity and inventiveness'.[5]

In the early 1930s government was already addressing itself to the problems of mobilising the country's industrial capacity in the event of war, and drawing upon businessmen's expertise to do so. A supply board organisation had been set up in Whitehall in 1929, and gauges and machine tools had early been identified as key strategic goods, and sub-committees were set up, with leading industrialists as chairmen, to survey capacity for production of gauges and machine tools in relation to official assumptions about wartime needs. These committees also made recommendations as to types of machines that should be manufactured, and which firms' capacity should be allocated to which defence departments. More general advice was forthcoming from the Weir Committee of industrialists, set up in 1933 to advise the principal supply officers of the three services on how to go about extending Britain's capacity to produce armaments and related goods. The industrialists were Lord Weir, of the Glasgow engineering firm of G. and J. Weir, Sir Arthur Balfour, the Sheffield steelmaker, who had been chairman of the Committee on Industry and Trade bearing his name in the 1920s, and Sir James Lithgow, the Glasgow shipbuilder, who had been president of both the National Confederation of Employers' Organisations and of the Federation of British Industries. The captains of industry were thus firmly established in the structure of defence policy-making, and this might be taken as justification of Marx's view of government as 'a committee for managing the common affairs of the whole bourgeoisie'.

However, there were political checks on the degree to which business could exploit the position that arose when the Government decided to rearm in the face of the threat of Hitler's Germany. For one thing, in the words of the Permanent Secretary of the Treasury, Sir Warren Fisher, 'the supreme interest of the stockholders is the integrity of the State . . . from destruction by external force'.[6] Moreover, while there was ample scope for disagreement over the level of profits that would be permissible on defence contracts, both government and leading businessmen were alert to the danger of alienating the public, with consequent loss of electoral support for government, and also, again in Fisher's words, the likelihood of stimulation of the workman 'to insistence on some improvement of his shabby lot in life'.[7] Chamberlain, when Chancellor of the Exchequer, wrote in 1937 of his fear of rising profits and prices leading to 'a series of crippling strikes, ruining our programme', followed by 'the defeat of the Government and the advent of an ignorant . . . Opposition'.[8] An intelligent businessman like Weir could see that even a Conservative-dominated government must take steps to control industry if profiteering appeared to endanger the government's survival. There must, he noted, be 'no jewing. . . . To blackmail the state in emergency is a present to Socialism, Communism and all evil movements. . . . No sector of Private Enterprise can do this by itself, risking all Private Enterprise.'[9] Undoubtedly business reaped benefits from being integrated with government, but it was hardly less subject to political checks and balances than government itself.

In the years of depression and retrenchment, between 1920 and 1934, arms manufacturers had been kept on short rations. Shipbuilding firms had ample spare capacity, and an examination of the published accounts of fifteen of the most important of them for 1934 showed that nine had made losses.[10] In the case of the aircraft industry, the Air Ministry, by doling out small orders, had contrived to keep a 'family' of sixteen firms alive, but even so some firms had had to have recourse to such work as making milk churns.[11] As for Army supplies, the arms industry, apart from Vickers and the Royal Ordnance Factories, had virtually ceased to exist. The task before the Government was to persuade industries, which had suffered severely from reductions in defence expenditure in the past, to expand capacity to cope with a rearmament programme which was explicitly stated to be temporary, being spread over five financial years from 1936/37. It was anticipated in 1936 that by 1942 the unusually high expenditure needed to make up for past deficiencies, and to raise the country's defences to a new level, would be complete, and defence expenditure would fall to more normal levels, and there would be every likelihood that defence contractors would once more find themselves with spare capacity, assuming, as most people did down to 1939, that no war had broken out in the interim. The prospect of surplus capacity was bound to make firms either reluctant to expand plant, or determined to make big profits to cover the cost of writing off capital over a few years. Yet already, in May 1935, there had been questions in Parliament about profiteering by aircraft companies.[12] The problem of firms' reluctance to expand plant was overcome by government providing capital, either paying the cost, and acquiring ownership, both of new factories and of extensions to existing premises, or, in the case of extensions, by providing special contributions to cover depreciation. The problem of securing an appropriate ceiling to profits, however, proved to be contentious, with no perfect solution being practical.

It is important to comprehend the degree of government dependence on business expertise. The rearmament programme, which had been drawn up in November 1935, called for expenditure of about £417 million over and above the original 1935/36 estimates (£124 million), or a total of £1038 million, to be spent over five years. In the event, the programme was accelerated, costs rose, and new items were added, so that about £400 million was spent in the financial year 1938/39 alone. Expressed as a proportion of gross domestic product, this meant that defence expenditure rose from about 3% in 1935/36 to over 7½% in 1938/39.[13] This programme involved a gigantic industrial effort, calling for the application of the latest techniques of mass production, yet government departments themselves were woefully short of experience of production techniques. The Air Ministry had no factories of its own, the original Royal Aircraft Factory having been limited to research, and renamed the Royal Aircraft Establishment, after the First World War. In the case of the Admiralty, there were the Royal Dockyards, but these were laid out primarily for repair work, and costs of ships built in the Royal Dockyards usually proved to be higher than those of ships built in private yards.[14] In the case of the War Office, there were only three Royal Ordnance Factories active before 1936, and although there was a remarkable expansion of the Royal Ordnance Factories thereafter – five new ones were in operation by the end of the financial year 1937/38; nine by the end of 1938/39, and forty by the end of 1941/42 – the difficulty in finding managerial staff proved to be a limiting factor. In the event it was necessary to ask private firms to take over the running of the last six factories on an agency basis.[15] Indeed, a shortage of men capable of managing large-scale undertakings appears to have been a general characteristic of British industry in the inter-war period.[16] Although in 1938 a Conservative MP, Colonel Moore-Brabazon – the future wartime Minister of Aircraft Production – called for national aircraft factories, on the lines of the Royal Dockyards,[17] he did not say where the men capable of managing such factories could be found, and the experience of the costs of production in the Royal Dockyards was not altogether encouraging, as matters turned out.

Shortages of orders before 1935 meant that even the existing management in the aircraft industry was short of production experience, and, in the case of some firms, it would seem, of managerial talent. Air Ministry surveys of nine leading aircraft manufacturers in 1936 and 1937 found that, from the point of view of production, three were 'incompetent' and two were 'disappointing', and the Air Ministry insisted upon, and secured, management changes.[18] The Air Ministry's programme could be carried out only through a switch from small-workshop methods to mass production techniques, and for experience in the field the Air Ministry looked to the motor vehicle industry. A scheme for wartime expansion of productive capacity bringing in selected motor-vehicle firms had been drawn up as far back as 1927, and in 1936 it was decided to implement the scheme for the rearmament programme. These firms managed state-owned factories as agents of the government, in return for fees. Meanwhile, in 1934, the Weir Committee had reported on the serious deficiency in production capacity for guns and ammunition, and recommended not only expansion of Royal Ordnance Factories and Vickers-Armstrong's capacity (Vickers was then the only firm with significant gun-making capacity), but also the introduction of selected engineering firms into arms production. These new entrants to the arms industry were intended to provide reserve capacity for war, but 'educational' orders were necessary in peace to give firms experience, and such orders, placed without competitive tenders, and with payment being made while work was in progress, were subsequently incorporated into the rearmament programme. Once more government was willing to pay a premium for the sake of gaining and extending managerial experience.

Government's dependence upon the businessman's 'know-how' extended to the highest level. Lord Weir's position as a wealthy industrialist, allied to his experience in government organisation of munitions production during the First World War, and the fact that he had been Secretary of State for Air in 1918, gave him unique standing in Whitehall. Even so, government's reliance upon him for advice – advice freely given without fees – was remarkable. His activity as chairman of the Weir Committee surveying munitions capacity in 1933/34 has already been mentioned. According to Baldwin's biographers, Weir was always Baldwin's choice when industrial problems came up, and, when the decision to expand the Air Force was taken in the spring of 1935, Weir was asked to assist the Air Ministry in an advisory capacity.[19] The records of the Secretary of State for Air's weekly progress meetings show that Weir was an active participant, and Lord Swinton, who was Secretary of State from 1935 to 1938, recorded later that he could hardly think of an important meeting with industrialists where he had not had Weir's help, and generally his presence.[20] At the beginning of 1936 Weir was invited to join an important Cabinet sub-committee, the Defence Policy and Requirements Committee, which considered the draft rearmament programme, which had been drawn up by officials. Ministers accepted uncritically Weir's advice that although bottlenecks in production of machine tools, gauges and all precision tools, and, above all, a lack of skilled labour, would prevent the whole programme being carried out on time, there could be no question of industry being subject to government controls, which he equated with 'the system in countries such as Germany and Russia, i.e. peace production with a war type of control'. Instead, he invited ministers to consider recasting defence policy in the light of what industry could accomplish without such controls – which, in his opinion, meant priority for the Air Force, at the expense of the Army, since he believed the latter to be a less cost-effective way of helping allies. Subsequently Chamberlain adopted the same position, and, as Prime Minister, enforced priority for the Air Force.[21] Weir did not have a high opinion of the War Office's supply organisation, and in 1937 he accepted the invitation of the new Secretary of State for War, Leslie Hore-Belisha, to sit in with his informal Army Council to advise on how munitions supply might be reorganised.[22] There is not the slightest evidence that the high-minded Weir ever sought to exploit his position for personal gain. It is true that his own firm was a major beneficiary from the rearmament programme, but Weirs were concerned mainly with naval rearmament, and had only a small direct interest in equipment for the Air Force. Weirs did develop a factory for field artillery, but, far from trying to 'corner the market', Weir was favourably inclined to the War Office looking abroad for suppliers, as the Defence Policy and Requirements Committee minutes show.[23]

The acceptance of no government interference with the organisation of industry was not, of course, solely the product of Weir's advice. The suggestion that government consider organising industry for speedy conversion to production for defence, if need be, had been made at the Conservative Party conference in 1935, and representatives of the Federation of British Industries had been quick to call on the Prime Minister, Baldwin, to seek assurances from him, and from the Chancellor of the Exchequer, Chamberlain, that organisation would not be imposed upon industry. Instead, the FBI offered co-operation, 'in every way', on the basis of 'organisation within and by industry',[24] although the FBI itself could not, of course, enforce such co-operation by industry. The National government does not seem to have had any intention of taking powers over industry in peace, partly because of a belief in the virtues of the market economy, partly on account of fears of what use a future Labour government might make of such powers, and partly because government lacked adequate organisation to impose controls if industry were unco-operative. Controls over industry in the First World War had only been possible through recruitment of businessmen into government organisation, and recruitment of business executives was once more to be a feature of wartime ministries in the Second World War.

Capital was not the only aspect of industry which government was chary about attempting to control. Government was no less cautious in the areas of labour supply and industrial relations. As noted above, Weir believed in January 1936 that the supply of skilled labour would be a limiting factor in the rearmament programme. From his own experience as an employer, he believed that, even before the programme had begun, there was an acute shortage of highly skilled men, and a growing shortage of lower grade skilled personnel in the engineering industry. He estimated that the programme would require 150,000 extra men in the engineering, shipbuilding and metallurgical industries, and he could not see how these men could be found except by diverting them from civilian production, which, government feared, might destabilise the economy. Ministers on the Defence Policy and Requirements Committee doubted whether government assistance, in the form of technical training schools, could be of any real assistance, and felt that it was 'better and quicker that men should be trained "on the job" '. The Ministry of Labour had plans in 1936 to train 10,000 semi-skilled engineers a year, but held the view that skilled workers could only be trained under factory conditions by the firms themselves.[25] Despite persistent high unemployment since 1920, the fact was that the state had not created an apparatus capable of maintaining the unemployed as a reserve of labour trained in the latest methods of production, and, given some trade union attitudes to the necessity for long apprenticeships, the situation in the 1930s was that an increase in demand was likely to lead to increases in wages and prices long before all the unemployed could be absorbed into industry. In many industries jobs which did not, in fact, demand much skill were reserved for members of craft unions, and there was scope for economising on skilled labour by allowing unskilled men to do part of their work. However, in practice skilled men seem to have resented such 'dilution' of labour. For example, at an Air Ministry progress meeting in March 1937 it was reported that there had recently been strikes at four different aircraft firms, and that three of these strikes had apparently arisen from unskilled men being put on to machines hitherto manned by time-served tradesmen.[26] Trade union attitudes were no doubt conditioned by memories of the First World War, when wage differentials between skilled men and unskilled men had been reduced, and also by a desire to hold on to jobs for members, given that government itself in 1936 described employment arising from rearmament as temporary.

Some employers, at least, saw the need to reassure trade unionists on employment prospects, and this implied more forward planning by government. In a letter dealing with the increasing shortage of skilled building labour in the summer of 1936, the Ministry of Labour recorded how Scottish employers in the Building Trades Federation had suggested that government should draw up a programme of building requirements for a period of years. The employers could then go to the unions and suggest to them that the programme justified an increase in the labour force.[27] The general union line in meetings with various employers' federations was to insist upon recruitment of skilled men first before agreeing to dilution. Although that process took months, government did not seek to interfere. Even after Hitler's occupation of Austria in March 1938, Sir Horace Wilson, the government's Chief Industrial Adviser, and Sir Walter Citrine, General Secretary of the Trades Union Congress, could agree in informal discussion that, while it would be a good thing for the Prime Minister to educate trade unionists in the facts of international relations, negotiations on the means to secure acceleration in rearmament were best left to employers and the trade unions directly concerned.[28] It remains an open question whether workers would have been more flexible in their attitudes towards restrictive practices had government been less dependent upon private manufacturers. The official historian of British war production suggested that one of the reasons why Royal Ordnance Filling Factories were among the relatively few industrial undertakings during the war to introduce three-shift working and time-and-motion studies may have been that superintendents in charge of the factories could claim that private profit would not accrue from greater exertions from the workforce.[29]

Government relied upon employers' organisations not only for negotiation of new industrial practices, but also for collective action to ensure that production of armaments did not have an unnecessarily detrimental effect on the economy. For example, the rearmament programme of 1936 could have absorbed the whole of the capacity of the machine tool trades currently used for exports, with the consequence that, by the time defence-related orders had been completed, export markets would have been lost, perhaps permanently. Again, rearmament came at a time when civil investment was recovering from depression, with consequent heavy and increasing demand for machine tools. Given that in 1936 rearmament requirements for machine tools were estimated to be worth £4 million to £5 million annually (an underestimate as it turned out), and that in 1935 total domestic output of machine tools had been only £6.5 millions' worth, it was not difficult for the newly-appointed Minister for Co-ordination of Defence, Sir Thomas Inskip, and representatives of the Machine Tool Trades Association, to agree on an increase in imports of machine tools free of duty to allow total British domestic demand to be met without diverting exports. Priority for government orders was not subject to formal agreement, but Sir Arthur Robinson, chairman of the Supply Board, was able to report to the Defence Policy and Requirements Committee at the beginning of 1937 that he understood that 'certain machine tool makers' were giving a 'gentleman's priority' to defence work. At the outbreak of war it was apparent that more than this was needed, and by issue of the Machine Tools Control Order in September 1939 all persons engaged in the 'production, keeping, distribution, disposal, acquisition or use of machine tools' had to comply with any directions of the Ministry of Supply.[30]

Generally, even in war, government preferred that businessmen should direct the affairs of particular trades where there was no pre-existing official machinery. For example, the Raw Materials Department of the Ministry of Supply was responsible for purchase, production, costing, distribution and pricing of the most necessary and scarcest materials, but the Department delegated much of its day-to-day work to agents. In one exceptional case, that of non-ferrous metals, the whole control operation was delegated to the British Metal Corporation. More usually an agent was required only to make purchases and to sell to licensed customers – examples being the United Molasses Company (for industrial alcohol) and the Cotton Importers and Distributers Ltd, representing the Liverpool and Manchester Cotton Associations.[31] Given the scarcity of competent civil servants, it no doubt made sense to make use of businessmen even in the exercise of state powers, but, as one historian employed as a temporary civil servant at the Board of Trade between 1940 and 1945 observed, there was a 'danger that a corporative state would grow up, as it were, "in a fit of absence of mind" '.[32] Certainly the use made by businessmen of these powers in wartime would seem to justify further research. Once again one is reminded of how inadequate the state apparatus was from the point of view of direct control of economic activities.

There was no lack of complaints about profiteering on aircraft contracts before the war, and these have been made the focus of a study of rearmament by Robert Shay, who describes profiteering as the final manifestation of the breakdown of co-operation between government and industry as regards rearmament.[33] However, it is easy to overemphasise the importance of profiteering in this respect. There was an official view on what profits should be: in 1935 a sub-committee of the defence departments' joint Contracts Co-ordinating Committee suggested that in an 'emergency', when wages and raw materials were controlled, profits should be limited to a standard of 10%, and a maximum of 15%, on capital employed.[34] Although there were no controls of any kind on wages or raw material prices before the war, officials in Whitehall seem to have taken the view that the use of non-competitive contracts and of government-supplied capital so reduced risk that profits above 15% on defence contracts would be excessive. Shay quotes Treasury or Inland Revenue estimates of the aircraft industry's average rate of profit on private invested capital at about 10% in 1936 and about 20% in 1937. In 1939 the Air Ministry calculated that if its existing agreement with the aircraft industry regarding pricing of contracts were not modified, the average rate of profit on private invested capital would be 21%. Under pressure of parliamentary criticism the Society of British Aircraft Constructors agreed to forgo a third of its forecast profits for 1939, which would have brought the average profit to between 14 and 15%. There were, then, some excess profits made by the aircraft industry from 1937, but those forecast for 1939 were handed back. Moreover, what did these excess profits amount to in the aggregate? Shay offers only one figure – £750,000 for 1937[35] – which, seen in relation to the turnover of the aircraft industry that year (£25½ million), does not seem very large.[36]

It is in any case difficult to draw general conclusions about the relationship between government and industry on the basis of profits in the aircraft industry alone. There was no uniformity of contract procedure between departments, and even within the Air Ministry's programme those motor manufacturers such as Sir Herbert Austin, who agreed to manage government-owned 'shadow' factories, received less generous treatment than members of the Society of British Aircraft Constructors. Weir calculated in 1936 that Austin would only be receiving a return of between 5 and 7% of the £4 million to £5 millions' worth of work he would be overseeing.[37] The source of the aircraft firms' profits lay in the terms agreed between the Air Ministry and the SBAC regarding pricing of contracts. These terms, embodied in the First McLintock Agreement (named after Sir William McLintock, the accountant who conducted negotiations between the Air Ministry and the SBAC) were applied from 1936, although the agreement was not signed until 1938. Although it was government policy to try to calculate profit as a rate on private capital employed, businessmen were in general unwilling to adopt this practice, partly because it was contrary to their normal practice in costing contracts of regarding profit as a rate on turnover, and partly because when a factory was employed turning out aircraft for civil and export orders, as well as government orders, it was not always easy to calculate the capital employed on individual contracts. Accordingly, the SBAC secured terms which related profit to costs, and guaranteed that profits should not normally be less than 5% of ascertained cost. As the turnover of the aircraft industry increased, however, (from £8½ million in 1935 to £42 million in 1938) and as the proportion of government-financed plant to private capital employed rose, it was inevitable that profits related to private capital employed should rise. A committee on contract procedure was appointed by the Treasury and, immediately following its report in March 1939, the Air Ministry notified the SBAC that the McLintock Agreement was to be terminated. A fresh agreement signed in July 1939 allowed for profit on cost-related contracts to be varied according to size of turnover, but even during the war firms' profits calculated on private capital employed tended to rise as turnover and efficiency increased, the highest profits of all (estimated at 29.74% for a group of aircraft firms) being made in 1944.[38] Profits were high, but where profits were owing to greater efficiency, the country benefited, since weapons were being produced with less expenditure of resources than had at first been expected.

It is as well to bear this last point in mind when considering the profits of the War Office and Admiralty's contractors. Whereas the Air Ministry aimed as far as possible at 'fixed price' contracts, whereby prices were negotiated as early as possible in the production process, with subsequent savings being shared between government and contractors, to encourage efficiency,[39] the War Office relied on costing after the contract was completed, with a fixed profit, and usually a maximum price, but otherwise with no financial incentive to efficiency. A Treasury 'guesstimate' in 1938 of average profits on private capital employed on War Office contracts in 1937 was 'not higher than 10%', and this figure receives some backing from a Ministry of Supply survey in 1943, which showed that Army contractors were then making average profits of less than 10%, on the same basis.[40] Whether the absence of high profits on Army contracts indicated efficient use of resources is another matter. The highest profits of all seem to have been made by shipbuilders, despite, or rather partly because of, the Admiralty's belief that the cost of work done in the Royal Dockyards would enable it to keep a check on private contractors' costs and prices. The costs in private yards were in fact lower, for the most part, than in the Royal Dockyards, and the Admiralty's costing methods seem to have allowed private builders to make average profits of 27% on cost, and presumably more on private capital employed, on contracts placed between 1936 and 1939.[41]

High profits gave rise to political scandal, which government had to guard against, but the real problem was one of efficient use of resources. The most serious charge against government contracts departments is not that they permitted profiteering, but that, by not insisting on relating profits to private capital employed, they may have allowed a 'cost plus' mentality to have developed in industry, with baleful effects on productivity. As a Treasury official, writing in February 1939, when charges of aircraft firms' profiteering were being made in Parliament, remarked:

> There is no evidence to show that the sums which the nation is having to find for rearmament have been appreciably inflated by profiteering. . . . If criticism proceeds on the lines that the country is not getting value for the money which it has spent because (apart from profits) costs are too high, it will be very difficult to meet. No one could say that the Air Ministry have had good value for their expenditure. It is, however, fair to point out that the acceleration which has been demanded and the pace at which the contractors have been required to work have been quite incompatible with economical production, even if all the firms had been, which they are not, skilled, competent and experienced.[42]

The later 1930s saw a helter-skelter rush for security after years of neglect of the country's defences – years during which aircraft firms, shipbuilders and munitions contractors had barely scraped a living – and neither defence departments nor their contractors were well placed to control costs. The Treasury, for its part, did not wish to discourage firms from contracting; hence Chamberlain's acceptance of the view – put forward by Fisher as well as by Weir – that statutory powers to inspect firms' books as a check on prices would be harmful, and that, instead, departments should aim at 'voluntary acceptance' by firms, and the right to inspect books should be written into contracts.[43] In general, while main contractors were willing to allow individual contracts to be costed, they refused to supply defence departments with trading accounts, which would have enabled profits on private capital employed to be calculated. The Inland Revenue could have provided information on profits, but felt constrained by its statutory obligation to treat individual tax returns in confidence, and would only provide the Treasury with aggregate figures for the profits of the aircraft industry as a whole.[44] Control of profits became even more complex when sub-contractors were taken into account. Not all of sub-contractors' work would be for defence contractors, and, even in wartime, when there were ample legal powers to investigate subcontract prices, defence departments' staffs were usually unable in practice to use these powers, being too busy dealing with main contractors. Before the war, departments had had less work to handle, but had had difficulty in recruiting technical costings staff.

The bureaucratic machine was better geared to using taxation to claw back high profits, but here, at least in peace, there were political limits. In his budget for 1937/38 Chamberlain proposed to impose a tax – called National Defence Contribution – on profits, in the belief that such a tax would anticipate political unrest which, he felt, was bound to occur as rearmament resulted in an increasing cost of living and charges of profiteering. However, businessmen were shocked at what seemed to them to be a 'socialist' measure, and both directly, in the form of deputations to the Chancellor, and, apparently through the Conservative party, pressure was brought to bear on the Treasury to modify the tax. Chamberlain felt that he had stirred up a 'hornets' nest', and reckoned the proposal of NDC to be 'the bravest thing I have ever done since I have been in public life, for I have risked the Premiership just when it was about to fall in my hands'.[45] (Chamberlain did, in fact, succeed Baldwin in May 1937.) Although Chamberlain tried to explain to businessmen that the tax was bound to be temporary, because it was dependent upon the growth of profits, and would be dropped as soon as there was a down-turn in the trade cycle,[46] he and his successor as Chancellor, Sir John Simon, had to substitute a straight tax of 5% on profits instead of a tax based on a variable scale. Even so, since income tax was also being raised over the period (from a standard rate of 4*s*. 6*d*. in the pound in 1935/36 to 7*s*. in the pound in September 1939), substantial sums *do* seem to have been clawed back from defence contractors. Indeed, according to the historian of Vickers, the largest contractor to defence departments, most of the increased profits of the firm before 1940 were absorbed by increased taxation.[47] After the outbreak of war an excess profits tax was introduced, levied originally at a rate of 60% and then, from 1940, at 100%, of all profits in excess of a standard fixed for each taxpayer on the basis of his profits in the period 1935–37. This tax effectively dealt with charges of profiteering, but, according to the Ministry of Aircraft Production, another result was that manufacturers were deterred from financing any part of their own expansion, and some considered that commercial production was not worthwhile, and asked to be relieved of risk by operating plant as government agents. This, of course, was quite contrary to the Government's general policy of relying as much as possible on commercial production of munitions.[48]

The influence of businessmen was felt in government over matters other than taxation. In the spring of 1938 pressure was brought to bear on the Secretary of State for Air, Swinton, as a result of personal contact between Bruce-Gardner, of the Society of British Aircraft Constructors, and the Prime Minister's confidential adviser, Wilson, as well as through inspired press attacks on the Air Ministry. The burden of the SBAC's complaints was that the Air Ministry, even while looking to America for aircraft, was failing to use the British industry's full capacity, by allowing gaps to appear between contracts, and by impeding the flow of production by persistently requiring modifications to be made to aircraft which were under construction. Bruce-Gardner claimed that unless the Air Ministry changed its ways, British aircraft production would continue to be far below that of Germany.[49] Although there seems to be some force in Swinton's defence that 'there were not wanting manufacturers who would like to have built a lot of old . . . death-traps which could have been turned out in quantity', whereas he wished to wait for up-to-date types,[50] Wilson advised Chamberlain that 'a wave of dissatisfaction with the Air Ministry is developing fast'. The dissatisfaction extended to the House of Commons, where Swinton, a peer, could not defend himself or the Government, and both Chamberlain and Swinton said that it was on this last ground that Chamberlain asked for, and Swinton offered, his resignation.[51] Directly or indirectly, however, the SBAC had helped to bring down the Secretary of State for Air. Shay has speculated, not improbably, that the root cause of the break between Chamberlain and Swinton was the former's continued belief in co-operation with business on a voluntary basis, while Swinton had come to believe in compulsion.[52] Too much can be claimed for business influence, however: in particular, there is a need to correct Keith Middlemas's statement that claims by the Federation of British Industry and the British Employers' Confederation that they could resolve all production problems without government interference 'may have strengthened Chamberlain in dismissing Inskip – together with [Ernest] Brown and Hore-Belisha, both persistent advocates of a Ministry of Supply'.[53] It is true that all three ministers in question did become advocates of a Ministry of Supply after Munich. However, Brown was never dismissed by Chamberlain! Hore-Belisha was dismissed by Chamberlain, but not until four months after war had broken out and the Ministry of Supply had been given powers over industry. As for Inskip's resignation, which Chamberlain requested in January 1939, Inskip's diary gives no grounds to support the hypothesis, favoured by Shay, that Chamberlain was moved by Inskip's support for a Ministry of Supply.[54] On the other hand, the reason Chamberlain gave for asking for Inskip's resignation – that there had been a loss of confidence in Inskip both in the House of Commons and in the country – can be supported by the First Sea Lord, Admiral Backhouse's, comment at the time that he had been 'rather expecting' a new Minister for Co-ordination of Defence for some time, 'as there has undoubtedly been a strong move to shift Inskip'.[55] The fact is that Swinton, Inskip and Hore-Belisha all lost their jobs when they lost the support of the House of Commons, and only in the case of Swinton can one detect the influence of pressure from a business organisation.

That relations between ministers and businessmen should be strained in 1938–39 is hardly surprising, but neither the extent of profiteering nor cabinet changes give much support to the view that there was a breakdown in co-operation between government and industry. That such co-operation should encounter problems was not surprising, but co-operation continued, as it had to do, since the parties concerned shared a fundamental interest in national security. Moreover, a recent international study of aircraft industries in 1939–45 suggests that the greater success of the British government, compared with the German government, in integrating businessmen into the organisation and planning of production was a major reason why Britain's aircraft production exceeded Germany's in the years 1940–43 inclusive. In Britain, as in America, the commercial interests of capitalism were respected; in Germany there was greater bureaucratic or military interference with industry, and there existed in the private aircraft industry a distrust of the state which led firms to resist the intervention of the state. Not until after Hitler accepted a policy of 'self-responsibility' of industry in order to get businessmen more involved in the running of the war economy did German aircraft production once more overhaul that of Britain.[56]

To conclude, British businessmen sought to use changing circumstances both to strengthen their position *vis-à-vis* government, and to make profits; but public opinion regarding profiteering was an important counterweight to business influence. Again, businessmen resisted government controls so long as peace lasted. They had no wish to see a command economy established, but then neither did the trade unions. The profit mechanism, with adequate contract procedure, could, in theory, have acted as a spur to efficient use of resources, but unfortunately, in the time available, government departments were unable to recruit the full range of trained staff capable of supervising all parts of industry involved directly or indirectly in defence contracts. Whether in such circumstances it would have been worth forcing controls on industry before businessmen were ready to co-operate seems unlikely, and, in any case, government, as then organised, was unwilling to do so, since businessmen were integrated with government. Government was simply unable to manage production in peace or war without goodwill of men with the necessary managerial expertise. Essentially government was bound to business by bureaucracy's lack of competence, or, less politely, by that ignorance which Spinoza called the 'essence of human bondage'.

9 The 'Old Aunts': Governments, Politicians and the Oil Business

Geoffrey Jones

I am quite willing to treat the Government nicely, and not be too impatient, but if an old aunt does not see her own interest, and is wasting precious time, I cannot refrain from constantly pushing her a bit.

Henri Deterding, April 1914[1]

I

Perhaps in reaction to the fact that the petroleum industry boasts some of the largest industrial enterprises in the world, writers on oil seem determined to maintain that it is really a family business. Anthony Sampson has made the description of the seven largest oil multinationals as the 'seven sisters' familiar to every browser in railway bookstalls.[2] In this paper, the process is taken a stage further by the introduction of some new and rather less glamorous characters in the old family. These are the 'old aunts'. The 'old aunts' are the governments, and the politicians who control them, who have been for decades a growing factor in the activities of oil companies.

There has never been much affection between the sisters and their aunts. In Europe and the United States businessmen have traditionally looked askance at interference by governments in their affairs, except when that interference increased their companies' profits. Oilmen have always been particularly vocal in their disapproval of state intervention in their industry. Henri Deterding, the Dutchman who was the dominant force in the Royal Dutch/Shell Group for nearly thirty years after its formation in 1907, was in a fairly affectionate mood when he referred to the colonial government in the Dutch East Indies as an 'old aunt'. He regularly expressed the view that governments were barely qualified to govern, let alone interfere in the petroleum business. 'Too often', he observed in 1934, 'the men who run countries have never run businesses, as the results of their government so painfully show.'[3]

It is ironical, from this point of view, that the oil business has attracted more intervention from the 'old aunts' than most industries in the modern capitalist world. The developments that have highlighted the 'politicisation' of the oil industry in recent years are familiar enough: the nationalisation throughout the Third World of the properties of Western oil companies; the political debate in both producing and consuming countries about the threat to national sovereignty posed by the oil multinationals; the Arab use of the 'oil weapon'; the rise to prominence of oil in the list of priorities of the United States, Western Europe and Japanese foreign policy-makers. It is less well-known, however, that these phenomena have a long historical pedigree.

Before the Second World War the governments of the leading oil-producing countries, with one exception, already exercised an extensive range of regulatory controls over the operations of foreign and domestic oil companies on their territories. In Tsarist Russia, which briefly at the turn of the century produced more oil than any other nation, the leasing of oil property was in the hands of the government, and foreign oil companies could not establish themselves in Russia without the permission of several government ministries. Romania, a relatively small oil producer with an exaggerated view of its overall importance in the world of petroleum markets, also developed an extensive system of State regulations after 1900.[4] In the United States, where the modern petroleum industry had begun and which was – with the exception of Russia's brief period of primacy – the leading oil producer in the world between 1870 and 1940, there was much less public regulatory activity. Even there, however, federal and state anti-trust laws could, and recent research suggests did, exercise a powerful influence on the structure of the industry.[5]

During the inter-war years 'host country' controls over oil companies increased. In Romania, the dominant Liberal Party conducted a sustained campaign to bring the oil industry under national control.[6] In Venezuela, whose oil industry developed rapidly after 1920, there began a progressive campaign to increase the Government's share of the profits from the oil business after the death of the dictator General Gomez in 1935. In 1948 Perez Alfonso, the Venezuelan oil minister who was later to become the architect of OPEC, negotiated an arrangement under which his government received 50% of the profits made by the oil companies.[7]

Meanwhile, expropriation, the most extreme form of political interference in the oil industry, had been used as early as 1918. The Bolshevik Revolution was followed by the nationalisation of the £25 million of foreign capital – nearly four-fifths of it British – invested in the Russian oil industry. After the Bolshevik nationalisation, the prospect of some government taking everything was always a threat, if sometimes rather a distant one, to the oil companies. The lightning struck next in Mexico. In 1915 a Committee on Nationalisation was established in Mexico, but it took the depression of the 1930s to make the subject a major issue in practical politics. In 1938 Mexico followed the example of Soviet Russia and nationalised the oil industry. This again involved a substantial loss of British capital.

It would be erroneous to suggest that oil companies working outside the United States before 1939 lived in terror of nationalisation and punitive state taxation. Under almost all concession agreements negotiated before the Second World War, host countries' shares of profits rarely exceeded 10 or 15%. The concession agreements signed in Persia in 1901 and Iraq in 1925 were extremely generous to the Western, predominately British oil interests, and provide support for those who would see a conspiracy between Western governments and oil companies.[8] Yet even in the politically weak Middle East some qualification is necessary. After 1920 an increasingly nationalistic Iranian government challenged the terms of the D'Arcy concession of 1901, which had given to the British oil interests which in 1909 became the Anglo Persian Oil Company (APOC) an extensive concession over most of Iran on very generous terms.[9] In 1932 the Iranian government cancelled APOC's concession. The dispute was taken to the League of Nations before a new agreement was signed in 1933, which reduced the size of APOC's concession area and increased the company's financial commitments to Iran.[10] Other governments in the Middle East, although officially under British 'influence' or 'guidance', succeeded in playing important roles in the negotiations for concessions on their territories. Even in British-mandated Iraq in 1924–5, the Iraqi ministers managed to secure some important benefits for their country during the negotiations to confirm the Turkish Petroleum Company's concession in 1924–5.[11]

If host governments were flexing their muscles well before the birth of OPEC, another phenomenon of the contemporary world was also firmly established before 1940 – state oil companies. The proclivity of the 'old aunts' to go directly into the oil business originated in the countries of Western Europe. The first 'state oil company' was in Britain, the European country with the least State intervention in its economy. In 1914 the British government, for reasons which will be examined below, acquired a majority shareholding in APOC. Under the terms of the agreement, the Government secured a right of veto over the political and strategic aspects of the company's decisions, and the right to appoint two Government directors to the Company board. After 1918 other Western Europe governments sought to emulate what they thought was the British example. In 1924 the French Government arranged the formation of the Compagnie Française des Pétroles (CFP), charged with pursuing France's national oil interests.[12] In Italy, the Fascist government established the Azienda General Italiana Petroli (AGIP) in 1926, which not only searched (without success) for oil in Italy, but conducted exploration and production operations in Albania and Romania.

Oil was also confirmed as a prominent foreign policy issue well before the Second World War. In March 1914 the question of who was to receive an oil concession in the Turkish Empire was settled by representatives of the British and German Foreign Offices.[13] Between 1919 and 1921 Britain and the United States engaged in a diplomatic dogfight over the question of Middle Eastern oil.[14] The dispute between the Persian government and APOC in the early 1930s rapidly escalated into an inter-governmental dispute and ended up at the League of Nations.

It will be obvious that in the above discussion the term 'politicisation' has been defined widely to cover a multitude of the 'old aunts' ways, from regulatory controls over oil exploration, to anti-trust laws, to nationalisation, to the founding of state oil companies, and even the participation of diplomats in oil concession negotiations. There is no suggestion of a coherent pattern in all this. The point being made is simply that by 1940, in many different ways and for many different reasons, governments had emerged as major factors in the world's oil industry.

The rest of this chapter puts forward some explanations for this phenomenon. It focuses especially on the British experience: the response of British-based companies to the 'politicisation' of the industry, and the role played by the British government in this 'politicisation'. During the forty years before 1940 the involvement of Britain in the world oil industry was transformed. In 1900 the United Kingdom had been merely a market supplied by American oil from American companies, especially the giant Standard Oil Company, or by Continental companies with eastern European oilfields, such as the Nobels and the French Rothschilds. Over the next four decades, however, British oil interests secured major stakes in the oil industries of Tsarist Russia, the East Indies, Mexico and the Middle East. By the late 1920s APOC and the Anglo-Dutch Shell Group had become major forces in the world industry, equals to the leading American companies. Both at home and abroad these British oil companies began to find themselves entangled with 'old aunts'.

II

The most important initial factor in prompting many governments to take a strong interest in the petroleum industry was the fact that in most countries the rights to the subsoil resources of liquid hydrocarbons are vested in the state. Only in a few countries, notably the United States, did subsoil go with the ownership of the surface land, and in some of these cases the law was changed after petroleum exploration began. In 1923 the Romanians made all mineral deposits state property, and a

British Act of Parliament in 1934 vested in the Crown all property rights over petroleum in the United Kingdom. The state ownership of subsoil rights brought oil companies and governments face to face. It meant that governments owned the raw material which the companies wished to exploit. The 'old aunts' were forced to have policies towards firms in the oil and similar natural resources industries, concerning matters such as terms of entry, conditions of work, etc., years before such regulations became standard for all industries in the economy.

Britain, until the discovery of North Sea oil, was not a host country for oil companies, but several British colonies or protectorates were in that category. These included Trinidad, Egypt and, most importantly, British India. After the annexation of Burma to the Indian Empire in 1886, the Crown acquired the primitive oil wells of the former Burmese king. It already possessed the mining rights over the territories of the Indian Empire. The officials of the Government of India, though frequently denounced by some contempories and many later historians for the adverse effects their free trade and *laissez-faire* views had in the development of the Indian economy, felt an obligation to encourage the development of the industry. There were various experimental borings for oil, and state geologists conducted pioneer geological work. A tariff, though imposed for revenue-raising purposes, encouraged the rapid expansion of Burmese oil in Indian markets. A policy towards oil companies evolved. The Government of India considered that the Indian oil industry would be most rapidly developed if several competing companies were allowed to operate. Thus the Burmah Oil Company, pioneer Glasgow-based oil company on the Burmese oilfields, was repeatedly denied all the leases it desired. Indeed, certain sections of the Burmese oilfields were 'reserved' against the company. Another dimension of this policy came in 1902, when Standard Oil was refused permission to explore for oil in Burma by the Government of India on the grounds that it might use its vast resources merely to acquire its competitors and then delay the development of the high-cost Burmese oilfields.[15]

It would be possible to make several comparisons between this policy and the policy of Indian governments towards foreign oil companies since 1947, but it would be a mistake to over-emphasise the coherence of official policy in the earlier period. The Government of India did want to avoid a monopoly over the Burmese oilfields; it also sought to maximise royalty payments. But specific policies fluctuated considerably according to the personalities and views of industrial officials. Moreover in 1095 the British Admiralty persuaded the Government of India that Imperial defence considerations required the replacement of the prohibition on potential 'monopolists' with one on all non-British companies. The result was to leave the Burmese oilfields very much in the hands of the largest of the British oil companies in the region, Burmah Oil. Nevertheless, for all the inconsistencies of Government of India 'policies' towards the oil industry, it is undeniable that its actions were a major influence on the structure of the Indian oil industry before 1947. The Burmah Oil Company could hardly have survived the competition from its larger foreign competitors without the 'protection' it received from the government of India.

In several other oil-producing countries before 1914, policies very similar to that of the Government of India had evolved. In the Dutch East Indies, colonial officials were extremely suspicious of any single oil company securing a monopoly over the oilfields. Indeed, as early as 1906 a member of the Dutch Parliament proposed that the government should set up a state oil company. In Tsarist Russia, the state also blocked the entry of Standard Oil, and encouraged the flow of British and French capital into the country's oil industry, with the dual aim of encouraging its growth and keeping out Standard Oil interests. The oil policies of the Dutch and Russian governments, however, were no more coherent or based on long-term planning than those of the Government of India. The Tsarist government arbitrarily set the levels of the freight rates on the Transcaucasian railway, which transported Russia's oil from the oilfields of Baku to the export port of Batum, according to the revenue requirements of the Treasury. The Russian oil producers struggled for years to achieve a lowering of these freight rates and a reduction in their fluctuations.

The fact that many governments controlled the giving and conditions of oil concessions forced oil companies into regular negotiations with them. In many countries in which oil was found, politicians and officials were incompetent, slow-moving or worse, and inevitably companies sometimes found themselves drawn into the web of political corruption and bribery. There are repeated allegations of bribery in the extensive partisan literature on the oil industry, but the number of proven cases is remarkably few. It was certainly used by both foreign and native oil companies in Tsarist Russia,[16] but there is no reason to believe that the oil business was any more corrupt – or corrupting – than any other commercial enterprise which came into contact with the Tsarist bureaucracy. The region where bribery was most endemic before 1939 was Latin America. The man whom President Wilson of the United States and a large section of American public opinion before 1914 regarded as the arch-paradigm of the corrupt oilman was Weetman Pearson, later Lord Cowdray. Cowdray had secured large grants of land from the Mexican dictator Diaz in the early twentieth century, and built a large oil empire after the discovery of huge oilfields in 1910. Many Americans came to believe firmly that this success was based on pure corruption. President Wilson pursued a vendetta against

Cowdray, not only in Mexico but elsewhere in Latin America wherever the firm attempted to secure concessions. In fact, Wilson's view of Lord Cowdray was profoundly mistaken. The idea of Cowdray as the corrupter of Mexico was largely based on propaganda originating from Cowdray's American and Standard Oil-associated rival in Mexico, Henry Clay Pierce. Diaz was not outstandingly corrupt, at least as far as Mexican rulers of this period went, and his favourable attitude to Cowdray stemmed from genuine respect for the harbour and engineering work carried out in Mexico by the firm of S. Pearson & Son before it even became interested in the oil industry.[17] Cowdray scrupulously refused to permit the use of bribery by his companies. During the brief flirtation of his firm with the Russian oil industry during the First World War, he rejected the proposals by Vickers, his partners in this venture, to secure more favourable concession terms from the Russian government by using bribery.[18]

It is difficult to believe that bribery had more than a marginal influence on occasional oil negotiations. Far more useful assistance to companies seeking oil concessions or operating such concessions abroad came from the diplomatic support of their home governments. In several countries in the early twentieth century, oil companies found it almost impossible to operate without the support of their home governments. Persia was such a country. The country was under Russian sway at the turn of the century, and the concession secured by William D'Arcy in 1901 was only secured through the direct intervention with the Persian government of the British ambassador. The small British oil company was subsequently faced by the task of searching for oil, and after it had been discovered in 1908, of developing an oilfield in a country which lacked both economic infrastructure and political stability. The Persian central government was unable to exercise sovereignty over the parts of the country in which the oil company was interested. The assistance of the British government was essential if the D'Arcy interests were to achieve anything. During the first years, before oil was located, the company ran out of money. The Admiralty persuaded another British oil company, Burmah Oil, to invest in Persia and save the concession for Britain. After the company ran into serious difficulties with local tribesmen in 1907, the company's request for British military support was granted in the shape of a small force of Indian troops. British consular officials meanwhile performed the very important function of managing some of the company's political and semi-political negotiations.

There was little consistency in the British government's support for APOC before 1914. The Admiralty in 1904–5 was concerned to protect a potential supplier of fuel oil to the Royal Navy. In contrast, the diplomatic and consular support given to the company stemmed entirely from political and diplomatic considerations. British officials were determined to challenge the Russian influence in Persia, and every British commercial enterprise was supported as a means of achieving this goal.

Nevertheless, it can be seen that having the support of one's parent government – for whatever reason it was given – could be a critical factor in the commercial success or failure of oil companies in areas of the world like Iran. Not surprisingly, oil companies, even in *laissez-faire* Britain, were to be seen jockeying with each other for the special favours of the 'old aunts'. Before 1914 several oil companies actively sought to establish close relations with the British government. APOC's location of oil in Persia in 1908 was only the beginning of its problems. The company needed a constant flow of funds to develop its prolific oilfields. It needed a distribution network to sell the oil it had discovered. And it was determined to keep rival companies such as Shell out of neighbouring areas which were suspected of bearing oil. All this led to a campaign by the company, led by its Managing Director, Charles Greenway, to persuade the British government to give the company exclusive diplomatic support, state money and admiralty contracts for one of its products, fuel oil. To try to prompt the British government to lend this very exceptional assistance to a private commercial enterprise, Greenway and his associates made the most of the alleged menace posed by its great rival, the Shell Group. Shell was portrayed as a set of rapacious, German, Jewish monopolists, an equal threat to British consumers and national security. This 'octopus', so the story went, was on the verge of taking over APOC unless state assistance were given. The tactic worked, and the company, with its skilful use of the 'monpolistic menace' scare, was mainly responsible for the British government's decision to 'acquire' it in 1914.[19]

After 1916 the Shell Group, the victim of APOC's campaigns, entered the competition for special support by the British government. Henri Deterding had little respect for 'old aunts'. Yet he fully recognised that governments were a fact of life in the oil industry; they controlled the granting of oil concessions, they had enormous powers of obstruction, and they therefore had to be taken into account. Deterding's view was that governments should assume the role of a contractor. They should make a contract with a large commercial oil company which, if given the right support, would be able to supply a country with a full range of petroleum products. Deterding attempted to put these views into practice in several Western European countries during and after the First World War. In France and Germany he tried to persuade governments to establish state petroleum monopolies, with Shell as the contracting company. In 1919 Deterding reached an agreement with the French government under which Shell established a

French-registered subsidiary, which was to be entrusted with France's recently acquired stake in the oilfields of Mesopotamia.[20]

Deterding attempted to reach a similar arrangement with the British government between 1916 and 1924. In 1913 the British Foreign Office had blocked Deterding's schemes to control the oil concession for Mesopotamia, and placed APOC in control of the embryonic Turkish Petroleum Company.[21] Shell's Dutch shareholding had been repeatedly referred to by Foreign Office officials. In order to prevent a re-occurrence of such difficulties, Deterding made a series of offers to the British government to rearrange the internal structure of the Shell Group (perhaps by merger with British companies such as APOC and Burmah Oil) so as to give British, rather than Dutch, interests 'control' of the company.[22] The *quid pro quo* was to be British diplomatic support, and, in particular, support in gaining privileged access to the oilfields of the Middle East which lay under British control after the defeat of the Turks and Germans during the First World War.

Deterding watched in growing frustration as this scheme sank over the next eight years. Deterding continually overestimated the role of rationality in political decision-making. As a man who ran his own company dictatorily, he found it hard to cope with inter-departmental wrangling, let alone the occasional and highly destructive interventions of Prime Minister Lloyd George – who knew nothing about the oil industry – in the Middle East oil negotiations of 1919 and 1920.[23] The scheme for a giant, all British oil company was finally abandoned in 1924. About the same time, Deterding's French plans were also wrecked following a change in the political climate, and a decision by the new French government to create a national oil company, the CFP. For Deterding, it was all confirmation for his views that the 'old aunts' could never see their 'own interests' and perenially wasted 'precious time'.

There is no evidence in inter-war Britain that leading politicians or senior civil servants (apart perhaps from the small but non-executive Petroleum Department) understood the complexities of the oil industry, or even the politics of oil. British oil interests rarely came near the top of the list of the Foreign Office's priorities. This was true even during 1914–28, identified by one writer as a period of particularly close relations between oil companies and their home governments.[24] There were short periods (1912–14, 1919–21) when some officials became quite excited about the subject, but the Foreign Office never put oil interests before, say, the far more important general policy aim of maintaining good relations with the United States. This was demonstrated in Mexico before the First World War, when the British oil interests of Lord Cowdray were refused support against the hostile policies of the American administration.[25] It was demonstrated even more conclusively in the Middle East after 1920, when Britain allowed American companies to secure the dominant share of the oil deposits around the Persian Gulf, even though the area was allegedly under British 'influence'.

In summary, the fact that many governments were in a position to give, or to influence the granting of, oil concessions, led inevitably to interaction between oil companies and governments from an early stage of the industry. Even governments which played very restricted roles in their economies, such as the Government of India, had to formulate some policies on the oil industry and the companies within it. These policies were frequently incoherent, transient or based on very short-term considerations. Nevertheless, such policies could and did have considerable effects in the oil industry. Oil companies sought to influence political decisions and control political uncertainty in a number of ways. In certain conditions, they became closely involved in local politics, sometimes buying favours. Moreover, British oil companies in foreign countries tried to secure diplomatic support from their home government for their operations.

III

The second factor which led the 'old aunts' to take a very strong interest in the petroleum business was the commodity produced by the industry, oil. Coal remained the dominant source of primary energy in both the United States and Europe before 1940. The consumption of oil grew fastest in the United States. In 1899 oil supplied less than 5% of the energy requirements of the United States. By 1930 this proportion had risen to perhaps a quarter. The growth in the relative importance of petroleum was much slower in Europe, and especially in Britain. In 1938 oil contributed only about 8% of the total consumption of primary energy in Western Europe. In Britain, King Coal remained dominant.

Yet, after 1900, oil products did assume a new significance. The first use of oil was as lamp oil or kerosene, a source of heating and lighting. Virtually all the oil imported into Britain before 1900 was in this form. Kerosene was unlikely to provoke great government or political interest. Unlike its rival fuels, gas and electricity, there was no 'natural monopoly' argument to invite state intervention or regulation. The price of kerosene to consumers was only a politically sensitive issue in some extremely poor countries, such as British India.

After 1900, new uses for petroleum began to develop, and these uses were of far more concern to governments. The growth of the automobile industry caused rapid increases in the demand for petrol. The motor industry was one of the much-acclaimed 'new' industries in inter-war Britain. The number of motor vehicles registered in Britain increased from under 40,000 in 1914 to over 1.5 million in 1925. In 1937 the British motor industry produced some 380,000 cars. Petrol was the vital fuel for the internal combustion engine, and the price of petrol was of concern to far more articulate groups within society than kerosene consumers. However, a more significant factor increasing state interest in the oil industry in the early twentieth century was the growth in the use of fuel oil. By the early twentieth century a number of navies were experimenting in using oil instead of coal under the boilers of their vessels, and the consensus soon emerged that oil was the preferable fuel. The Royal Navy took the lead in these developments and in 1912 the decision was taken to convert Britain's battleships to burn fuel oil. The French laid down their first vessels to employ successfully oil burning machinery, the *Brumaire* class of submarine, in 1911.

These moves had considerable political repercussions. Britain and the other Western European nations were devoid of domestic oil industries. The Royal Navy had for decades drawn its supplies from the coalfields of South Wales, which produced the best steam coal. The only threat to supplies came from militant labour. The switch to oil, however, meant that supplies of the new fuel would have to be drawn from countries such as the United States, Russia, Romania, the Dutch East Indies, which were all a long way away, foreign, and, in some cases, politically unfriendly. The political repercussions of the Royal Navy's dependence on a foreign country were driven home to British policy-makers during the First World War. During 1917 German submarines nearly managed to cut off supplies of fuel oil to Britain, and British national security rested on the goodwill of the United States in supplying more oil in more oil tankers.[26]

The desire to preserve the limited reserves of oil in the Empire for British interests lay behind the Admiralty's pressure on the Government of India in 1904–5 to exclude all foreign oil companies from the Indian Empire. More spectacularly, the Royal Navy's fuel oil requirements were the primary factor in Winston Churchill's decision in 1914 to respond favourably to APOC's requests to be placed under State 'control'. This step, probably the single most important act of British oil policy in the period 1900 to 1940, was prompted by short-term, *ad hoc* considerations. Although the conversion of the Navy from coal to oil made the Admiralty greatly concerned about oil supplies, until the spring of 1913 civil servants strictly ruled out suggestions of a government financial involvement with any oil company. The year 1913, however, saw a sharp upward trend in fuel oil prices, and the growth in the number of consumers for the available quantities of fuel oil. APOC's offer of a large supply of oil on a long-term basis at a reasonable price was irresistable, both to the First Lord of the Admiralty,

Churchill, and his officials.[27]

The use of fuel oil by navies had a similar effect elsewhere in provoking the 'old aunts' to take an interest in the oil business. During 1913 the United States Secretary of the Navy, Josephus Daniels, proposed that the United States government should go into business as an oil producer, a proposal which was to surface periodically in American military and navy circles for at least the next three decades.[28]

Paradoxically, the emergence of oil as a 'defence industry' also encouraged many oil companies to take a closer interest in governments. The state in every country with an army and navy became a market for oil products. It was the prospect of Royal Navy fuel contracts which particularly attracted APOC to a special relationship with the British government before 1914. The company had no markets for the oil it discovered in Persia. In the short term, therefore, it could sell the oil either to its rival, the Shell Group, or to the British government. The company did make a marketing agreement with Shell in 1912 for the sales of its petrol, kerosene and much crude oil, but an Admiralty contract held out the prospect of the company retaining some independence in its sales policies. A major naval fuel oil contract formed an essential part of the 1914 Agreement with the British government.

IV

The third factor which encouraged the old aunts of both oil-producing and consuming countries to take an interest in oil was the structure of ownership of the industry. There is a parallel here with other energy industries such as gas and electricity. From the late nineteenth century onwards the view that these industries were 'natural monopolies' had prompted central or municipal governments in many countries to regulate them closely, or even take them into public ownership. There were similar thoughts about the oil industry, but in this case many governments suspected that the monopoly was anything but 'natural'. Since its inception in the United States the petroleum industry has exhibited strong tendencies towards concentration, the ownership of its vast wealth by a few companies or even individuals. The early history of the American industry is associated with the name of J.D. Rockefeller. E.L. Drake drilled the first commercial oil well in 1859. By 1870 J.D. Rockefeller had formed a million dollar corporation, the first Standard Oil Company. During the following decade Rockefeller consolidated the American oil industry under his influence, obtaining control of pipelines and making secret contracts with railway companies. By 1881 Rockefeller-dominated companies refined over 90% of the oil refined in the United States. During the 1880s and 1890s Standard Oil further extended its monopolistic position by becoming a major crude oil producer. Although most American industries of this period had their robber barons, Rockefeller soon emerged as the arch-demon. Standard Oil accumulated a reputation for dishonesty and corruption in its relentless pursuit of monopolistic control over the American oil industry. It became a favourite target for radicals and journalists. By the turn of the century Standard Oil was a major political issue. A number of state governments launched law suits against the company. In 1907 the federal government itself took Standard Oil to court on charges of having violated the anti-trust laws of the United States. In 1911 the great Standard Oil trust was broken up by the Supreme Court.[29]

A number of points deserve emphasising in this story. It is clear that many of the suspicions of the 'old aunts' about the behaviour of oil companies began in the United States, the home of the oil industry. The federal and state governments of the United States have continued ever since to intervene in the oil business, mainly on anti-trust grounds. Moreover, many of the criticisms of the large oil companies had their origins from inside the petroleum industry. Anti-trust attacks on Standard Oil's use of railways and trunk pipelines to control oil transportation were often initiated by the smaller independent oil companies and were not disinterested.[30] It is now generally conceded that Standard Oil was losing its monopolistic hold on the industry well before it was broken up by the federal government, as new companies based in areas such as Texas, which Standard Oil failed to penetrate, broke into the industry.[31]

Nevertheless, the myth of Rockefeller, of 'trusts' and 'octopuses', was exported from the United States alongside American oil. Standard Oil and its reputation was well-known by the time the company tried to find oil overseas, and its limited attempts to establish itself as an overseas producer caused fierce political controversy. It was shut out of both Tsarist Russia and British India. Standard Oil did manage to establish a subsidiary, Romana Americana, in Romania in 1903, but this immediately became a major issue in local politics.[32] The language of the American 'trust busters' soon began to be used, often inappropriately, in Europe. In 1914 Winston Churchill dressed up the British government's remarkable decision to acquire a majority shareholding in APOC in terms of the need to defend the national interest against the ravages of the 'oil trusts'. The Admiralty had experienced, Churchill observed, a 'long steady squeeze by the oil trusts all over the world'.[33]

This was not, however, the beginning of an 'anti-trust' crusade in Britain to match that of the United States, and over the next three decades the two countries followed divergent paths. In the United States the phase of anti-trust activity before the First World War abated in the inter-war years. The Federal government's acquiescence and participation in plans for the price-fixing of refined products, the exploration and development of foreign crude resources, and favourable tax policies for the petroleum industry, were all aspects of growing government–industry co-operation. Anti-trust, however, continued to lurk, and prosecutions began to start again in the late 1930s. In October 1940, the Anti-trust Division of the Justice Department charged twenty-two integrated oil companies with participating in a range of activities aimed at fixing prices and restricting competition.

In Britain, there was some support in government circles after 1914 for using the state investment in APOC to challenge the hold of the large 'foreign' oil companies on the British market. This policy was a non-starter. Although the terms of the APOC Agreement gave the government formidable powers to influence the company's policy, it was clear from the start that these powers would not be used. Officials were unwilling to be involved in such a commercial enterprise as an oil company. In June 1914 the Permanent Secretary of the Treasury had expressed his uncertainty about 'the precise length of spoon which Government Departments need when engaged in the unaccustomed pursuit of supping in the City'.[34] The spoon the government chose was a long one. APOC was left remarkably free of state control, and during the First World War pursued policies some ministers and officials regarded as at variance with the interests of the state.[35] APOC and its successor company, British Petroleum, have ever since acted as a private company, giving the British government the cold shoulder over a wide range of issues from – during the 1970s – Rhodesian sanctions busting to refusing to allow its North Sea interests to be hived off into the British National Oil Corporation.

After 1916 the emphasis in the British government's policy changed from challenging the 'trusts' to trying to get hold of one of them, the Shell Group. The government's pursuit of British 'control' of the Shell Group between 1916 and 1924 revealed a considerable lack of understanding of the realities of the world oil industry. The Shell management regarded the whole affair as a simple business matter, a necessary pandering to the naive ideas of governments in order to secure very real commercial benefits. The company, unlike the British government, knew full well that the government's influence over the Shell Group would be no greater (or smaller) if the Group had a majority of British shareholders than if it had a majority of Dutch ones. 'The whole question of control', a Shell director observed in 1923, was 'very largely nonsense. It is a matter of sentiment, but if by transferring control to the Hottentots we could increase our security and our dividends I don't believe any of us would hesitate for long.'[36]

After the abandoning in 1924 of the last attempt to create a giant 'all-British' oil company, British governments for the rest of the inter-war period adopted the policy of welcoming the growth of co-operation between the large oil companies. This was a reflection of the government's general faith in concentration and rationalisation in British industry.[37] APOC was allowed to participate with the other oil companies in international cartels and joint ventures. The leaders of Jersey Standard, APOC and the Shell Group met in 1928 in a Scottish castle, Achnacarry, to plan a world oil cartel. The administration of this cartel was subsequently based at Shell in London, and Britain was one of the few countries where it was really effective. By the mid-1930s the British market had become the most regulated in Europe. The three largest companies sold 90% of Britain's petrol.

The dislike of the 'foreign' nature of oil companies was not confined to the British government. Although multinational oil has always been regarded as predominantly American, international companies developed in Western Europe earlier than in the United States. Western European entrepreneurs were forced to explore and develop the oilfields of foreign countries because they had no oil on their own soil. By the eve of the First World War, the Shell Group had oilfields in the United States, Russia, Dutch Borneo, Romania and Egypt. The Paris Rothschilds and the Swedish Nobels had large integrated oil companies, based on the oilfields of Russia. The Deutsche Bank of Imperial Germany possessed production companies and concessions in Romania, Austria-Hungary and the Turkish Empire.

However, the incipient multinational oil companies of the Nobels, Rothschilds and the Deutsche Bank were wrecked by the First World War and the Russian Revolution. European oil companies were British and Anglo-Dutch. The British government-owned APOC and the Shell Group both expanded rapidly in the 1920s. By that decade all the major international oil companies were either American, British or Anglo-Dutch. To the major consuming countries of Western Europe, and to the producing nations apart from the United States and Soviet Russia, oil companies were large, 'monopolistic' and run by foreigners. The unaccountability of foreign companies, their largeness and foreign ethos, have always provoked criticisms of multinational enterprises in general, and of the oil industry in particular. The 'foreignness' of most oil companies became increasingly important after 1918, and primarily accounts for the emergence of 'oil' as an important political issue in the Middle East and Latin America. Post-1918 Romania, however, probably deserves the distinction for taking the first significant measure against foreign oil companies, not because they had committed some misdemeanour, or were 'capitalists', but simply because they were foreign.[38]

The ability of the great oil companies to respond to this situation was strictly limited. The Shell Group was in a better position than the

American companies or APOC, and it carefully cultivated its dual British–Dutch nationality in order to differentiate itself, when required, from the Anglo-Saxon oil 'empire'. Yet this tactic had only marginal success. During the early 1920s Deterding tried hard to convince the French government that Shell was essentially Dutch, and not a part of the 'Anglo-Saxon oil empire'.[39] But he failed, and the pressures of economic nationalism led to the establishment of CFP.

V

The 'politicisation' of the world petroleum industry was, then, already widespread by 1939. This can be ascribed to a number of special factors which encouraged the governments of both producing and consuming countries to take an interest in the industry's affairs. One was the ownership by many governments of subsoil rights. Another was the growing economic and strategic importance of oil products after 1900. A third was the oligopolistic ownership structure, and its concentration after 1918 in Anglo-Saxon hands. In addition, some oil men encouraged State 'intervention' in their industry, for the commercial benefits accruing to an oil company from a friendly relationship with a government were considerable.

The British government, like most governments of the period, showed little understanding of the oil business. Governments looked upon the industry as a source of revenue; or as a legal or political problem because of its corporate structure; or as an instrument of foreign policy. It was hardly surprising, therefore, that the forays of the 'old aunts' into oil were rarely consistent or well-informed. British politicians such as Winston Churchill and Lloyd George intervened sporadically in the oil industry's affairs at certain crucial moments, even though neither of them knew or cared much about the industry. Official policies were frequently based on incomplete information or even popular myths. Foreign Office and Admiralty officials readily succumbed to – and for a time based policy-decisions on – APOC's mischievous propaganda describing the Shell Group as a foreign, pro-German, Jewish menace. Similarly, President Wilson of the United States pursued policies against Lord Cowdray which were entirely based on misconceptions.

The fact, however, that the policies of 'old aunts' were frequently ill-conceived, based on short-term considerations and ill-informed, did not prevent governments from exercising a powerful influence on the development of the petroleum industry, often more by accident than design. The British government, through a combination of foreign policy aims in Persia and concern about the short-term fuel requirements of the Royal Navy, ended up as the moving spirit behind the rapid growth of APOC into one of the 'seven sisters'. Moreover, oil companies – contrary to popular mythology – had only a limited capacity to thwart the designs of governments. Certainly, when inter-war Mexican politicians proved 'difficult' in their negotiations with the British and American oil companies, the companies were able to respond by slowing down the development of Mexico's oilfields and expanding production in friendly Venezuela. The companies, however, were powerless to prevent the final act of nationalisation in 1938. Moreover, they were rarely able to act collectively for long. The Shell Group and the American oil companies financed several campaigns during the 1920s against the 'stolen oil' being marketed in the West by the Soviets, but they were unable to refrain from secretly bidding against each other for the exclusive right to buy this 'stolen' oil. 'In the fullness of their hatred for one another', a contemporary writer observed, 'the capitalists have never been able to discuss their differences and combine in a common hatred against the expropriating Soviets.'[40] Perhaps this factor, above all others, allowed most of the 'old aunts' of the period to very much retain the upper hand when it came to relations with the 'sisters'.

Notes

Chapter 1

1. Harold Lasswell, *Politics: Who Gets What, When, How* (New York: McGraw-Hill, 1936).
2. German historiography is particularly rich. See e.g. Hartmut Kaelble, *Industrielle Interessenpolitik in der wilhelminischen Gesellschaft* (Berlin: De Gruyter, 1967); Dirk Stegmann *et al.*, *Industrielle Gesellschaft und politisches System* (Bonn: Verlag Neue Gesellschaft, 1978).
3. Stephen Blank, *Industry and Government in Britain: the Federation of British Industries in politics, 1945–1965* (Farnborough: Saxon House, 1973); Keith Middlemas, *Politics in Industrial Society* (London: André Deutsch, 1979).
4. See e.g. Keith Burgess, *The Challenge of Labour* (London: Croom Helm, 1980); Ralph Miliband, *The State in Capitalist Society* (London: Weidenfeld and Nicolson, 1969).
5. Charles Lindblom, *Politics and Markets* (New York: Basic Books, 1977).
6. See the typology of 'corporatisms' in P. Schmitter, 'Still the century of corporatism?', in P. Schmitter and G. Lehmbruch, eds., *Trends Toward Corporatist Intermediation?* (Beverly Hills, Calif.: Sage, 1979), pp. 7–52.
7. Gerald D. Feldman, 'German interest group alliances in war and inflation, 1914–1923', in Suzanne Berger, ed., *Organizing Interests in Western Europe* (Cambridge: Cambridge University Press, 1981).
8. Samuel Beer, *Modern British Politics* (London: Faber and Faber, 1965).
9. Ulrich Nocken, 'Corporatism and pluralism in modern German history', in Stegmann *et al.*, *Industrielle Gesellschaft und politisches system*, pp. 37–56.
10. Bernard Semmel, *Imperialism and Social Reform* (London: George Allen and Unwin, 1960), pp. 74–117; Alan Sykes, *Tariff Reform in British Politics* (Oxford: Clarendon Press, 1979), pp. 115–144.
11. R.P.T. Davenport Hines, 'Dudley Docker', in L. Hannah and D. Jeremy, eds., *Dictionary of Business Biography* (forthcoming).
12. *Supra*, p. 132.
13. J.M. McEwen, 'Unionist and Conservative Members of Parliament, 1914–1939' (University of London Ph.D. thesis, 1959), p. 83.
14. W.L. Guttsman, *The British Political Elite* (London: MacGibbon and Kee, 1963), p. 82.
15. Philip Stanworth and Anthony Giddens, 'An economic elite: company chairmen', in Stanworth and Giddens, eds., *Elites in British Society* (Cambridge: Cambridge University Press, 1974), pp. 81–101.
16. See e.g. Derek Fraser, *Urban Politics in Victorian England* (Leicester: Leicester University Press, 1976).
17. J.P. Cornford, 'The transformation of Conservatism in the late nineteenth century', *Victorian Studies*, **vii** (1963), 35–66.

18. A.J. Heeson, 'The northern coal-owners and the opposition to the Coal-Mines Act of 1842', *International Review of Social History* **xxv** (1980), 236–271; A.H. Yarmie, 'Employers' organisations in mid-Victorian England', *ibid.*, 209–235; N. Soldon, 'Laissez-faire as dogma: the Liberty and Property Defence League', in K.D. Brown, ed., *Essays in Anti-Labour History*, (London: Macmillan, 1974), pp. 208–233.
19. A.R. Ilersic and P.F.B. Liddle, *Parliament of Commerce*, (London: Newman Neame, 1960), pp. 93–102.
20. John Turner and Jim Gillespie, 'Trade associations in the chemical industry, 1863–1939', unpublished, Bedford College, 1981.
21. J.C. Carr and W. Taplin, *History of the British Steel Industry*, (Oxford: Basil Blackwell, 1962), pp. 93–97, 119–122, 255, 243; British Electrical and Allied Manufacturers' Association, *The BEAMA Book* (BEAMA, 1926).
22. See evidence to the Devonshire Commission in e.g. *Parliamentary Papers* 1893–94, Cd 7063, **xxix**, *passim*.
23. G. A. Alderman, *The Railway Interest* (Leicester: Leicester University Press, 1976), pp. 165–169; G.A. Alderman, 'The railway companies and the growth of trade unionism in the 19th and early 20th centuries', *Historical Journal*, **xiv** (1971).
24. Soldon, 'Laissez-faire as dogma'; E. Bristow, 'The Liberty and Property Defence League and individualism', *Historical Journal* **xviii** (1975), 761–789.
25. J.R. Hay, 'Employers' attitudes to social policy and the concept of social control, 1900–1920', in P.M. Thane, ed., *The Origins of British Social Policy* (London: Croom Helm, 1978).
26. Cf. Clive Trebilcock, 'War and the failure of industrial mobilisation: 1899 and 1914', in J.M. Winter, ed., *War and Economic Development* (Cambridge: Cambridge University Press, 1975), pp. 139–164; R.S. Sayers, *The Bank of England* (Cambridge: Cambridge University Press, 1975), **i**, 1–53; V. Vale, 'The Government and the Cunard Contract of 1903', *Journal of Transport History*, n.s., **v** (1979), pp. 26–45.
27. *Report of the Committee on Trusts, Parliamentary Papers* 1918, Cmd 9236, **xii**, 789; Carr and Taplin, *British Steel Industry*, pp. 343–5; Public Record Office, Air Ministry Papers, AIR 2/124.
28. *Reports* of the Committee on Industrial Relations, P.P. 1917–18, Cd 8606, **xviii**, 415; 1918, Cd 9001, **xiv**, 951; Cd 9002, **x**, 659; Cd 9153, **viii**, 629.
29. *Parliamentary Papers* 1924–5, Cmd 2327, **xv**, 573.
30. Sir Herbert Hutchison, *Tariff Making and Industrial Reconstruction* (London: Harrap, 1965).
31. L.P. Carpenter, 'Corporatism in Britain, 1930–1945', *Journal of Contemporary History*, **xi** (1976), 3–25.
32. Anthony Slaven, 'Self-liquidation: National Shipbuilders Securities Ltd and British Shipbuilding in the 1930s', unpublished, University of Glasgow, 1981.
33. M.W. Kirby, 'Government intervention in industrial organisation: coal-mining in the nineteen-thirties', *Business History*, **xv** (1973), 160–173; 'The control of competition in the British coal-mining industry in the thirties', *Economic History Review*, 2s, **xxvi** (1973), 273–284.
34. Turner and Gillespie, 'Trade associations in the chemical industry', pp. 12–15.

35. PEP, *Industrial Trade Associations* (London: George Allen and Unwin, 1957), pp. 38–44.
36. H.F. Gospel, 'Employers' organisations: their growth and function in the British system of industrial relations in the period 1918–1939' (University of London Ph.D. thesis, 1974), pp. 141–144, 162–164, 210–216.
37. Eric Wigham, *The Power to Manage* (London: Macmillan, 1973), p. 119.
38. This is based on unpublished research in the papers of the NFBTE, held at its London headquarters, and on conversations with a former official; but the NFBTE itself bears no responsibility for the view expressed.
39. Wayne Lewchuk, 'Technology, pay systems and the motor companies', paper presented at the SSRC Conference on Business and Labour History, Business History Unit, March 1981.
40. G.W. Macdonald and Howard Gospel, 'The Mond-Turner Talks, 1927–1933', *Historical Journal*, **xvi** (1973), 807–829; Howard F. Gospel, 'Employers' labour policy: a study of the Mond-Turner Talks', *Business History*, **xxi** (1979), 180–197.
41. Peter Mathias, *The Federation of British Industries*, unpublished typescript deposited at the Business History Unit, LSE, chapter 1.
42. Rodney Holland, 'The Federation of British Industries and the international economy, 1929–1939', *Economic History Review*, 2s, **xxxiii** (1981), 287–300; budget submissions are in Public Record Office, Treasury Papers, T172, *passim*.
43. Rodney Lowe, 'Hours of labour: negotiating industrial legislation in Britain, 1919–1939', *Economic History Review*, 2s, **xxxv** (1982), 254–271.
44. Middlemas, *Politics in Industrial Society*, pp. 128, 183, 191, 211, 222.
45. Kathleen Burk, ed., *War and the State* (London: George Allen and Unwin, 1982), pp. 7–56; E.M.H. Lloyd, *Experiments in State Control* (Oxford: Oxford University Press, 1924).
46. J.M. Hinton, *The First Shop Stewards Movement* (London: George Allen and Unwin, 1973).
47. W.A.S. Hewins, *Apologia of an Imperialist*, (2 vols, London: Constable, 1929), **i**, *passim*; see also the UBC papers in the Hewins collection deposited in the Sheffield University Library.
48. On the separation, see Bernard Semmel, *Imperialism and Social Reform*, pp. 93–4; see also R.P.T. Davenport Hines, 'Dudley Docker' and J.A. Turner, 'Sir Vincent Caillard', in Hannah and Jeremy, eds., *Dictionary of Business Biography*.
49. Paul Barton Johnson, *Land Fit For Heroes* (Chicago: Chicago University Press, 1968).
50. Jim Tomlinson, *Problems of British Economic Policy* (London: Methuen, 1981), esp. pp. 62–105.
51. Martin Gilbert, *Winston S. Churchill*, **v**, companion part i (London: Heinemann, 1979), p. 437.
52. Chris Cook, *The Age of Alignment* (London: Macmillan, 1971), esp. pp. 140–179; Maurice Cowling, *The Impact of Labour* (Cambridge: Cambridge University Press, 1971), esp. pp. 388–389.
53. Forrest Capie, 'The pressure for tariff protection in Britain, 1917–31', *Journal of European Economic History*, **ix** (1980), 431–447.
54. Federation of British Industries, *Memorandum on Industrial Policy* (The Federation, 1930).
55. Holland, 'The Federation of British Industries', pp. 294–298.

56. President of the Board of Trade to the Prime Minister, 8 January 1919 and Chancellor of the Exchequer to the President of the Board of Trade, 10 January 1919, Treasury Papers, T172/1073.
57. Leslie Hannah, *Electricity before Nationalisation* (London: Macmillan, 1979), pp. 71–73.
58. *Ibid.*, pp. 100–102, and personal communication.
59. Sayers, *Bank of England*, pp. 321–327.
60. W.J. Reader, 'Imperial Chemical Industries and the State', in B.J. Supple, ed., *Essays in British Business History* (Oxford: Oxford University Press 1977), pp. 226–243.
61. Correspondence and papers in Ministry of Aviation Papers, AVIA 2/1830 and AVIA 2/1908.
62. Reader, 'Imperial Chemical Industries and the State', p. 241.
63. Federation of British Industries, 'Report of the Labour Sub-Committee on Industrial and Commercial Efficiency', Engineering Employers Federation Archives.
64. Helen Jones, 'Employers' welfare schemes and industrial relations in inter-war Britain,' *Business History*, **xxv** (1983).
65. Paul Addison, *The Road to 1945* (London: Jonathan Cape, 1975), pp. 214, 218.
66. *Supra*, note 47.
67. Minutes of the Balfour of Burleigh Committee, 9 November 1916, 19 January and 1 and 2 February 1917, Board of Trade Papers, BT 55/8.
68. J.A. Ramsden, personal communication.
69. Addison to Lloyd George, 8 March 1917, Bodleian Library, Addison Papers, Box 66.
70. McEwen, 'Conservative and Unionist Members of Parliament', pp. 44 ff. and tables *passim*.
71. Cf. *Industrial Peace* (an organ of the BCU), September 1923.
72. Minutes of the Empire Industries Association, House of Lords Record Office, Hannon Papers.
73. John Barnes and David Nicholson, eds., *The Leo Amery Diaries* (London: Hutchinson, 1980), pp. 439, 449, 542; Philip Williamson, ' "Safety First": Baldwin, the Conservative Party and the 1929 General Election', *Historical Journal* **xxv** (1982), 385–404.
74. Untitled memorandum by J. Walker Smith, February 1934, NFBTE Archives.
75. *Infra*, p. 142; R.P. Shay, *British Rearmament in the 1930s: Politics and Profits* (Princeton: Princeton University Press, 1977), pp. 147–155.
76. J.A. Ramsden, *The Making of Conservative Party Policy* (London: Longman, 1980), pp. 80–82, and personal communication.
77. Simon Haxey, *Tory M.P.* (London: Gollancz, 1939), esp. pp. 32–116. Despite Haxey's prejudices and lack of system, there is substantial evidence here of the growing diversity of Tory wealth-holding.
78. See chapter 6 below and John Turner, 'Public administration and private enterprise: the industrial policy community between the wars', paper presented at a colloquium at Birkbeck College on 2 April 1982.
79. See Howard F. Gospel and Craig Littler, *Managerial Strategy and Industrial Relations* (London: Heinemann Educational Books, 1983); and the thesis in progress by Mr R. Fitzgerald, of Bedford College, on 'The politics of welfare capitalism'.

Chapter 2

1. G.B.S. Shaw, *The Common Sense of Municipal Trading* (London: Constable, 1904), p. 1.
2. D. Knoop, *Principles and Methods of Municipal Trading* (London: Macmillan, 1912), p. 2.
3. *Parliamentary Papers* 1900, **vii**, Joint Select Committee on Municipal Trading, *Evidence*, Appendix VI; H.J. Gibbons, 'The opposition to municipal socialism in England', *Journal of Political Economy*, **ix** (1900–1901), 245.
4. D.H. Davies, *The Cost of Municipal Trading* (Industrial Freedom League, 1903), p. 10.
5. A.V. Dicey, *Law and Public Opinion in England*, 2nd edn. (London: Macmillan, 1914), pp. 284–288.
6. E. Bristow, 'The Liberty and Property Defence League and Individualism', *Historical Journal*, **xviii** (1975), 761–789; N. Soldon, 'Laissez-Faire as dogma: the Liberty and Property Defence League', in K.D. Brown, ed., *Essays in Anti-Labour History* (London: Macmillan, 1974), pp. 208–233.
7. *Manchester Times*, 25 January 1834, quoted in W. Robson, 'The public utility services', in H. Laski, ed., *A Century of Municipal Progress, 1835–1935* (London: George Allen and Unwin, 1935), p. 310.
8. F. Dolman, 'Joseph Chamberlain's municipal career', *Fortnightly Review*, **lvii** (1895), 904–912; E.P. Hennock, *Fit and Proper Persons* (London: Edward Arnold, 1973), pp. 116–124.
9. A.M. McBriar, *Fabian Socialism and English Politics, 1884–1918* (Cambridge: Cambridge University Press, 1962), pp. 191–193.
10. *Ibid.*, pp. 194–195.
11. *Ibid.*, p. 175.
12. S.J. Webb, 'The course of municipal socialism', *Labour Annual*, **iii** (1896), 77–84.
13. Details of business interests from E. Garcke, *Garcke's Manual of Electrical Undertakings*, **v** (1900–1901).
14. 'Municipal trading', *Municipal Journal*, 7 December 1900.
15. 'The Industrial Freedom League', *Municipal Journal*, 22 July 1904; 'The Anti-Municipal Trading League', *ibid.*, 17 March 1905; Industrial Freedom League, *Report of Annual Meetings on 24th June, 1903*, p. 22.
16. British Electric Traction Company, Board Minutes, quoted in R. Fulford, *Five Decades of BET* (BET, 1946), p. 42.
17. BET Board Minutes, 18 September 1902, cap. 706, p. 244.
18. H.G. Hutchinson, *Life of Sir John Lubbock, Lord Avebury* (2 vols, Macmillan, 1914), p. 114.
19. Bristow, 'Liberty and Property Defence League', p. 784.
20. C.J. Kauffman, 'Lord Elcho, trade unionism and democracy', in Brown, ed., *Essays in Anti-Labour History*, p. 207.
21. Earl Wemyss, *The Dangers of Municipal Trading* (Liberty and Property Defence League, 1899), p. 7.
22. *British Electric Traction Company Gazette*, May 1902, p. 111.
23. *Chamber of Commerce Journal*, April 1900, p. 56.
24. R.P. Porter, *The Conflict over Municipal Trading* (Industrial Freedom League, 1903), p. 19.

25. W.G. Towler, *Socialism in Local Government* (London: George Allen and Unwin, 1909), p. 140.
26. R. Donald, 'Municipal trading – a defence', *Contemporary Review*, **lxxviii** (1900), 277.
27. R. Donald, 'Recent attacks on municipal ownership in Britain', *Municipal Affairs*, **vi** (1902), 585.
28. Shaw, *Common Sense of Municipal Trading*, pp. x–xii.
29. A. Maude, *Municipal Trading* (1908), p. 19.
30. Lord Rosebery speaking on 1 March 1898, quoted McBriar, *Fabian Socialism*, p. 195.
31. Donald, 'Recent attacks on municipal ownership', 39.
32. J.R. Kellett, 'Municipal socialism, enterprise and trading', *Urban History Yearbook*, 1978, p. 39.
33. *Chamber of Commerce Journal*, April 1900, supplement, p. 23.
34. E. Garcke, *The Progress of Electrical Enterprise* (Electrical Press, 1907), p. 30.
35. *Parliamentary Papers*, 1918, **viii**, 4–5. *Report* of the Committee Appointed by the Board of Trade on Electricity Supply; R. Donald, 'The case for municipal trading', *Contemporary Review*, **lxxxiii** (1903), 486.
36. *Chamber of Commerce Journal*, February 1899, p. 22.
37. D.H. Davies, *The Cost of Municipal Trading* (P.S. King, 1899).
38. *Parliamentary Papers*, 1899, **lxxxviii**, *Return Relating to Municipal Corporations (Reproductive undertakings)*.
39. *Hansard*, Commons, 21 February 1899; 23 February 1899; 28 February 1899; 2 March 1899; *Hansard*, Lords, 3 March 1899; Bristow, 'Liberty and Property Defence League', 784.
40. *Hansard*, Commons, 2 March 1899, col 1053 (A.J. Balfour).
41. R.H. Gretton, *A Modern History of the English People, 1899–1910* (Grant Richards, 1913), p. 108.
42. *Hansard*, Commons, 29 March 1900, col 757, motion of Mr Anstruther.
43. *Ibid*., 5 April 1900, col 1369 (Lord Balcarres).
44. *Ibid*., 29 March 1900, col 760 (Mr Ritchie).
45. *Ibid*., 29 March 1900, col 764 (Mr J. Burns).
46. *Ibid*., 5 April 1900, col 1351 (Sir Albert Rollitt).
47. *Parliamentary Papers*, 1900, **vii**, 1. *Report* of the Joint Select Committee on Municipal Trading.
48. 'The murder out', *Municipal Journal*, 17 March 1905; 'Attempt to cripple municipal borrowing', *ibid*., 6 January 1905.
49. *The Economist*, 12 December 1903.
50. *Parliamentary Papers*, 1906, **xxvi**, **lv**, *Annual Report of the Local Government Board for 1906*; M. Schultz, 'The control of municipal borrowing', in C. Wilson ed., *Essays in Local Government* (Oxford: Basil Blackwell, 1948), pp. 188–189; Knoop. *Principles and Methods of Municipal Trading*, p. 153.
51. *Hansard*, Commons, 19 April 1904, cols 554–555 (Mr Chamberlain); 'Industrial freedom', *Municipal Journal*, 22 April 1904.
52. R.P. Porter, 'European and American methods and results compared', *Municipal Affairs*, **vi** (1902), 542.
53. 'Municipal expenditure', *The Economist*, 19 May 1906.
54. *Municipal Socialism: A Series of Articles Reprinted from The Times* (*The Times*, 1903), p. 6.

55. A.K. Cairncross, *Home and Foreign Investment, 1870–1913* (Cambridge: Cambridge University Press, 1953), pp. 144–145; J. Blackman and E.M. Sigsworth, 'The Home Boom of the 1890s', *Yorkshire Bulletin of Economic and Social Research*, **xvii** (1965), 82–83.

Chapter 3

The author would like to thank the Confederation of British Industry and the Engineering Employers' Federation for access to records and permission for their publication here. He is also indebted to Leslie Hannah for comments on an earlier draft, and to Terence Rogers for advice and guidance on sources, but he is solely responsible for the interpretation offered here.

1. Stephen Blank, *Industry and Government in Britain* (Farnborough: Saxon House, 1963); Keith Middlemas, *Politics in Industrial Society* (London: André Deutsch, 1979).
2. H.H. Asquith to King George V, reporting Cabinet discussions, Public Record Office, Cabinet Papers, CAB 41/36/10.
3. e.g. R.J.Q. Adams, *Arms and the Wizard* (London: Cassell, 1978).
4. Middlemas, *Politics in Industrial Society*, pp. 76–77.
5. Information from Terence Rodgers.
6. *Supra*, pp. 5–6.
7. 'Proposed Central Association of Employers' Organisations', 3 December 1915, Engineering Employers' Federation Archives.
8. List of persons present at the meeting, *ibid.*; on the Midlands Employers' Federation see G.R. Askwith, 'Memorandum on Employers' Associations', 30 August 1917, Public Record Office, Ministry of Reconstruction Papers, RECO 1/376.
9. Guildhall Library, ABCC Archives, Guildhall MSS 14476/6, *passim*.
10. ABCC Executive Council, 11 May 1915, Guildhall MSS 14476/7.
11. ABCC Executive Council, 9 November 1915, *ibid.*
12. ABCC Annual and Special General Meetings, 29 February 1916, Guildhall MSS 14476/8.
13. ABCC Executive Council, 9 May 1916, *ibid.*
14. 'Extension of Policy and Programme', enclosed with Stafford Ransome to Allan Smith, 23 March 1916, EEF Archives.
15. ABCC Executive Council, 9 June 1916, Guildhall MSS 14476/8.
16. J. Thorneycroft to Allan Smith, 5 February 1916, EEF Archives.
17. R.P.T. Davenport Hines, 'Dudley Docker' in Hannah and Jeremy, eds., *Dictionary of Business Biography*, vol I (forthcoming).
18. *The Globe*, 1 May 1916.
19. R.T. Nugent to Richardson, 11 January 1917. University of Warwick Modern Records Centre, Confederation of British Industries Predecessor Archives, FBI/D/Nugent/2.
20. ABCC Executive Council, 9 May 1916, Guildhall MSS 14476/8.
21. *United Manufacturers Journal*, i (May, 1919).
22. Percy Reid to Allan Smith, 27 September 1916, EEF Archives.
23. Nugent to Docker, 9 November 1916, FBI/Nugent/D/3.
24. *Manchester Guardian*, 27 January 1917.
25. Nugent to F.R. Davenport, 21 August 1917, FBI/D/Nugent/2.
26. Nugent to V. Caillard, 9 November 1916, *ibid.*

27. The FCSDA was a combine, not a trade association.
28. N.d. circular in FBI/D/Nugent/2.
29. J. Hinton, *The First Shop Stewards Movement* (London: George Allen and Unwin, 1973).
30. EEF Emergency Committee, 28 April 1916, EEF Minute Book 12.
31. EEF Emergency Committee, 29 September 1916, *ibid*.
32. EEF M.B. 12, *passim*.
33. EEF Emergency Committee, 28 July 1916, EEF Minute Book 12.
34. EEF Emergency Committee, 27 October 1916; J. McKie Bryce to local associations, 1 November 1916, EEF Archives.
35. Nugent to Docker, 28 October 1916, FBI/D/Nugent/2.
36. Nugent to Docker, 1 November 1916, *ibid*.; cf. FBI Organising Sub-Committee, 5 and 12 December 1916 and 5 January 1917, FBI/C/10.
37. EEF Management Committee, 21 December 1916, EEF Minute Book 12; circular withdrawing the proscription, 13 January 1917, EEF Archives.
38. R.T. Nugent, 'Employers' Advisory Council', n.d. memo., FBI/D/Nugent/2; Meetings of the EAC in FBI/C/19/48.
39. E.L. Hill to Nugent, 31 August 1917, FBI/D/Nugent/2.
40. Minutes and Agenda in Public Record Office, Ministry of Munitions Papers, MUN 5/53.
41. EEF Management Committee, 29 June 1917, EEF Minute Book 13.
42. EEF Management Committee, 27 July 1917, *ibid*.
43. EEF Management Committee, 31 August 1917, *ibid*.; Employers' Advisory Council, 26 July 1917 and 9 August 1917, FBI/C/19/48.
44. Employers' Consultative Committee, 17 July 1917, MUN 5/53.
45. Employers' Consultative Committee, 29 November 1917 and 26 January 1918, MUN 5/53.
46. EEF Management Committee, 5 October 1917, EEF Minute Book 13.
47. EEF Management Committee, 27 July and 30 November 1917, *ibid*.
48. EEF Management Committee, 31 August 1917 and 22 February 1918, *ibid*.
49. 'Report of the Labour Sub-Committee on Industrial and Commercial Efficiency', FBI Circular, 6 December 1917, EEF Archives.
50. 'Observations' (on the report of the Labour Sub-Committee), EEF Archives.
51. EEF Management Committee, 25 January and 22 March 1918, EEF Minute Book 13; Notes of a meeting with the FBI Labour Sub-Committee, 15 March 1918, EEF Archives.
52. Notes of a meeting with the FBI Labour Sub-Committee, 10 April 1918, *ibid*.
53. Minutes of Special Committee, 14 March 1918 and 19 April 1918, National Maritime Museum, BSRA Predecessor Papers, SEF Minutes.
54. EEF Management Committee, 17 May 1918, EEF Minute Book 14; Terms of Agreement, n.d., *ibid*. pp. 145–146; EEF Management Committee 30 April 1918, *ibid*. In the deal, the EEF absorbed fourteen specialised associations which had been in the NEF.
55. Eric Wigham, *The Power to Manage* (London: Macmillan, 1973), p. 98;
56. Cf. Rodney Lowe, 'The failure of consensus in Britain: the National Industrial Conference, 1919–21', *Historical Journal* **xxi** (1978), 647–675.
57. Hiley to Nugent, 20 February 1917, FBI/D/Nugent/3.
58. Nugent to Hadfield, 14 May 1917, FBI/D/Nugent/5a.

59. J.A. Turner, 'The British Commonwealth Union and the General Election of 1918', *English Historical Review*, **xciii** (1978), 528–558.
60. Untitled memorandum by Nugent, 7 June 1917, FBI/D/Nugent/5a; Terrell to Nugent, 16 May 1917, FBI/D/Nugent/3.
61. *Bulletin* of the Federation of British Industries, June 1917.
62. Parliamentary Sub-committee of the Executive Council, 16 January 1918, FBI/C/16, vol 37.
63. House of Commons Committee, 11 March 1919, FBI/C/19/50.
64. Nugent to E.L. Hill, 4 August 1917, FBI/D/Nugent/2.
65. Turner, 'The British Commonwealth Union', 535–537.
66. Management Committee, 22 February 1918, EEF M.B. 13.
67. Turner, 'The British Commonwealth Union', 542–543.
68. Middlemas, *Politics in Industrial Society*, p. 132.
69. John Haworth (EPA Secretary) to Nugent, 8 January 1917, FBI/D/Nugent/3; Nugent to Docker, 30 January 1917, FBI/D/Nugent/1.
70. Unsigned memorandum on the NAEE and the Industrial League, 8 June 1920, EEF Archives; Nugent to F. Huth Jackson, 7 May 1917, FBI/D/Nugent/2.
71. Nugent to Rylands, 17 May 1917, FBI/D/Nugent/1; Appleton to Nugent 4 August 1917, FBI/D/Nugent/2.
72. FBI Organisation and Management Committee, 14 December 1917, FBI/C/10.
73. 'Report No. 735', 10 April 1918, EEF Archives.
74. National Stability League, 'List of Subscribers', *ibid*.
75. See e.g. Balfour of Burleigh Committee evidence no. 18, 16 February 1917, BT 55/10; Stanley to Lloyd George, 10 January 1919, T172/1073; and the records of the ineffectual Board of Trade Advisory Council in BT 197.
76. J.T. Walton Newbold, *The Gang Behind the Government: or Capital's case for Industrial Unionism* (Glasgow: n.d.), p. 3.

Chapter 4

1. See in particular J. Ramsden, *The Age of Balfour and Baldwin, 1920–1940* (London: Longman, 1978); T.F. Lindsay and M. Harrington, *The Conservative Party, 1918–1970* (London: Macmillan, 1974); M. Cowling, *The Impact of Labour 1920–1924* (Cambridge: Cambridge University Press, 1971); C. Cook, *The Age of Alignment* (London: Macmillan, 1975); B. Semmel, *Imperialism and Social Reform* (George Allen and Unwin, 1960); N. Blewett, 'Free Fooders, Balfourites, Whole Hoggers: factionalism within the Unionist Party, 1906–10', *Historical Journal*, **xi** (1968), 95–124; R.A. Rempel, *Unionists Divided* (Newton Abbot: David & Charles, 1972); A. Sykes, *Tariff Reform in British Politics, 1903–13* (Oxford: Clarendon Press, 1979).
2. Cf. D.H. Aldcroft and H.W. Richardson, *The British Economy 1870–1939* (London: Macmillan, 1969), pp. 62–101. On steel see D.L. Burn, *Economic History of Steelmaking, 1867–1939* (Cambridge: Cambridge University Press, 1940); F. Capie, 'The British tariff and industrial protection in the 1930s', *Economic History Review*, 2s, **xxxi** (1978), 399–409.
3. R. and K. Macleod, 'War and economic development: government and the optical industry in Britain, 1914–18', in J.M. Winter, ed., *War and*

Economic Development (Cambridge: Cambridge University Press, 1975); D.C. Coleman, 'War demand and supply: the "Dope Scandal", 1915–1919', *ibid*.; G. Jones, *The State and the Emergence of the British Oil Industry* (London: Macmillan, 1980); W. Reader, 'Imperial Chemical Industries and the State', in B. Supple, ed., *Essays in British Business History* (Oxford: Oxford University Press, 1977).

4. C. Trebilcock, 'A "special relationship" – Government, rearmament and the Cordite firms', *Economic History Review*, 2s, **xix** (1966), 364–379; G. Jones, *op. cit*. (n. 3 *supra*).
5. M.W. Kirby, *The British Coalmining Industry 1870–1946. A Political and Economic History* (London: Macmillan, 1977).
6. P.J. Cain, 'Railway combination and government, 1900–1914', *Economic History Review*, 2s, **xxv** (1972), 623–641; L. Hannah, *Electricity before Nationalisation* (London: Macmillan, 1979); and see below, pp. 56–57.
7. D. Burn, *The Economic History of Steelmaking, 1867–1939* (Cambridge: Cambridge University Press, 1940); K. Warren, 'The steel industry', in D. Aldcroft and N. Buxton, eds., *British Industry Between the Wars* (London: Scolar Press, 1979); S.W. Tolliday, 'Industry, finance and the state: an analysis of the British steel industry in the inter-war years' (Cambridge University Ph.D. thesis, 1979), henceforth Tolliday thesis, pp. 37–56.
8. Tolliday thesis, pp. 45–52.
9. On locational problems see K. Warren, *The British Sheet Steel Industry since 1840* (London: Bell, 1970) and *The Geography of British Heavy Industry since 1800* (Oxford: Oxford University Press, 1976); see also D.W. Heal, *The Steel Industry in Post-War Britain* (Newton Abbot: David & Charles, 1974).
10. For case studies see Tolliday thesis, pp. 63–164, 169–211, 321–331.
11. P.L. Payne, *Colvilles and the Scottish Steel Industry* (Oxford: Oxford University Press, 1980); K.L. Warren, 'Locational problems of the Scottish steel industry since 1780', *Scottish Geographical Magazine*, **lxxxi** (1965).
12. Tolliday thesis, pp. 125–164.
13. *Ibid*., pp. 45–52.
14. Public Record Office, Cabinet Papers, Cabinet Conclusions 22 April 1933, CAB 24/66; 'Notes on evidence of the Heavy Steelmakers to the Sankey Committee', 24 October 1929, CAB 58/128.
15. 'Notes on the evidence of NFISM on heavy steel', October 1929, CAB 58/128, cf. Sir Peter Rylands speech as retiring chairman, British Steel Records Centre, National Federation of Iron and Steel Manufacturers papers, AGM Minutes, 19 April 1931.
16. J.A. Turner, 'The British Commonwealth Union and the General Election of 1918', *English Historical Review*, **xciii** (1978), 551–553.
17. P.K. Cline, 'Eric Geddes and the "experiment" with businessmen in government, 1915–1922', in K.D. Brown, ed., *Essays in Anti-Labour History* (London: Macmillan, 1974); P.J. Cain, 'Railway combination and government'; Jones, *The State and the Emergence of the British Oil Industry*.
18. Cf., Macleod and Macleod, Coleman, and Jones as cited *supra* note 3.
19. *Report* of the Departmental Committee appointed by the Board of Trade to consider the position of the iron and steel trade after the War (the Scoby-Smith Report), *Parliamentary Papers*, 1918, Cd 9071, **xiii**, 423.

20. J.C. Carr and W. Taplin, *The History of the British Steel Industry* (Oxford: Oxford University Press, 1962), p. 376.
21. British Steel Records Centre, Cargo Fleet Minute Books, 24 June 1925; Dorman Long AGM Report, 1925; C. Smith (Consett Iron Co.) in *Daily Telegraph*, 14 August 1928.
22. A. Steel-Maitland, 'Notes on discussion with a delegation of heavy steel-makers to the Prime Minister', 21 June 1928, Scottish Record Office, Steel-Maitland Papers. GKN's attitude was probably influenced by their considerable overseas investments. See L. Hannah, *The Rise of the Corporate Economy* (London: Methuen, 1975), p. 133.
23. Carr and Taplin, *British Steel Industry*, p. 375.
24. David Colville and Sons Minute Books (hereafter DCS MINS), 10 March 1925; 6 April 1925; 11 April 1928, 8 August 1930. British Steel Records Centre.
25. Steel Co. of Scotland Minute Books, 9 June 1925; 21 April 1925; 16 September 1930. British Steel Records Centre.
26. Evidence of F. Scraf (President of the Re-Rollers Association) to the Balfour Committee, 10 December 1924, Evidence vol 1, pp. 84 *seq.*, BT 55; L.D. Whitehead to *Iron and Coal Trades Review*, 4 December 1935, p. 925.
27. B.W.E. Alford, *Depression and Recovery? British Economic Growth 1918–1939* (London: Macmillan, 1972), p. 61.
28. Semmel, *Imperialism and Social Reform*; Sykes, *Tariff Reform*.
29. This has been extensively covered in the works cited by Cook, Cowling and Ramsden, note 1 *supra*.
30. Lindsay and Harrington, *The Conservative Party*, p. 60.
31. Tolliday thesis, pp. 419–440.
32. Hannah, *Electricity, passim*.
33. W.S. Churchill, 'Memorandum on steel industry', 30 October 1925, CAB 58/10, pp. 4 and 9.
34. W. Larke (President of the NFISM) Evidence to Balfour Committee, vol 1.
35. Larke at Q. 6200, *ibid.*, 'We have never had a full run on that new plant.'
36. 'Summary of evidence and of memoranda submitted to the Committee on Civil Research', 16 November 1925, CAB 58/10.
37. 'Stenographic notes on the evidence of the heavy steel industry, 24 October 1929', p. 3, CAB 58/128.
38. Churchill, 'Memorandum', 30 October 1925.
39. Tolliday thesis, pp. 26–30.
40. Cain, 'Railway combination', 624–625.
41. *Ibid.*, pp. 633–638.
42. See e.g. P. Cunliffe-Lister, 'Possibilities of amalgamations', 21 July 1925, CAB 58/10. The Sankey Committee guessed at an overall figure of £15m for the reconstruction of the steel industry.
43. C. Bruce Gardner: 'Confidental report on the structure of the iron and steel industry of Great Britain, incorporating plans for rationalisation', 1930, Bank of England Archives, Securities Management Trust Papers (hereafter SMT).
44. Cunliffe-Lister, 'Possibilities of amalgamations'.
45. Sir Hugo Hirst to S. Baldwin, 31 July 1925, CAB 58/10.
46. Sankey Committee, *Report*, p. 35.

47. A. Steel-Maitland, 'Memorandum', July 1928, CAB 24.
48. A. Steel-Maitland, 'Draft memorandum on the iron and steel trades', 10 December 1928. Cambridge University Library, Baldwin Papers, vol 29.
49. Economic Advisory Council, Minutes 21 July 1930, CAB 58/143.
50. P. Snowden to J.R. MacDonald, 3 July 1930, Public Record Office, Ramsay MacDonald Papers, 1/164.
51. Steel-Maitland to Norman, 21 November 1928, Steel-Maitland Papers; Steel-Maitland, 'Draft memorandum', 10 December 1928, Baldwin Papers.
52. Cunliffe-Lister to Steel-Maitland, 11 December 1928, Baldwin Papers, vol. 29.
53. Tolliday thesis, pp. 254–289.
54. *Ibid.*, pp. 290–364.
55. *Ibid.*, pp. 254–258 and 276–289.
56. *Ibid.*, pp. 254–258.
57. *Ibid.*, part III *passim*, esp. pp. 237–250.
58. M. Norman, marginal note on E.R. Peacock to Norman, 21 August 1925, reporting his conversation with the Chancellor, SMT 2/72.
59. Steel-Maitland to Norman, 21 November 1928; Norman to Steel-Maitland, 28 November 1928, both Steel-Maitland Papers.
60. Steel-Maitland, 'Draft memorandum', pp. 56–57, Baldwin Papers 29; Steel-Maitland to Baldwin, July 1928, Steel-Maitland Papers; H. Goschen (Lloyds Bank) to Steel-Maitland, 7 December 1928, Steel-Maitland Papers.
61. C. Bruce-Gardner, 'Memorandum on a visit to the President of the Board of Trade', 13 July 1931, SMT 2/73; Tolliday thesis, pp. 287–289.
62. 'Private meeting between Sir Guy Granet, Bruce Gardner and Cunliffe-Lister at 7 Lygon Place', 30 July 1930, SMT 3/19. At the same time Cunliffe-Lister was giving various steelmakers personal assurances that the Tories would introduce tariffs when elected: A. Pam to A. Dorman, 29 July 1930, SMT 3/19.
63. Tolliday thesis, pp. 259–275.
64. See e.g. Norman to Sir Guy Granet, 18 December 1930, SMT 2/55.
65. Mosley Memorandum, 23 January 1930, CAB 24/209
66. Cf. C. Attlee, 'The problems of British industry', 29 July 1930, CAB 24/124; and discussions in the Unemployment Committee, 25 October 1930.
67. Snowden to MacDonald, 1 May 1931, Public Record Office, Treasury Papers, T172/1772.
68. *Ibid.*
69. Unsigned memorandum, 'The rationalisation of industry', 1931, T175/41. Internal evidence suggests that it was prepared in close conjunction with Snowden and Thomas.
70. *Ibid.*
71. *Recommendations of the Import Duties Advisory Committee, Parliamentary Papers* 1931–32, Cmd 4066, **xiv**, 693.
72. SMT 23 November 1931, House Meeting Minutes (hereafter SMT. HM. MINS).
73. SMT. HM. MINS, 30 May 1932.
74. SMT. HM. MINS, 6 June 1932.
75. 'Note of a meeting of the IDAC with the Steel Conference at Caxton

House', 7 September 1932, T172/1772; Import Duties Advisory Committee, 'Report of Conference with representatives of the iron and steel industry', 3 June 1932, T172/1773.

76. Minutes of a Meeting of the Executive Committee of the National Committee, 14 September 1932, NFISM Papers.
77. A. Hurst, 'Reorganisation of the iron and steel industry: an analysis of the present position', 9 February 1933, T172/1773.
78. SMT. HM. MINS, 18 July 1932; Hurst, 'Reorganisation', *supra* note 77.
79. Minutes of Executive Committee of the National Committee, 10 October 1932, NFISM Papers.
80. SMT.HM.MINS, 19 September 1932.
81. A. Hurst, 'Reorganisation of the iron and steel industry; an analysis of the present position', 9 February 1933, T172/1773.
82. *Recommendations of the Import Duties Advisory Committee*, *Parliamentary Papers* 1931–32, Cmd 4181, **xiv**, 811.
83. W. Runciman to N. Chamberlain, 5 October 1932, T172/1772.
84. P. Snowden to J.R. MacDonald, n.d. (October 1932), *ibid*.
85. Minutes of the Executive Committee of the National Committee, 27 October 1932, p. 5, NFISM Papers.
86. C. Bruce Gardner, 'Notes on the iron and steel industry', 24 February 1933, SMT 3/89.
87. Horace Wilson, 'Memorandum on the iron and steel organisation scheme', 6 March 1933, T172/1773.
88. Bruce Gardner, 'Notes on the iron and steel industry'.
89. SMT.HM. MINS, 17 October 1932.
90. *Ibid*., 20 February 1933.
91. Bruce Gardner, 'Notes . . .'; Runciman to Chamberlain, 30 March 1933, T172/1773; Minutes of National Committee, 10 March 1933, NFISM Papers.
92. *Correspondence between the National Committee for the Iron and Steel Industry and the Import Duties Advisory Committee* (HMSO, 1933), February 1933.
93. A joint drafting committee with two sub-committees ('A' and 'B') sat from July to November 1933. In November 1933, their proposals were partially adopted by the National Committee. In February 1934 a Revision Committee was set up which produced the final BISF Constitution, which was adopted in April 1934.
94. Minutes of Sub-committee A, 21 July, 1 August and 21 September 1933, NFISM Papers.
95. Skinner, 'Note on William Firth's views', June 1934, SMT 2/73.
96. Stewart and Lloyds were represented on sub-committee B by S.C.E. Lloyd. For his views see Minutes of Sub-Committee B, 11 August 1933, NFISM Papers.
97. Craig in Minutes of Executive Committee, 18 May 1933, NFISM Papers.
98. Beale in Minutes of Special General Meeting of NFISM, 22 February 1934.
99. Bruce-Gardner, 'Notes on the iron and steel industry', 24 February 1933, SMT 3/89.
100. Talbot in Minutes of Executive Committee, 18 May 1933, NFISM Papers.
101. Cf. Minutes of Sub-committee A, 21 July and 21 September 1933; and

Talbot's comments to Executive Committee, 18 May 1933 (Both NFISM Papers): 'was his [Talbot's] company prevented from going into the wire trade without the prior consent of a body sitting in London . . . he certainly would be no party to such a scheme'.

102. McCosh in Minutes of National Committee, 10 March 1933 and Whitehead in Minutes of NFISM Executive Committee, 18 May 1933 (both NFISM Papers).
103. Minutes of Joint Meeting of Executive and General Standing Committees of NFISM, 21 December 1933, NFISM Papers. On this group see also Minutes of the Executive Committee of the National Committee, 16 November 1932, Minutes of National Committee, 10 March 1933, both NFISM Papers, and A.W. Hurst to D. Ferguson, 3 April 1933, T172/1773.
104. Minutes of Sub-committee B, 11 August 1933, NFISM Papers.
105. Minutes of Special General Meeting, 22 February 1934.
106. Cf. A.W. Hurst, 'Reorganisation of the iron and steel industry: report on the present position', 31 October 1933, T172/1773.
107. See comments of Bruce Gardner in Bruce Gardner to Pam, 21 April 1934 and 'Notes' n.d. SMT 3/89.
108. Sir Herbert Hutchison, *Tariff Making and Industrial Reconstruction* (Harrap, 1965), p. 78.
109. Cf. 'Record of a conversation between the Chancellor of the Exchequer and Sir George May', 2 November 1933, T172/1773.
110. A.W. Hurst, 'Reorganisation of the iron and steel industry: report on the present position', 31 October 1935, T172/1773.
111. D. Ferguson, 'Note accompanying Hurst's report to the Chancellor of the Exchequer', 1 November 1935, T172/1773.
112. 'Memorandum by W. Runciman', 11 November 1933, T172/1773.
113. Minutes of Special General Meeting of MTSM, 19 April 1934. Hurst described the post of Chairman as the 'linchpin of the industry'. and cf. Report of Independent Chairman Committee, 11 July 1934.
114. SMT.HM.MINS, 20 February 1933.
115. Bruce Gardner in SMT.HM.MINS, 14 April 1934.
116. E.g. SMT.HM.MINS, 19 September 1932.
117. SMT.HM.MINS, 13 March 1933.
118. SMT.HM.MINS, 16 April 1934.
119. SMT.HM.MINS, 13 March 1933.
120. SMT.HM.MINS, 16 April 1934.
121. Larke to Craig, 6 June 1933, British Steel Records Centre, Colville Papers, JCB XVIII (iv) Craig Personal Papers.
122. SMT.HM.MINS, 17 July 1933.
123. Sir Horace Wilson, 'Iron and Steel Trade – Chairman', 26 June 1934, SMT 2/73, and 'Memorandum on iron and steel reorganisation', 6 March 1933, *ibid*. 2/215.
124. M.W. Kirby, 'The Lancashire Cotton Industry in the interwar years: a study in organisational change', *Business History* **xvi** (1974), 145–174.
125. Hannah, *Electricity before Nationalisation*, esp. pp. 107–121.
126. For a Marxist analysis of the post-war steel industry in terms of government action 'in the interests of capital as a whole', see D. MacEachern, *A Class Against Itself* (Cambridge: Cambridge University Press, 1980).

127. See esp. MacEachern, *op. cit.* and D.L. Burn, *The Steel Industry 1939–1959* (Cambridge: Cambridge University Press, 1961).

Chapter 5

1. Robert Currie, *Industrial Politics* (Oxford: Clarendon Press, 1979), p. 45.
2. *Ibid.*, pp. 49–56.
3. J.M. Keynes, *The Collected Writings*, vol IV (London: Macmillan, 1971), pp. 17–36.
4. Robert Skidelsky, *Oswald Mosley* (London: Macmillan, 1975), pp. 141–145, 299–315.
5. Sidney Pollard, 'The great disillusionment', *SSLH Bulletin* 16 (Spring 1968), pp. 34–36, and Pollard, ed., *The Gold Standard and Employment Policy Between the Wars* (London: Methuen, 1970), p. 6. See also John Foster, 'British imperialism and the labour aristocracy', in Jeffrey Skelley, ed., *The General Strike 1926* (London: Lawrence and Wishart, 1976), pp. 9–17.
6. Keith Middlemas, *Politics in Industrial Society: The Experience of the British System Since 1911* (London: André Deutsch, 1979), pp. 18–22, 214.
7. The 'corporate bias' argument has been advanced by Middlemas in *Politics in Industrial Society*, pp. 137–141, 207–213, while the 'unsuccessful variations' approach was articulated by G.W. McDonald and Howard F. Gospel in 'The Mond–Turner talks, 1927–1933: a study in industrial co-operation', *Historical Journal*, **16** (1973), 807–829.
8. For the National Industrial Conference, see Rodney Lowe, 'The failure of consensus in Britain: the National Industrial Conference, 1919–1921', *Historical Journal*, **21** (1978), 649–675 and for the Mond–Turner talks, see McDonald and Gospel, 'The Mond-Turner Talks'.
9. Middlemas, *Politics in Industrial Society*, pp. 13–23, 214, 234–243.
10. I am indebted to Dr John Turner for pointing out to me the importance of producers' alliances at the local level and in particular trades. Of course, he bears no responsibility for my interpretation of their constitutional significance.
11. It is arguable that welfare provision is only properly understood in the context of social control. See Joseph Melling, 'Employers, industrial welfare and the struggle for workplace control in British industry' in Howard Gospel and Craig Littler, eds., *Managerial Strategy and Industrial Relations*, for the view that the analytical separation of social control and social welfare is untenable.
12. In this paragraph and the two that follow I have relied upon the account provided in McDonald and Gospel, 'The Mond–Turner Talks', pp. 810–826.
13. For a discussion of the composition of the Mond group, see Howard F. Gospel, 'Employers' labour policy: a study of the Mond–Turner talks 1927–1933', *Business History*, **XXI** (1979), 180–197.
14. McDonald and Gospel, 'The Mond–Turner Talks', pp. 822–826.
15. Stephen Blank, *Industry and Government in Britain: The Federation of British Industries in Politics, 1945–65* (Lexington, Mass.: Lexington

Books, 1973), pp. 17–18, and Eric Wigham, *The Power to Manage* (London: Macmillan, 1973), p. 103.

16. Robert Skidelsky, *Politicians and the Slump: The Labour Government of 1929–1931* (Harmondsworth: Penguin Books, 1970), pp. 136–137.
17. Charles Loch Mowat, *Britain Between the Wars* (London: Methuen, 1968), p. 357.
18. Skidelsky, *Politicians and the Slump*, pp. 137–138.
19. Minutes of the TUC General Council, 18 December 1929; Minutes of the GC Economic Committee, 25 February 1930; and *TUC Annual Report* 1930, p. 161.
20. TUC *Annual Report* 1931, pp. 273–275.
21. *Report of the Committee on Finance and Industry*. Minutes of Evidence, vol I, pp. 186–197.
22. Director's Report to the Organisation and Management Committee, 21 May 1930. FBI/c/16, vol 36, p. 14; TUC *Annual Report* 1930, p. 162.
23. *Report of the Committee on Finance and Industry*. Minutes of Evidence, vol II, pp. 239–240.
24. See the Minutes of Grand Council Meeting, 12 March 1930. FBI/c/1, vol. I, pp. 251–252.
25. See, for example, *Industry and the Nation* (1931) and the 1932 *Report on Industry and Monetary Policy*.
26. *Ibid*.
27. For statements along these lines by prominent FBI members, see *Report of the Committee on Finance and Industry*. Minutes of Evidence, vol II, pp. 244–245; and Minutes of Grand Council Meeting, 16 September 1931. FBI/c/2, vol 3, pp. 2–9.
28. *Report of the Committee on Finance and Industry*. Minutes of Evidence, vol I, p. 189.
29. TUC *Annual Report* 1931, p. 278.
30. *Ibid*.
31. *Ibid*.
32. Minutes of Meeting of Joint Committee of TUC and NCEO, 19 May 1931. TUC File 310; Minutes of General Council Meeting, 20 May 1931.
33. NCEO, *The Industrial Situation* (1931).
34. TUC *Annual Report* 1931, p. 278.
35. Minutes of Meeting of Joint Committee of TUC and NCEO, 19 May 1931. TUC File 310; Minutes of General Council Meeting, 20 May 1931.
36. Minutes of Joint Meeting, 26 May 1930. FBI/S/Walker/102/22.
37. Alan Bullock, *The Life and Times of Ernest Bevin*, vol I (London: Heinemann, 1960), pp. 442–443, and TUC *Annual Report* 1930, pp. 212–217, 257–287.
38. TUC *Annual Report* 1930, pp. 208–212.
39. *British Economic Policy with Respect to the Dominions* in FBI/S/Walker/102/22.
40. Minutes of Joint Meeting, 16 June 1930. FBI/S/Walker/102/22.
41. Letter from J. Ramsay MacDonald to Sir James Lithgow, dated 26 September 1930. FBI/S/Walker/102/22. Lithgow was then president of the FBI.
42. Minutes of Cabinet Meeting, 17 September 1930. CAB 23/76.
43. See Report on 'Imperial Economic Machinery' of Inter-Departmental Economic Preparatory Committee, CAB 27/474, and Minutes of Meeting

of Cabinet, 31 May 1933, CAB 23/76.

44. Minutes of Meeting of GC Economic Committee, 27 January 1931, p. 1.
45. Minutes of General Council Meeting, 22 April 1931.
46. Minutes of Cabinet Committee on Proposed Economic Conference at Ottawa, 22 April 1931. CAB 27/441.
47. Minutes of Meetings of the Grand Council of the FBI, 13 October 1930, FBI/C/1, vol 2, pp. 269–274, and 14 January 1931, FBI/C/1, vol 2, pp. 277–278.
48. Minutes of the GC Economic Committee Meetings, 11 February 1932 and 2 March 1932.
49. Cabinet Committee on Proposed Economic Conference. CAB 27/474.
50. CAB 32/106.
51. The FBI's services to the Board of Trade are documented in various memoranda on Customs Tariffs in the Dominions in CAB 27/473.
52. See the letter from J.H. Thomas to W. Runciman, dated 21 December 1931 in BT 11/50 and the Board of Trade's Commercial Relations and Treaties Department's report on the nomination of industrial advisers to UK delegations to international conferences in BT 11/141. See also the memo on 'Proposed Attachment of Business Advisers to the Ottawa Conference' in CAB 27/473.
53. GC Economic Committee's Minutes of its First Meeting with the Federation of British Industries' Empire Committee, 16 June 1932.
54. TUC *Annual Report* 1932, pp. 220–222.
55. See Minutes of GC Economic Committee's Meeting with the FBI's Empire Committee, 13 July 1932.
56. *The Times*, 8 July 1933.
57. Minutes of Cabinet Committee on Imperial Economic Co-operation, 13 July 1933. CAB 27/553.
58. TUC *Annual Report* 1923, p. 396 and TUC *Annual Report* 1925, pp. 166–170.
59. Minutes of Grand Council, 8 October 1924. FBI/C/1, vol 2, p. 81.
60. Minutes of Meeting of Grand Council, 10 July 1929, FBI/C/1, vol 2, pp. 224–228.
61. Mowat, *Britain Between the Wars*, p. 374.
62. Minutes of Cabinet Meeting, 22 April 1931. CAB 23/66, p. 409.
63. Minutes of Meeting of Grand Council, 14 October 1931. FBI/C/2, vol 3, pp. 17–18.
64. Minutes of Meeting of the Executive Committee of the FBI, 9 November 1932. FBI/C/6, vol 13, pp. 115–116.
65. Minutes of Meeting of Joint Committee on Russian Trade, 22 November 1932, FBI/S/Walker/43/10, pp. 1–3, and Minutes of Meeting of Special Sub-Committee of FBI Russian Trade Committee, 15 December 1932, FBI/C/35, vol 80, pp. 75–77.
66. Minutes of Meeting of FBI Main Russian Trade Committee, 18 January 1933. FBI/C/35, vol 80, p. 67.
67. Cmd 4513. *Temporary Commercial Agreement Between His Majesty's Government in the United Kingdom and the Government of the Soviet Socialist Republic*.
68. Cmd 5253. *Agreement with Soviet Trade Representatives Relating to Guarantees in Connection with the Export to the Soviet Union of Goods Manufactured in the United Kingdom*.

69. Derived from B.R. Mitchell, *European Historical Statistics 1750–1970* (London: Macmillan, 1975), pp. 496–497 and Political and Economic Planning, *Britain and World Trade* (London: PEP, 1947), p. 125.
70. See Lord Citrine, *Men and Work: An Autobiography* (London: Hutchinson, 1964), p. 238 and Bullock, *Ernest Bevin*, p. 368.
71. R.F. Holland, in 'The Federation of British Industries and the international economy, 1929–39', *Economic History Review*, **XXIV** (May 1981), pp. 287–300, maintains that such an increase in influence upon decision-making as the FBI won in the late 1930s owed a great deal to the technical expertise which it could provide decision-makers.
72. Middlemas, *Politics in Industrial Society*, pp. 13–23, 214, 234–243. For a sceptical discussion of this aspect of Middlemas's argument, see my review of *Politics in Industrial Society* in *SSLH Bulletin* (Autumn, 1980).

Chapter 6

Research for this essay was undertaken with support from the Social Science Research Council. I would also like to thank Messrs Basil and Christopher Streat for permission to quote from their father's diary; and Professor Leslie Hannah and Mr S.R. Stacey for comments on an earlier draft.

1. R.K. Snyder, *The Tariff Problem in British Politics, 1917–1923* (Stanford: Stanford University Press, 1944).
2. 'Safeguarding of Industries', *Parliamentary Papers* 1921, **xxxi**, p. 563, Cmd 219; 'Safeguarding of Industries: Memorandum on Procedure', *Parliamentary Papers* 1924–5, **xv**, p. 573, Cmd 2327.
3. Cf. 'Deputation from the users to the President of the Board of Trade, April 1926' [on packing and wrapping paper], Public Record Office, Board of Trade papers, BT55/99/SOI/177.
4. E.g. H.W. Richardson, *Economic Recovery in Britain,* 1932–9 (London: Weidenfeld and Nicolson, 1967).
5. J.H. Porter, 'Cotton and Woollen Textiles', in N.K. Buxton and D.H. Aldcroft, eds., *British Industry Between the Wars* (London: Scolar Press, 1979), p. 39.
6. One of the leading advocates of this idea was Henry Clay, Economic Adviser to the Bank of England. See Henry Clay, *The Cotton Industry* (privately printed, 1930).
7. 'Report on the Cotton Industry', *Parliamentary Papers* 1929–30, **xii**, p. 825, Cmd 3615.
8. For Preston's discussions with officials see BT64/6/IM700/34 and BT64/13/IM175/36.
9. H. Quigley, 'Industrial power survey', *World Power*, **xii** (1928), pp. 13–17.
10. For a full study of Wilson's views on the cotton industry see my forthcoming D.Phil. thesis for Oxford University, 'The Board of Trade, 1925–39', chapter 4.
11. Raymond Streat Diary, 17 February 1931, Nuffield College, Oxford, Streat Papers. Streat was Secretary of the Manchester Chamber of Commerce.
12. Streat diary, 9 September 1931.
13. 'Papers relating to the "Informal Committee" on cotton, 1931–2', Bank of

England, Securities Management Trust Papers, SMT3/43.
14. *Manchester Guardian*, 15 May 1931.
15. *H.C. Debs*, 5s., (308), 4 February 1936, cols 73–87.
16. Memorandum by Hale, 23 June 1930, Wilson to C. Bruce Gardner, 26 June 1930, BT56/31/CIA/1768/4; C. Bruce Gardner to Wilson, 27 June 1930, 'Memorandum on Egyptian Cotton Spinning Companies', 2 October 1930, Bank of England, Bankers' Industrial Development Corporation papers, BID1/43. Bruce Gardner was at this time Managing Director of the Securities Management Trust.
17. Note of a meeting, 28 September 1932, BT64/2/IM4881/32.
18. Wilson to President of the Board of Trade, 25 July 1934, BT64/7/IM2988/34.
19. F.E. Hyde, *Cunard and the North Atlantic* (London: Macmillan, 1975), pp. 206–209; Lord Salter, *Memoirs of a Public Servant* (London: Faber, 1961), p. 92.
20. Bates to the Prime Minister, 15 February 1932, Public Record Office, Ministry of Transport Papers, MT9/2714/M5119/32. Sir Percy Bates was Chairman of Cunard.
21. Bates to Chamberlain, 2 March 1932, Public Record Office, Treasury Papers, T160/1313/F11798/01.
22. Note of a meeting, 18 February 1932, MT9/2714/M5119/32; 'Memorandum', 18 February 1932, University of Liverpool Library, Cunard Papers, C3/6/WS/5.
23. H.J. Dyos and D.H. Aldcroft, *British Transport* (Harmondsworth: Penguin Books, 1974), pp. 343–355.
24. Chamber of Shipping of the United Kingdom, *Annual Report, 1933–4*, (Privately printed, 1934).
25. E.J. Foley to Lord Essendon, 25 October 1932, MT9/2170/M13442/32. Foley was in charge of the Board of Trade's marine department: Essendon was chairman of the Shipping Policy committee of the Chamber of Shipping.
26. 'Chamber of Shipping: Confidential Memorandum, Oct. 1932', MT9/2170/M13442/32.
27. Notes by E. Marker, 19 November 1932, *ibid*.
28. Chamber of Shipping, Committee minute book for 1934, vol 2, General Council of British Shipping, St Mary Axe, London, Chamber of Shipping Papers.
29. W.J. Reader, *Imperial Chemical Industries: A History* (Oxford: Oxford University Press, 1975), ii, 75–79.
30. Jose Harris, *Unemployment and Politics* (Oxford: Oxford University Press, 1972), pp. 272–347.
31. P. Abrams, 'The failure of social reform, 1918–21', *Past and Present*, no. 24 (1963), 43–63.
32. E.g. Sir Stephen Demetriadi, *Inside a Government Office* (London: Benn & Co., 1921). Demetriadi had been a temporary wartime official.
33. The *locus classicus* being Lord Hewart, *The New Despotism*, (London: Benn & Co., 1921).
34. Keith Middlemas and John Barnes, *Baldwin: A Biography* (London: Weidenfeld and Nicolson, 1969).
35. P.W.L. Ashley was head of the Industries and Manufactures department of the Board of Trade from 1918 to 1932, and later the secretary of the

Import Duties Advisory Committee. His elder brother was the 'fair trade' economist, W.J. Ashley.

36. TAC 1, Report of an Inter-departmental conference, 15 November 1923, BT232/2.
37. PMC 5, Notes on an Economic General Staff, 3 December 1929, Public Record Office, Cabinet Office Papers, CAB 58/15.
38. E.G. W. Eady to H.D. Henderson, n.d. (1929), Nuffield College, Oxford, Henderson papers, Box 22A.
39. David Marquand, *Ramsay MacDonald* (London: Jonathan Cape, 1977), pp. 533–542, 555.
40. Keith Middlemas, *Politics in Industrial Society* (London: André Deutsch, 1979), p. 372.
41. Buxton and Aldcroft, *British Industry*, pp. 19–22.
42. Dyos and Aldcroft, *British Transport*, p. 354.
43. *Parliamentary Papers*, 1928–9, **viii**, p. 413, Cmd 3282, 'Committee on Industry and Trade: Final Report'.
44. The work of Walter Carter, the Board of Trade principal who was the secretary to the committee, in persuading government departments to contribute draft chapters can be followed in T160/247/F9585/1.
45. CP 101 (29), Memorandum on the Industry and Trade committee, 27 March 1929, CAB 24/203.
46. EAC (H) 92, Effect of Rationalisation on Unemployment, 18 June 1930, CAB 58/10.
47. Susan Howson and Donald Winch, *The Economic Advisory Council, 1930–1939* (Cambridge, Cambridge University Press, 1977).
48. Memorandum sent to F.W. Leith Ross, BT56/37/CIA/1770; memorandum by Hopkins, 1 February 1930, T175/42.
49. CP 134 (30), Unemployment Policy (1930) Committee: Report, 1 May 1930, CAB 24/211.
50. For the immediate circumstances of Wilson's appointment, see W.H. Janeway, 'The Economic Policy of the Second Labour Government' (Cambridge University Ph.D. thesis, 1976).
51. See 'The Relations between the State and Industry', 19 July 1934, Bodleian Library, Oxford, Conservative Research Department Papers, files on the state and industry, 1934–5.
52. Minutes of the Conservative Cabinet Committee, sub-committee A, 25 October 1934, Conservative Research Department Papers.
53. Officials had stressed these arguments against an Enabling Bill since the summer of 1934. See 'Brief for Mr Colville', by W.B. Brown, September 1934, BT64/7/IM3653/34.

Chapter 7

I am grateful to Kathleen Burk for obtaining material for me from American bankers' archives, and for much encouragement and advice; to Mr G.W. Mackworth-Young, chairman of Morgan Grenfell & Co, for permission to cite papers in his company's archives; to Marguerite Dupree for kindly showing me extracts from her forthcoming edition, *Lancashire and Whitehall: the Diary of Sir E. Raymond Streat 1931–1957*; to Messrs Basil and Christopher Streat for permission to quote from their father's diary; and to Professor Sayers for giving me valuable advice at an early stage of my research. My greatest thanks are to Christine Woodhead, who helped at all stages in the preparation of this essay.

1. Sir Henry Clay, *Lord Norman* (London: Macmillan, 1957); R.S. Sayers, *The Bank of England 1891–1944*, 3 vols (Cambridge: Cambridge University Press, 1976); S.V.O. Clarke, *Central Bank Co-operation 1924–31* (New York: Federal Reserve Bank of New York, 1967); D.E. Moggridge, *British Monetary Policy 1924–1931* (Cambridge: Cambridge University Press, 1972); Susan Howson, *Domestic Monetary Management in Britain 1919–1938* (Cambridge: Cambridge University Press, 1975).
2. See, however, Donald Winch, *Economics and Policy* (London: Fontana, 1972), pp. 99–101; Sidney Pollard (ed.), *The Gold Standard and Employment Policies between the Wars* (London: Methuen, 1970), p. 25; and Roger Middleton, 'The Treasury in the 1930s: political and administrative constraints to acceptance of the "new" economics', *Oxford Economic Papers*, vol 34 (1982), 64–65.
3. Moggridge, *British Monetary Policy*, pp. 64–78; F.W. Pethick-Lawrence, *Fate Has Been Kind* (London: Hutchinson, 1943), p. 141; Snowden, 4 May 1925, *Parliamentary Debates. House of Commons*, 5 s., vol 183, cols 625–633.
4. Wallhead and Stephen, 5 May 1925, *Parliamentary Debates*, vol 183, cols 818–821, 826–829. *Pace* Moggridge, p. 95, only Mond opposed with them: Horne and Boothby merely expressed reservations.
5. Sayers, *Bank of England*, vol 2, p. 387.
6. Unfortunately this frequently quoted statement appears to be apocryphal.
7. Pollard, *The Gold Standard and Employment Policies*, pp. 13–14, 16, 22–23.
8. Layton to Morrow, 20 April 1925. Amherst College Library, Amherst, Mass., Morrow papers, 'Layton' folder.
9. *The Economist*, 24 and 31 January 1925; Sayers, *Bank of England*, vol 1, pp. 135, 141–144; Moggridge, *Monetary Policy*, pp. 42–47, 60–61, 63, 73.
10. McKenna at Midland Bank meeting, 27 January 1925, *The Economist*, 31 January 1925, and reported in P.J. Grigg, *Prejudice and Judgment* (London: Hutchinson, 1948), p. 184.
11. Committee on Currency and Foreign Exchanges after the War (Cunliffe Commitee), *First Interim Report, Parliamentary Papers* 1918, Cd 9182, **viii**, 853, paras 15, 47; Committee on Financial Facilities, *Report*, *Parliamentary Papers* 1918, Cd 9227, **x**, 25, para 23; Goodenough at Barclays Bank meeting, 21 January 1925, *The Economist*, 24 January 1925; Addis, 27 June 1924, Norman and Niemeyer, 2 February 1925, quoted in Moggridge, *British Monetary Policy*, pp. 41–42, 262–272.
12. W. Stewart, Committee on Finance and Industry (Macmillan Committee), *Minutes of Evidence* (HMSO, 1931), 3 July 1930, qu. 7770; cf. Kindersley, 6 February 1930, qu. 1652–1653.
13. Cunliffe Committee, *First Interim Report*, paras 6, 15, 47; Committee on Financial Facilities, *Report*, paras 17–23; Moggridge, *British Monetary Policy*, pp. 77, 86, 267, 275.
14. Bradbury reported in March 1925, in Grigg, *Prejudice and Judgment*, p. 183.
15. Middleton, 'The Treasury in the 1930s', pp. 56–63.
16. McKenna at Midland Bank meeting, 27 January 1925, *The Economist*, 31 January 1925.
17. Macmillan Committee, *Evidence*, 28 November 1929, qu. 3, 95; Clay,

Norman, pp. 274, 276, 278; Sayers, *Bank of England*, vol 1, chap. 11; vol 2, pp. 552–560, chap. 22, Appendixes, pp. 90–91.

18. Clay, *Norman*, pp. 144–145, 239–240, 277–282; Sayers, *Bank of England*, vol 1, pp. 148, chap. 11; Moggridge, *British Monetary Policy*, chap. 9.
19. Macmillan Committee, *Evidence*, 28 November and 12 December 1929, qu. 3, 454.
20. Clay, *Norman*, pp. 136–137, 188–193, 202–203, 283–285; Sayers, *Bank of England*, vol 1, chap. 8, vol 2, pp. 512–527, Appendixes, pp. 74–75.
21. Sayers, *Bank of England* vol 1, pp. 159–160; Clay, *Norman*, p. 289.
22. Andrew Boyle, *Montagu Norman* (London: Cassell, 1967), p. 247; Clay, *Norman*, pp. 297, 365; Sayers, *Bank of England*, vol 1, pp. 352–356.
23. Moggridge, *British Monetary Policy*, p. 159; Committee on Industry and Trade (Balfour Committee), *Final Report, Parliamentary Papers* 1928–29, Cmd 3282, **vii**, 413, p. 56.
24. Macmillan Committee, *Evidence*, 16 May 1930, qu. 5321. Cf. Chalmers and Bradbury to Leith-Ross, both 6 December 1925; Blackett, Bradbury and Niemayer to Phillips, 17 and 18 February 1929, T176/13; Pethick-Lawrence, *Fate Has Been Kind*, p. 159.
25. *Parliamentary Debates*, vol 181, cols 141–142, 1518–1519; vol 225, cols 221–223, 546–547, 952–953; *Labour Party Conference Report*, 1929, pp. 227–228.
26. *Labour Party Conference Report*, 1928, pp. 199, 231; Committee on Finance and Industry (Macmillan Committee), *Report, Parliamentary Papers* 1930–31, Cmd 3897, **xiii**, 219, p. 240.
27. Macmillan Committee, *Evidence*, 12 December 1929, qu. 454.
28. *Ibid.*, and Clay, *Norman*, pp. 286, 289; Sayers, *Bank of England*, vol 2, pp. 598 and 597.
29. For Grenfell and the Morgan corrections, see Kathleen Burk, 'The diplomacy of finance: British financial missions to the United States 1914–1918', *Historical Journal*, **xxii** (1979), esp. p. 352.
30. 3 February 1930, *Parliamentary Debates*, vol 234, col 1581.
31. Norman memorandum, 4 September 1929, in Clay, *Norman*, pp. 295–297.
32. Clay, *Norman*, pp. 290–291.
33. *Ibid.*, pp. 116–125; Sayers, *Bank of England*, vol 1, pp. 112–115.
34. Harvey, Macmillan Committee, *Evidence*, 12 December 1929, qu. 454; Sayers, *Bank of England*, Appendixes, p. 90; Clay, *Norman*, pp. 295–296; Pethick-Lawrence, *Fate Has Been Kind*, p. 159.
35. Moggridge, *British Monetary Policy*, pp. 161–164. See Sayers, *Bank of England*, vol 2, pp. 650–651.
36. Keith Middlemas, ed., *Thomas Jones. Whitehall Diary*, vol 2 (Oxford: Oxford University Press, 1969), 12 April 1927, p. 98.
37. 'A plea for the removal of restrictions upon European trade', *The Economist*, 23 October 1926.
38. Sir Frederick Leith-Ross, *Money Talks* (London: Hutchinson, 1968), p. 95; Clay, *Norman*, p. 293; Leith-Ross memo., 3 December 1925, T176/13; Moggridge, *British Monetary Policy*, p. 162; Sayers, *Bank of England*, vol. 1, p. 222 (note 2); and generally, Grigg, *Prejudice and Judgment*, p. 193.
39. Clay, *Norman*, pp. 223–224; Macmillan Committee, *Evidence*, 26 March 1930, qu. 3319, 3360–3361, 3458, 3466–3467, 3491, and Kindersley, 24

January, 6 February 1930, esp. qu. 1551–1553, 1570, 1588, 1592–1598, 1623–1624, 1679.

This interpretation differs in emphasis from the conventional accounts, in Moggridge, *British Monetary Policy*, chap. 7; Howson, *Domestic Monetary Management*, pp. 34–35, 142; Sayers, *Bank of England*, vol 1, pp. 216–217, 222, 305.

40. Suggested also in David Williams, 'Montagu Norman and banking policy in the nineteen twenties', *Yorkshire Bulletin of Economic and Social Research*, vol 11, 1959, p. 39, note 2. For expedients see Moggridge, *British Monetary Policy*, chaps. 7–9; Norman quoted in Clay, *Norman*, pp. 223–224, 244–245, and Sayers, *Bank of England*, vol 1, p. 312; and Harvey, Macmillan Committee, *Evidence*, 2 July 1930, qu. 7597.
41. Norman notes, summer 1928, in Clay, *Norman*, p. 310.
42. Norman, Macmillan Committee, *Evidence*, 26 March 1930, qu. 3339, 3458; and Harvey, 2 July 1930, qu. 7534, 7596–7597. Sayers, *Bank of England*, vol 1, pp. 218–219, 224–225.
43. Norman, Macmillan Committee, *Evidence*, 26 March 1930, qu. 3351, and 3335–3347, 3375, 3454; and Harvey, 2 July 1930, qu. 7597. Lubbock to Brand, 1 January 1931, Bodleian Library, Brand papers, 28.
44. Norman, Macmillan Committee, *Evidence*, 26 March 1930, qu. 3334–3362, 3392; Niemeyer, 4 June 1930, qu. 6672–6675; and W. Stewart, 3 July 1930, qu. 7611–7636, 7679–7680, 7702, and 4 July, qu. 7880–7893.
45. Speeches at Midland Bank meetings, 26 January 1926 and 28 January 1927, *The Economist*, 30 January 1926 and 29 January 1927.
46. Sayers, *Bank of England*, vol 1, pp. 360–361; *Britain's Industrial Future* (London: Benn, 1928), chap. XXVIII, and *Labour and the Nation* (Labour Party, 1928), 'Report on Currency, Banking and Credit'.
47. Harvey, Macmillan Committee, *Evidence*, 2 July 1930, qu. 7597. Clay, *Norman*, pp. 241–249. Moggridge, *British Monetary Policy*, pp. 136–137. Sayers, *Bank of England*, vol 1, pp. 225–226.
48. Lubbock to Hopkins, Phillips to Hopkins, and Hopkins note, respectively 9, 18 and 19 February 1929, T176/13. Cabinet 5(29) of 7 February 1929, Public Record Office, CAB 23/60. For parliamentary statements, note 25 above.
49. 25 April 1929, *Parliamentary Debates*, vol 227, col 1110.
50. Grenfell to Leffingwell, telegram no. 4942, 15 August 1929, Morgan, Grenfell & Co papers, Box P 421, file 'Gold'.
51. Clay, *Norman*, p. 296; Sayers, *Bank of England*, vol 1, pp. 132, 228, 362; Grigg, *Prejudice and Judgment*, pp. 136–137; Snowden in *Reynold's News*, 24 March 1929 and *The Daily Herald*, 18 May 1929.
52. Sayers, *Bank of England*, vol. 1, p. 362. Snowden, 15 July 1929, *Parliamentary Debates*, vol. 230, col. 60–61.
53. Mansion House speech, 24 July 1929, *The Times*, 25 July 1929.
54. Hopkins to Grigg, undated draft, 16 and 19 August 1929, T176/13; and in J.P. Morgan, and Grenfell, to Leffingwell, nos. 4936, 4942, 13 and 15 August 1929, Morgan, Grenfell papers, P 421, 'Gold'; Sayers, *Bank of England*, vol 1, pp. 228, 293; Clay, *Norman*, pp. 252–253; Clarke, *Central Bank Co-operation*, p. 162.
55. MacDonald diary note, 11 August 1929, Public Record Office, MacDonald papers, PRO 30/69/1753; Lamont to Young, no. 4929, 12 August 1929, Morgan, Grenfell papers, Bundle 213, file 'International Bank

(BIS)'; MacDonald telegram in Philip, Viscount Snowden, *An Autobiography*, vol 2 (London: I. Nicholson & Watson, 1934), p. 799.

56. Norman memo, 4 September 1929, Clay, *Norman*, pp. 296–298.
57. For examples, Bevin interview in *The Daily Herald*, 28 September 1929; and Melchett article in *The Sunday Express*, 29 September 1929 (copies in T176/13).
58. Margaret Cole, ed., *Beatrice Webb's Diaries 1924–32* (London: Longman, 1952) 2 October 1929, pp. 222–223. Trevelyan to his wife, 30 September 1929, Newcastle University Library, Trevelyan papers, Ex 123 (i).
59. Sayers, *Bank of England*, vol 1, pp. 362–363; *Labour Party Conference Report*, 1929, pp. 227–230.
60. E.g. Macmillan Committee, *Evidence*, 5 December 1929, qu. 332; and Lubbock to Ismay, 9 March 1931, quoted in Lubbock to Brand, same date, Brand papers, 30; Sayers, *Bank of England*, vol 1, p. 363, records that Norman discussed the committee's membership with Snowden on 14 October.
61. Brand to André Lazard, 22 October 1929, (copy) Brand papers, 27.
62. Grigg to Snowden, 11 October 1929, T160/426/F11548.
63. Lord Macmillan, *A Man of Law's Tale* (London: Macmillan, 1952), pp. 196–197; Snowden to Sankey, 22 October 1929, T172/1652.
64. Clay, *Norman*, pp. 335, 358. Sayers, *Bank of England*, vol 1, p. 319; Worthington-Evans memorandum 'The steel trade', July 1928, Bodleian Library, Worthington-Evans papers, MS Eng. Hist. c.896/35–40; Baldwin in *Jones Diary*, 5 March 1929, p. 174.
65. Norman memorandum, 4 September 1929, in Clay, *Norman*, pp. 296–298. Snowden note, 8 April 1930, EAC(H) 83, Cab 58/10.
66. Clay, *Norman*, p. 325; Sayers, *Bank of England*, vol 1, p. 321.
67. For Thomas, CP 287, 345(29) of 23 October, 29 November 1929, Cab 24/206, 207; *Webb Diary*, 2, 21 December 1929, pp. 230, 232; *Jones Diary*, 9, 23 December 1929, pp. 222, 229; Garvin note, 15 January 1930, The Humanities Research Centre, University of Texas, Austin, Garvin papers, notebook 42. Clay, *Norman*, pp. 326, 329. Sayers, *Bank of England*, vol 1, pp. 322–323. Memorandum, Norman, Snowden, Graham meeting, 11 May 1931, MacDonald papers, PRO 30/69/412.
68. *Manchester Guardian*, 11 January 1930; CP 21(30) of 20 January 1930, Cab 24/209; Cabinet 4(30) of 22 January 1930, Cab 23/63; 3 February 1930, *Parliamentary Debates*, vol 234, cols 1570–1572.
69. MacDonald to Graham, 2 October 1930, (copy) MacDonald papers, PRO 30/69/676.
70. Clay, *Norman*, p. 336; Cabinets 24, 27, 36, 40(31) of 22 April, 6 May, 1 and 30 July 1931, Cab 23/66, 67; Memorandum, Norman, Snowden, Graham meeting, 11 May 1931; Snowden to MacDonald, 12 May 1931, MacDonald papers, PRO 30/69/412, 677.
71. Strakosch, 'The economic consequences of changes in the value of gold', *The Economist*, special supplement, 5 July 1930; Interim Report, Gold Delegation of the League of Nations Financial Committee, summarised *ibid.*, 27 September 1930; Sayers, *Bank of England*, vol 1, pp. 346–351.
72. *The Times*, 12 and 18 December 1930, 2 January 1931; Webb diary, 14 October 1930, British Library of Political and Economic Science, Passfield papers. McKenna broadcast, reported in *The Times*, 29 November 1930, and speech at Midland Bank meeting, 21 January 1931, *The*

Economist, 24 January 1931; Leith-Ross memorandum, 'Possibilities of Government action in regard to the recent fall in world prices' (July) 1930, MacDonald papers, PRO 30/69/257; Leith-Ross to Strakosch, 5 January 1931, (copy) T188/15B.

73. Boothby, 18 March, 25 November; Morley, 24 July, 1 and 4 December; Falle, 30 October, Mander, 4, 11, 25 November; A.M. Samuel, 5 November; Kenworthy, 18 December, all 1930: *Parliamentary Debates*, vol 236, col 1909; vol 241, col 2397; vol 244, cols 202–203, 663, 850, 1503; vol 245, cols 1087, 1819–1820; vol 246, col 1433.
74. Angell to Murray, 8 December 1930, (copy) and Angell, Benson, Church, D. Grenfell, Leach, Malone, Philips Price, Phillips, Taylor notice, 2 December 1930, Ball State University Library, Muncie, Indiana, Angell papers, K9–35, E 63–25.
75. Graham, 3 November 1930, *Parliamentary Debates*, vol 244, cols 516–517. Thomas speech, *The Times*, 3 January 1931. MacDonald interview, *The Daily Herald*, 1 January 1931.
76. MacDonald to US ambassador Dawes, 20 February, 4 March 1931, in *Papers Relating to the Foreign Relations of the United States 1931*, vol 1 (Washington: Government Printing Office, 1946), pp. 609–611. Cabinet 16(31) of 4 March 1931, Cab 23/66. Rosenberg to H. D. Henderson, 4 March 1931 (copy) MacDonald papers, PRO 30/69/5.
77. Amery diary, 1, 10, 19, 22, 25, 27 July 1931, and Amery to Lord Bessborough, 15 July 1931, (copy) Amery papers, H 113, in the possession of the Rt Hon Julian Amery MP. Letters from Hunsdon, Amery, Horne, Darling, Lambert, and Wardlaw Milne, Waterhouse, Boothby, Hacking, Salmon, Vaughan-Morgan, and Buchan, in *The Times*, 22, 23, 24, 25, 27 July 1931.
78. Brand memorandum, 'Unemployment', late 1930, Scottish Record Office, Lothian papers, GD 40/17/133, fols. 25–87. Goodenough at Barclays Bank meeting, 20 January 1931; Beckett at Westminster Bank meeting, 28 January; Goschen at National Provincial Bank meeting, 29 January, *The Economist*, 24, 31 January 1931.
79. Niemeyer, Macmillan Committee, *Evidence*, 4 June 1930, qu. 6744, also 6720, 6727–6730; W. Stewart, 3 July 1930, qu. 7636–7638. Norman's total rejection of monetary explanations on 26 March at qu. 3342, 3354 was probably not an accurate reflection of his views but an over-reaction to hostile questions.
80. Clay, *Norman*, pp. 138–139, 370; Clarke, *Central Bank Co-operation*, pp. 36–40; Sayers, *Bank of England*, vol 1, pp. 160–162, 346–351; Snowden and Keynes at EAC 9th meeting, 7 November 1930, Cab 58/2. More generally, Niemeyer, Macmillan Committee, *Evidence*, 4 June 1930, qu. 6720–6722.
81. Leith-Ross to Brand, 21 July 1930, Brand papers, 28; to McKenna, 1 November 1930, and to Keynes 24 October 1930, (copies) T188/15B, 274; Leith-Ross memorandum, 28 July 1930, MacDonald papers, PRO 30/69/257. Snowden at EAC, 7th and 9th meetings, 24 July, 7 November 1930, Cab 58/2; Clay, *Norman*, pp. 269–370.
82. Stamp, and Keynes at EAC 9th meeting, 7 November 1930; MacDonald at 13th meeting, 16 April 1931, Cab 58/2.
83. MacDonald to Norman, 29 June 1931, (copy) MacDonald papers, PRO 30/69/677.

84. Charles Dawes, *Journal As Ambassador to Great Britain* (New York: Macmillan, 1939), 23 May 1931, p. 345.
85. 'Political Notes', *The Times*, 19 December 1930, and also Goodenough at Barclays Bank meeting, 21 January 1930, *The Economist*, 25 January 1930. For McKenna, Elibank notes, 2 March 1930, Scottish Record Office, 2nd Viscount Elibank papers, GD 32/25/74.
86. *The Times*, 4, 5 and 10 July 1930; Clay, *Norman*, p. 368.
87. Beaverbrook to Rothermere, 4 July 1930, (copy) House of Lords Record Office, Beaverbrook papers, C/284. Cf. Neville to Arthur Chamberlain, same date, (copy) Birmingham University Library, Neville Chamberlain papers, NC 7/6/18.
88. Amery diary, 4 July 1930. Amery to Baldwin, same date, Cambridge University Library, Baldwin papers, 31/133–34.
89. Resolution of 'National Association of Merchants and Manufacturers', *The Times*, 1 September 1930.
90. Grenfell at City of London Conservative Association, 22 July; Schuster at Lincoln Chamber of Commerce, 23 October; Holland-Martin, Institute of Bankers presidential address, 5 November; *The Times*, 23 July, 24 October, 6 November 1930; Sir A Lewis at EAC 8th meeting, 11 September 1930, Cab 58/2.
91. Garvin to Reading, 19 January 1931, India Office Library, Reading papers, MSS Eur F 118/24.
92. FBI council resolution, 13 October 1930; NCIC foundation meeting, 25 September, and NCIC committee statement, 9 October 1930, *The Times*, 26 September, 10, 14 October 1930; Hannon to Beaverbrook, 7 October 1930, (copy) House of Lords Record Office, Hannon papers, 17.
93. Goodenough at Barclays Bank meeting, 17 January 1929, *The Economist*, 19 January 1929.
94. Goschen, Paton and Dewhurst speeches, *ibid.*, 1 February 1930. Ashfield, Beale, Colwyn, Duncan, Sir F Lewis, McGowan, Sir K Stewart, Weir, May and Stamp to Thomas, 30 January 1930, MacDonald papers, PRO 30/69/477.
95. Goschen and Beckett respectively at National Provincial and Westminster Bank meetings, 28, 29 January 1931, *The Economist*, 31 January 1931.
96. Presidential address, Institute of Bankers, 5 November 1930, *The Times*, 6 November 1930.
97. NCIC resolutions, and Schuster at Lincoln Chamber of Commerce, *The Times*, 26 September, 24 October 1930; Brand memorandum, 'Unemployment', late 1930, Lothian papers, GD 40/17/133, fols. 25–87.
98. Norman to Keynes, 20 May 1930, in Donald Moggridge, ed., *The Collected Writings of John Maynard Keynes*, vol XX (Cambridge: Cambridge University Press, 1981), p. 349; Leith-Ross to Waley, 30 May 1930, to Hopkins and Ferguson, and to Hopkins and Snowden, undated but June 1930, T160/430/F 12317/1. Moggridge, *British Monetary Policy*, pp. 240–241.
99. Lamont reported in *Jones Diary*, 19 May 1930, p. 257. Grenfell, 3 June 1930, *Parliamentary Debates*, vol 239, cols 2067–2069. W Stewart, Macmillan Committee, *Evidence*, 3 July 1930, qu. 7777, also 7770.
100. 'The money market', *The Economist*, 14 June 1930; *ibid.*, Monthly Supplement, 27 September, and Banking Supplement, 11 October 1930; Moggridge, *British Monetary Policy*, pp. 174–175.

101. Sprague, 14 October 1930, in Sayers, *Bank of England*, vol 1, p. 233.
102. 'The Money Market', *The Economist*, 8, 24 November 1930, and 'Money in 1930', *ibid.*, 3 January 1931.
103. Sprague and Cariguel, in Sproul memorandum, 'Record of certain conversations in London and Paris, November 11–December 17, 1930', 21 January 1931, Federal Reserve Bank of New York (FRBNY) papers. Cariguel in 'Memo. of M.H.'s visit to Paris on 10 December 1930', Morgan, Grenfell papers, Box P 665 'Morgan et Cie Misc. File 13B'. Harrison in Clay, *Norman*, p. 369. Clarke, *Central Bank Co-operation*, pp. 175–177.
104. T160/430/F 12317/1, 2 *passim*; Leith-Ross to Hopkins, Snowden, 16 December 1930, *ibid.*, file 1; Quesnay, 21 November, in Sproul memorandum, 'Record of certain conversations', FRBNY papers; Clarke, *Central Bank Co-operation*. Generally, Clay, *Norman*, pp. 370–371.
105. *The Economist, passim* for January, February 1931; Snowden, CP 3(31) of 7 January 1931, Cab 24/219; Bondfield, CP 31(31) of 5 February 1931, Cab 23/90B; Cabinets 6, 12, 13(31) of 14 January, 5 and 11 February 1931, Cab 23/66; 'Memorandum submitted by the Treasury', 29 January 1931, Royal Commission on Unemployment Insurance, *Minutes of Evidence* (HMSO, 1931), pp. 381–383.
106. Bankers' speeches, *The Economist*, 24, 31 January, 7 February 1931; 'Friends' in *The Times*, 28 January 1931.
107. *Parliamentary Debates*, vol 247, cols 2255–2258; Grigg, *Prejudice and Judgment*, p. 344; Keynes to Case, 21 February 1931, in *Collected Writings of Keynes*, vol XX, pp. 485–486. Lewis and EAC staff report, at EAC 11th meeting, 12 February 1931, Cab 58/2. McKenna to Steel-Maitland, 5 January 1931, Scottish Record Office, Steel-Maitland papers, GD 193/254.
108. Brand to Keynes, 30 January 1931, (copy) Brand papers, 30.
109. Waley memorandum, 'Notes of a conversation between Leith-Ross, Sprague and Siepmann', 30 January 1931, T160/430/F 12317/2. Macmillan Committee, *Evidence*, 19 February 1931, qu. 9285–9298, and 18 February, qu. 9230–9267.
110. Sir Raymond Streat diary, 11 and 24 February, 17 and 31 March 1931, by courtesy of Dr M. Dupree, Emmanuel College, Cambridge.
111. Leith-Ross memo., 'Note of a talk with Hopkins and Norman', 17 February 1931, T160/430/F 12317/2.
112. Clay, *Norman*, p. 371.
113. de Trafford reporting a January conversation, *Lockhart Diary*, 13 September 1931, p. 185. Snowden, *Autobiography*, pp. 890–895.
114. Clay, *Norman*, p. 371; *The Economist*, 31 January, 7 February 1931.
115. Sayers, *Bank of England*, vol 1, pp. 233–234.
116. Harvey to Leith-Ross, 20 March 1931, T188/274. Lubbock to Ismay, extract in Lubbock to Brand, both 9 March 1931, Brand papers, 30. Cf. Sayers, *Bank of England*, vol 1, p. 372.
117. Moggridge, 'The 1931 financial crisis: a new view', *The Banker*, vol cxx, 1970, p. 837.
118. E.g. Sprague speeches to English Speaking Union, 12 May, and to Royal Statistical Society, 16 June 1931, *The Times*, 13 May, 17 June 1931.
119. Norman and Sprague insisted upon secrecy at these meetings; but see Angell, 'Notes on visit of Montagu Norman', 8 June (misdated May)

1931, Angell papers, M 37–3; J.M. Kenworthy, *Sailors, Statesmen – and Others* (London: Rich & Cowans, 1933), pp. 303–304; M. Philips Price, *My Three Revolutions* (London: George Allen and Unwin, 1969), p. 267; Sayers, *Bank of England*, vol 1, p. 382; on Sprague see Lansbury memorandum, 'The Cabinet crisis of 1931', c. September 1931, British Library of Political and Economic Science, Lansbury papers, 25. III. m. fol. 7; and D'Abernon in Hankey diary, 13 September 1931, in Stephen Roskill, *Hankey. Man of Secrets*, vol 2 (London: Collins, 1972), p. 552.

120. MacDonald to Norman (copy) and *vice versa*, 18 and 25 June 1931, MacDonald papers, PRO 30/69/677.
121. See Philip Williamson, 'A "bankers' ramp"? Financiers and the British political crisis of August 1931', *English Historical Review*, forthcoming.
122. Clay, *Norman*, p. 385. Sayers, *Bank of England*, vol 2, p. 393; Joint Committee, and clearing bank chairmen, to MacDonald and Snowden, respectively 30 July and 6 August 1931. MacDonald papers, PRO 30/69/260.
123. Siepmann reported in Governor Harrison memorandum, 'Telephone conversation with Lacour-Gayet', 8 August 1931, Columbia University Library, New York, Harrison papers, 3125.2; cf. Sayers, *Bank of England*, vol 2, p. 936. Harvey to Snowden, 6 August 1931 (copy) MacDonald papers, PRO 30/69/260.
124. MacDonald dairy, 11 August 1931: N. Chamberlain to Cunliffe-Lister, 15 August 1931, Churchill College, Cambridge, Swinton papers, 174/2/1, fol. 11–12.
125. *Ibid.*
126. Thomas Jones, *A Diary with Letters 1931–1950* (Oxford: Oxford University Press 1954), 14 September 1931, p. 11.
127. Harvey to Snowden, 6 August 1931 (copy) MacDonald papers, PRO 30/69/260; Peacock in MacDonald Diary, 11 August 1931;
128. Harrison memorandum, 'Telephone conversation with Governor Norman', 23 August 1931, Harrison papers 3115.2 (partly printed in Clarke, *Central Bank Co-operation*, p. 211).
129. Cabinet 46(31) of 23 August 1931, Cab 23/67.
130. Sayers, *Bank of England*, vol 2, pp. 399–400.
131. Hopkins notes (two), 25 August, 1931, T160/435/F 12568/1 and 557/F 1270/1; Peacock to Steel-Maitland, same date, Steel-Maitland papers, GD193/20/3.
132. Chamberlain diary, 27 August and 3 September 1931; Lothian to Samuel, 25 and 31 August 1931 (copies) Lothian papers, GD 40/17/143, fols. 13–17, 26–28.
133. Cabinet Financial Situation Committee, 14 and 17 September 1931, Cab 27/462.
134. Steel-Maitland 'Diary of events during the crisis of 1931', written 29 August 1931, Steel-Maitland papers, GD 193/20/3; Lord Citrine, *Men and Work* (London: Hutchinson, 1964), pp. 280–281.
135. Cabinet, 3 September 1931, 'Secretary's Notes', Cab 23/68; Cabinet Financial Situation Committee, 17 September 1931, Cab 27/462; Lamont (New York) to Grenfell, no. 2413, received 31 August 1931, and vice versa, no. 4968, 1 September 1931; Morgan, Grenfell papers, file 'British Government Credit 1931'; Morgan Grenfell memorandum on crisis for

Grenfell and Kindersley, *ibid.*, file 'Gold Standard'; Harrison memorandum, 16 September 1931, Harrison papers, 3117.2.

136. E.g. Hoare to Willingdon, 17 September 1931 (copy) India Office Library, Templewood papers, MSS Eur. E. 240/1.
137. Sayers, *Bank of England*, vol 2, pp. 406, 408, 410, 412; Public Record Office, Notes of meetings, 18 and 19 September 1931, Prem. 1/97.
138. *Ibid.*, Cabinet Financial Committee, 17 September 1931, Cab 27/462; Harrison memoranda 19 September 1931, Harrison papers, 3117.1; J.P. Morgan & Co to Morgan, Grenfell & Co, no. 2461, and *vice versa*, no. 5012, both 20 September 1931, Morgan, Grenfell papers, file 'Gold Standard 1931'.
139. Howson, *Domestic Monetary Management*, pp. 80–86, 173–179.

Chapter 8

1. See Ralph Miliband, *The State in Capitalist Society* (London: Quartet Books, 1973), pp. 7ff.
2. Alan Bullock, *The Life and Times of Ernest Bevin*, vol 2 (London: Heinemann, 1967), pp. 188ff.
3. J.D. Scott, *Vickers, A History* (London: Weidenfeld and Nicolson, 1962), pp. 215ff.
4. Stephen Roskill, *Hankey, Man of Secrets*, vol 3 (London: Collins, 1974), pp. 246–248.
5. *Royal Commission on the Private Manufacture of and Trading in Arms* (1935–36), *Report*, Cmd 5292, pp. 27–33.
6. Fisher to Chancellor of the Exchequer (Neville Chamberlain), 2 December 1935, Public Record Office Treasury Papers, T171/324.
7. Fisher to Chancellor of the Exchequer (Sir John Simon), 3 January 1939, T171/341.
8. Chamberlain to his sister Hilda, 25 April 1937, University of Birmingham Library, Neville Chamberlain papers, N.C. 18/1/1003.
9. Notes by Weir (no date), Churchill College, Cambridge: Weir Papers 19/24.
10. William Ashworth, *Contracts and Finance* (HMSO, 1953), p. 199.
11. Peter Fearon, 'The British airframe industry and the state, 1918–35', *Economic History Review*, 2nd series, **xxvii** (1974), 243–251.
12. *H.C. Deb.*, 5th series, vol 302: 754 and 1112, 27 and 29 May 1935.
13. G.C. Peden, *British Rearmament and the Treasury: 1932–1939* (Edinburgh: Scottish Academic Press, 1979), pp. 74 and 205.
14. Ashworth, *Contracts and Finance*, pp. 107 and 109.
15. William Hornby, *Factories and Plant* (HMSO, 1958), pp. 83, 91 and 143.
16. Leslie Hannah, 'Managerial innovation and the rise of the large-scale company in inter-war Britain', *Economic History Review*, 2nd series, **xxvii** (1974), 254.
17. *H.C. Deb.* 5th series, vol 341: 1161, 17 November 1938.
18. Peter Fearon, 'Aircraft manufacturing', in Neil Buxton and Derek Aldcroft, eds., *British Industry Between the Wars* (London: Scolar Press, 1979), pp. 235ff.
19. Keith Middlemas and John Barnes, *Baldwin, A Biography* (London: Weidenfeld and Nicolson, 1969), pp. 816ff.
20. Lord Swinton, *I Remember* (London: Hutchinson, 1948), p. 110.

21. Memorandum by Weir, 9 January 1936, and minutes of Committee of Imperial Defence Sub-Committee on Defence Policy and Requirements (hereafter cited as DPRC), 13 January 1936, pp. 86–99, Public Record Office, Cabinet Office papers, CAB. 16/123.
22. Minutes of Informal Army Council, item 1, 28 October 1937, Public Record Office, War Office papers, WO 163/47.
23. W.J. Reader, *The Weir Group* (London: Weidenfeld and Nicolson, 1971), pp. 121ff. and 129; minutes of DPRC, 10 December 1936, p. 7, CAB 16/137.
24. Note of a meeting between Prime Minister, Chancellor of the Exchequer and representatives of the Federation of British Industry, 17 October 1935, CAB 16/112.
25. Minutes of DPRC, 13 January 1936, pp. 86ff., and report DPR (DR) 9, 6 February 1936, p. 10, with memorandum by Ernest Brown, Minister of Labour, 21 February 1936, pp. 78 ff., CAB 16/123.
26. Minutes of Secretary of State's Progress Meeting, 2 March 1937, AIR 6/29.
27. Extract of letter from Humbert Wolfe, Ministry of Labour, to Chairman of the Supply Board, 16 July 1936, CAB 16/140: DPR 107.
28. Wilson to Prime Minister (Neville Chamberlain), 21 March 1938, Public Record Office, Prime Minister's Office papers, PREM 1/251. For more information on the problem of skilled labour see R.A.C. Parker, 'British rearmament 1936–9: Treasury, trade unions and skilled labour', *English Historical Review*, **xcvi** (1981), 318–343.
29. M.M. Postan, *British War Production* (HMSO, 1952), pp. 431ff.
30. Hornby, *Factories and Plant*, pp. 321 and 345ff.; minutes of DPRC, 21 January 1937, p. 35, CAB 16/137.
31. Ashworth, *Contracts and Finance*, pp. 142–145. As early as 1925 the Principal Supply Officers' Committee, advising the Committee of Imperial Defence, commended the work of the Board of Trade in assisting the setting up of trade associations 'on the principle that they should be the general headquarters of their particular trade' in war – See J. Hurstfield, *The Control of Raw Materials* (HMSO, 1953), p. 67.
32. Richard Pares, 'The work of a departmental priority officer', in D.N. Chester, ed., *Lessons of the British War Economy* (Cambridge: Cambridge University Press, 1951), p. 166.
33. Robert Shay, Jr., *British Rearmament in the Thirties: Politics and Profits* (Princeton: Princeton University Press, 1977), pp. 289ff.
34. Ashworth, *Contracts and Finance*, p. 86.
35. Shay, *British Rearmament in the Thirties*, pp. 252, 255 and 261.
36. Ashworth, *Contracts and Finance*, p. 87.
37. Shay, *British Rearmament in the Thirties*, pp. 111ff.
38. For an authoritative account of changes in aircraft contracts and profits between 1936 and 1944, see Ashworth, *Contracts and Finance*, pp. 87–93 and 117–122.
39. Swinton, *I Remember*, p. 119. But see Peden, *British Rearmament and the Treasury*, p. 51.
40. E.G. Compton to B.W. Gilbert, 1 December 1938, T161/922/S40730/04, and Ashworth, *Contracts and Finance*, p. 91.
41. Ashworth, *Contracts and Finance*, p. 108.

42. 'Charges of profiteering. A possible line of Government reply', memorandum by J.A. Barlow, 17 February 1939, T161/922/S40730/04.
43. Minutes of DPRC, 30 January 1936, pp. 195–201, and Annex D to report, DPR (DR) 9, CAB 16/123.
44. 'Note of discussions on profits of firms with armament contracts', by J.A. Barlow, 18 October 1937, T161/922/S40730/04.
45. Chamberlain to his sister Hilda, 25 April 1937, NC 18/1/1003.
46. Deputation to Chancellor of the Exchequer from Special Committee of Industrial Organisations, 13 May 1937, p. 3, T172/1856. The Committee included representatives of the Association of British Chambers of Commerce, the Chamber of Shipping, the Federation of British Industries, and the Mining Association of Great Britain. The Chancellor had earlier received a separate deputation from representatives of the shipbuilding industry.
47. Scott, *Vickers*, p. 263.
48. Ashworth, *Contracts and Finance*, pp. 84–86, 231.
49. Wilson to Prime Minister, 15 March 1938; Bruce-Gardner to Wilson, 17 March 1938, and memorandum by Bruce-Gardner (copy to Wilson), 20 April 1938, PREM 1/236.
50. Lord Swinton, *Sixty Years of Power* (London: Hutchinson, 1966) p. 119.
51. Wilson to Prime Minister, n.d., but about 22 April 1938, PREM 1/236; Swinton, *I Remember*, pp. 146ff.
52. Shay, *British Rearmament in the Thirties*, pp. 220ff.
53. Keith Middlemas, *Politics in Industrial Society* (London: André Deutsch, 1979), p. 260.
54. Shay, *British Rearmament in the Thirties*, p. 267.
55. Backhouse to Admiral Sir Frederic Dreyer, 29 January 1939, PRO, Admiralty papers, ADM 205/3.
56. R.J. Overy, *The Air War 1939–1945* (London: Europa Publications Ltd, 1980), pp. 180–183.

Chapter 9

I would like to thank Mr T.A.B. Corley, Professor L. Hannah, Dr M. Pearton and Dr J. Turner for their helpful comments on earlier drafts of this paper.

1. H. Deterding to H. Colijn, 9 April 1914, Shell Archives. I would like to thank the Shell Group for permission to use their archives.
2. A. Sampson, *The Seven Sisters: The Great Oil Companies and the World they Made* (London: Hodder and Stoughton, 1976).
3. H. Deterding, *An International Oilman* (London: Ivor Nicolson & Watson, 1934), p. 13.
4. M. Pearton, *Oil and the Romanian State* (Oxford: Clarendon Press, 1971).
5. This view, which is still very far from general acceptance, is strongly argued in Joseph A. Pratt, 'The petroleum industry in transition: antitrust and the decline of monopoly control in oil', *Journal of Economic History*, **xl** (1980).
6. Pearton, *Oil and the Romanian State*.
7. On the politics of Venezuelan oil see E. Lieuwen, *Petroleum in Venezuela* (Berkeley: University of California Press, 1954); B.S. McBeth, *Juan*

Vicente Gomez and the Oil Companies in Venezuela, 1908–1935 (Cambridge: Cambridge University Press, 1983). On Latin America generally, George Philip, *Oil and Politics in Latin America* (Cambridge: Cambridge University Press, 1982).

8. Z. Mikdashi, *A Financial Analysis of Middle Eastern Oil Concessions 1901–1965* (New York: Praeger, 1965).
9. The early history of APOC is reviewed in Geoffrey Jones, *The State and the Emergence of the British Oil Industry*, (London: Macmillan, 1981). The references for the subsequent discussion of APOC's history in this paper are given in that book, unless otherwise stated. Since this paper was written the first volume of a scholarly official history of British Petroleum has been published: R.W. Ferrier, *The History of the British Petroleum Company. Volume I. The Developing Years 1901–1932* (Cambridge: Cambridge University Press, 1982). Ferrier provides fresh evidence about APOC's relationship with the British government, and differs from this paper in his interpretation of certain events in the company's early history.
10. P.J. Beck, 'The Anglo-Persian oil dispute 1932–3', *Journal of Contemporary History*, **ix** (1975), 123–151.
11. C. Davies, 'British oil policy in the Middle East 1919–1932', Unpublished Ph.D. thesis, Edinburgh University, 1973), esp. chapter 7. The Turkish Petroleum Company had been formed in 1912 with the aim of securing a Mesopotamian oil concession. Its composition changed a number of times, but by 1925 it comprised a group of American companies, a French company, APOC, the Shell Group, plus a small shareholding by Calouste Gulbenkian.
12. A. Noushi, 'L'état Francais et les pétroliers anglo-saxons: la naissance de la Compagnie Francaise des Pétroles (1923–1924)', *Relations Internationales*, **xxxii** (1976). A general survey of French oil policy is given in Eric D.K. Melby, *Oil and the International System: The Case of France, 1918–1969* (New York: Arno Press, 1981).
13. M. Kent, *Oil and Empire* (London: Macmillan, 1976).
14. Jones, *The State and the Emergence of the British Oil Industry*, pp. 219–221, 231–233.
15. Geoffrey Jones, 'The state and economic development in India, 1890–1947: the case of oil', *Modern Asian Studies*, **xiv** (1979), 353–375.
16. A. Fursenko, 'Parizhkie Rotshildy i Russkaia Neft', *Voprosy Istoril* (1962).
17. P. Calvert, *The Mexican Revolution 1910–1914* (Cambridge: Cambridge University Press, 1968).
18. 'Memorandum of Conference at Messrs. Vickers, May 22, 1914', Science Museum Library, Pearson Papers, Box C15.
19. Jones, *The State and the Emergence of the British Oil Industry*, pp. 151–154.
20. *Ibid.*, p. 213.
21. Kent, *Oil and Empire.*
22. Jones, *The State and the Emergence of The British Oil Industry*, pp. 201–202, 208–209.
23. *Ibid.*, pp. 214–215.
24. L. Turner, *Oil Companies in the International System*, (London: George Allen and Unwin, 1978), pp. 83–86.
25. Calvert, *Mexican Revolution*, *passim*.
26. Geoffrey Jones, 'The British government and the oil companies, 1912–

1924: the search for an oil policy', *Historical Journal*, **xx** (1977), 657–658.
27. Jones, *The State and the Emergence of the British Oil Industry*, chapter 6.
28. J.A. DeNovo, 'Petroleum and the United States Navy before World War I', *Mississipi Valley Historical Review*, **xli** (1955), 641–656.
29. R.W. and M.E. Hidy, *Pioneering in Big Business* (New York: Harper Bros., 1955), chapter 23; Bruce Bringhurst, *Antitrust and the Oil Monopoly: The Standard Oil Cases, 1890–1911* (Westport, Conn.: Greenwood Press, 1979).
30. Arthur M. Johnson, *Petroleum Pipelines and Public Policy, 1906–1959* (Cambridge, Mass.: Harvard University Press, 1967), p. 466.
31. H. Williamson *et al.*, *The Age of Energy, 1899–1959* (Evanston, Ill.: Northwestern University Press, 1963), p. 5.
32. Pearton, *Oil and the Romanian State*, pp. 62–67.
33. *Parliamentary Debates* (Commons), 17 June 1914.
34. J. Bradbury to E. Montagu, 6 June 1914, Public Records Office, Treasury Papers, T1/11953/20174.
35. Jones, *The State and the Emergence of the British Oil Industry*, pp. 199–201.
36. Waley Cohen to August Phillips, 27 December 1923, Shell Archives.
37. British governments in the inter-war period were generally in favour of mergers and 'rationalisation' in all industries. L. Hannah, *The Rise of the Corporate Economy* (London: Methuen, 1976), pp. 46–60.
38. Pearton, *Oil and the Romanian State*.
39. H. Deterding to Minister of Commerce, December 1921. Archives Economiques (Paris), F30 1402.
40. L. Fischer, *Oil Imperialism* (London: George Allen and Unwin, 1927), p. 150.

Index